OUR
OWN
WORST
ENEMY

OUR
OWN
WORST
ENEMY

▼

Asking the Right Questions About Security to Protect You, Your Family, and America

by Randall J. Larsen, Colonel, U.S. Air Force (Ret.),
Director, Institute for Homeland Security

GRAND CENTRAL
PUBLISHING

NEW YORK   BOSTON

Grand Central Publishing
Hachette Book Group USA
237 Park Avenue
New York, NY 10017

Visit our Web site at www.HachetteBookGroupUSA.com.
Printed in the United States of America
First Edition: September 2007
10 9 8 7 6 5 4 3 2 1

Grand Central Publishing is a division of Hachette Book Group USA, Inc. The Grand Central Publishing name and logo is a trademark of Hachette Book Group USA, Inc.

Library of Congress Cataloging-in-Publication Data
Larsen, Randall J.
  Our own worst enemy : asking the right questions about security to protect you, your family, and America / Randall J. Larsen.—1st ed.
      p. cm.
  "A White House advisor poses a critical and prescriptive look at America's security, revealing what we as individual citizens, community and business leaders, and parents must do."—Provided by publisher.
  Includes bibliographical references and index.
  ISBN-13: 978-0-446-58043-4
  ISBN-10: 0-446-58043-0
  1. Terrorism—United States—Prevention.   2. National security—United States.   I. Title.
HV6432.L3685   2007
613.6'9—dc22
                                                                                    2007006028

Book design by Charles Sutherland

This book is dedicated to the men and women who serve on the front lines of homeland security—those who work to prevent attacks and those who stand ready to respond. The criticisms in this book are not directed at these dedicated professionals. It is America's political leaders who deserve the criticism—and, of course, those of us who elect them.

Contents

Foreword ix

Chapter 1
Introduction
Wrong Questions Produce Wrong Answers 1

Chapter 2
Perceptions
Wrong Questions Spring from Wrong Perspectives 18

Chapter 3
Dangers
Understanding the Weapons of Terrorism 37

Chapter 4
Strategy
The Long View 78

Chapter 5
Priorities
Where Do We Focus the Spending? 92

Chapter 6
Key Issues
New Thinking, New Rules, and New Organizations 136

Chapter 7

Corporate America
Their Responsibilities   189

Chapter 8

Local Communities
911 Is a Local Call   226

Chapter 9

Your Family
Be Prepared   246

Chapter 10

Conclusions
For the Oval Office, the Front Office, and Your Family   269

Family Preparedness List   281

List of Acronyms   283

Bibliography   285

Acknowledgments   289

Index   293

Foreword

THIS BOOK WAS WRITTEN FOR AMERICANS WHO ARE INTERESTED IN THE security of their families and local communities, and for those who take the time and effort to vote. It was not written for policy wonks. (Policy wonks are those in the nation's capital whose life's focus is policy. They are the ones at their kids' soccer games who are discussing the latest Beltway buzz, and who watch C-SPAN in bed.)

Since 9/11, my efforts have focused on attempting to shape the thinking of senior administration and congressional leaders, in addition to the army of policy wonks here in the nation's capital. After four and a half years on this path, I decided it was time for a change. This new focus developed over a six-month period, but the precipitating event was the Dubai Ports "scandal" in February 2006.

I work very hard to maintain my nonpartisan credentials because many homeland security issues quickly divide into Republican and Democratic "positions." In the Dubai Ports issue, I didn't have to face that problem—it was the epitome of bipartisan lunacy coupled with bipartisan vote pandering, compounded by media hyperbole and downright media incompetence. Do you remember hearing, "U.S. to turn over port security to Arab nation—details at eleven"? It was at this point that I decided the best way to change the course of homeland security in America was to help inform and educate the American public on the subject. Frankly, I don't know if I will succeed. It is an ambitious goal, but one that is worth the risk. Perhaps I was inspired by my third-grade teacher, Mrs. Jordon, who taught me that Thomas Jefferson believed the best way to improve government was to have a better-informed public.

This book, along with my op-ed articles, seminars, workshops, and speeches, is now the central focus of my educational efforts. I want to take this discussion directly to the American people, because elected officials here in Washington are interested in public opinion. (Keep in mind my perspective on this "interest." My favorite political commentator, P. J. O'Rourke, said: "Politicians are always interested in people. Not that this is always a virtue. Fleas are interested in dogs.") Politicians are interested in your votes and, even more importantly, your campaign contributions, so you can influence how they think. My goal is to ensure that your influence leads them down a path that will create a more secure America at a cost (in terms of dollars, privacy, and convenience) that you are willing to pay. If we, the American public, do not improve our thinking on homeland security, and properly influence the decision makers we send to Washington and state capitals to represent us, then we will most certainly be our own worst enemy. We will do more damage to our nation and its economy than any terrorist organization ever could.

This book is written for people who care about the security of America, and who vote, regardless of party affiliation. In 2008, America will conduct one of the most important elections since 1952, or perhaps even 1932. A new president and new Congress will provide us the opportunity to make some important changes in our approach to homeland security. If the voting public and the press start asking the right questions of those who seek elected office, perhaps it will encourage those newly elected officials to do the same as they develop the policies and spending priorities that will determine the future security of your children and grandchildren.

The focus of this book will be quite broad. It is the first book on homeland security that will attempt to connect the dots from the Oval Office to the front office to your kitchen table. It is important that you understand the big picture, but this book will also provide very practical advice for you and your family. It may be the only book on homeland security most Americans will need to read, and one that all voting Americans should read. This book will tell you what you can do to better protect your family, your local community, and your financial future, and it will teach you to ask the right questions for your corporations, organizations, and nation's security. You can make a difference.

We can secure our homes and homeland, and we can do it at an affordable cost, if we just ask the right questions.

Examples of Wrong Questions

How do we win the war on terror?

What can we do to ensure that al Qaeda does not smuggle a nuclear weapon into the United States through one of our ports?

What can we do to prevent a biological attack on a U.S. city?

Shouldn't we put the military in charge of logistics for disaster response?

Shouldn't we put missile defense systems on airliners?

How can we build a system to inspect every shipping container that enters the United States?

What will FEMA—the Federal Emergency Management Agency—do for my family during a crisis?

Why are American cities unprepared for mass evacuations?

Terrorists have never used bioweapons to attack a city. Why should we make biodefense a high priority?

How can we secure America if we can't prevent illegal immigrants from crossing our border?

How much more money must Congress provide to ensure sufficient manpower for crisis response?

How do we improve congressional oversight of intelligence operations in this highly partisan environment?

OUR
OWN
WORST
ENEMY

Wherefore, security being the true design and the end of government, it unanswerably follows, that whatever form thereof appears most likely to ensure it to us, with the least expense and greatest benefit, is preferable to all others.

—Thomas Paine
Common Sense, February 14, 1776

Chapter 1

Introduction

Wrong Questions Produce Wrong Answers

JUST NINE DAYS AFTER THE 9/11 ATTACKS, TWO MEN AND A WOMAN CROSSED Pennsylvania Avenue and approached the northwest entrance to the White House. All three carried briefcases. Security was incredibly tight, and it took them nearly fifteen minutes to clear the metal, explosives, and radiological detectors, and a physical search of their bags. These were not regular times at the White House, and these were not regular guests.

Everything appeared normal, but a uniformed Secret Service agent asked one of the men why he had a surgical mask in his briefcase. The man replied, "Just for demonstration. You saw Mayor Rudy Giuliani wear one at Ground Zero, right?" The three were permitted to enter. They walked down two corridors and up two flights of stairs. After waiting for several minutes in a small room, Vice President Dick Cheney and several of his senior staff members walked into the room. In the same briefcase that contained the surgical mask, not more than ten feet from where the vice president was seated, was a test tube filled with weaponized *Bacillus globigii*. None of the security devices had detected it.

During that meeting, Vice President Cheney asked the question: "What does a biological weapon look like?"

I pulled the test tube from my briefcase and said, "Sir, it looks like this, and by the way, I did just carry this into your office." I went on to explain that *Bacillus globigii* is harmless, but physically and even genetically it is nearly identical to *Bacillus anthracis*—the bacterium that causes anthrax. If you can make the former, you will have no difficulty making the latter.

Two weeks later, Dr. Tara O'Toole, the director of the Center for Biosecurity–University of Pittsburgh Medical Center and I walked into CIA Headquarters in Langley, Virginia, to meet with the chief of indications and warning. While going through the security checkpoint, I noted the presence of a guard in full battledress uniform and armed with a machine gun (something not often seen at CIA Headquarters). After making eye contact with him, I took the test tube from one pocket, looked at it for a moment to make sure he could see it, and gently placed it in the other. The guard said nothing. Once again, a test tube of weaponized *Bacillus globigii* was carried into one of the most secure buildings in America.

Three weeks later, the office of Tom Daschle, the Senate minority leader, received an envelope filled with a far smaller quantity of weaponized and dangerous *Bacillus anthracis*. The young intern running the automatic letter-opening machine saw a fine mist of powder emerge from the envelope, and the Capitol Police were summoned. Later that day, all members of Congress and their staffs were evacuated from the Capitol Building and the six congressional office buildings. The Senate Hart Office Building, home to Tom Daschle and his staff, would remain closed for ninety days. It was contaminated with anthrax.

It would be easy to place the responsibility for the two earlier security lapses on the men and women entrusted with guarding the White House and CIA Headquarters. After all, if they can't protect their own house, how can we expect them to protect ours? But centering the blame on these individuals is both unjust and inaccurate. The failure was not one of execution, but of education. This lack of education and understanding of homeland security is the root of our problems. The Secret Service agent saw the test tube in my briefcase, but he asked about the surgical mask. He asked the wrong question. He is not alone.

Since 9/11, the business of homeland security has experienced unprecedented growth, creating a boom market for disciplines such as nuclear, chemical, and biological science, security and intelligence services, and information technology. While American taxpayers continue to pour hundreds of billions of dollars into the homeland security machine, media reports inundate us with daily proof of our failures despite our most valiant efforts. My admittance into two highly secure government buildings with a test tube of *Bacillus globigii* was just one small (fortunately benign) and unreported example. Throughout history, America has proven to be a resilient and formidable world force capable of meeting any challenge head-on and emerging triumphant. So what, if anything, has changed? Why are we struggling with this so-called War on Terror? Certainly it can be argued that the world stage has changed dramatically over the past several decades, due to the end of the Cold War, the emerging threat from previously nonnuclear players, and the advent of state-sponsored terrorism. But in examining the trends and reactions of Congress, the administration, and the homeland security community over the past several years, it has become abundantly clear where America's problem lies. *The most formidable military force in the history of mankind, the most brilliant scientists employing the most sophisticated technology available today, the most dedicated civil servants and the most committed, united citizens in the world cannot provide the answers to our problems so long as we continue to ask the wrong questions.*

The number one problem of homeland security is that the majority of leaders in the public and private sectors, academics, self-appointed experts, and pundits rush to provide answers before they have properly constructed the questions. *This is because they assume the questions have not changed. They are wrong. The questions have changed.* The reason for these changes is not al Qaeda or 9/11; the reason is technology. Weapons formerly restricted to the arsenals of large industrialized nation-states are now within reach of small states and some nonstate actors.

In the twenty-first century, biotechnology will change our lives even more than nuclear technology did in the twentieth century. Thirty years ago we didn't have to struggle with the ethical dilemmas of stem cell research and cloning or the threat of genetically engineered bioweapons. But change has not been limited to new types of weapons; it is the entire international environment that has changed.

When I use the term al Qaeda in this book, I am not limiting it to the terrorist group commanded by Osama bin Laden. I use it to describe a loose affiliation of fanatical Islamic terrorists. They go by many names: Jemaah Islamiyah (Indonesia), Islamic Jihad (West Bank and Gaza), Al-Gama al-Islamiyya (Egypt), Harkat-ul-Mujahideen al-Alami (Pakistan), and the Armed Islamic Group (Algeria). The State Department identifies two dozen Islamic terrorist organizations. Some operations are under the strict command and control of bin Laden, such as the attacks on our embassies in Kenya and Tanzania, the USS *Cole*, and 9/11. Other operations, such as the attacks in Bali, Spain, and London, were planned and executed by al Qaeda affiliates. These affiliates endorse al Qaeda religious guidance that allows for the killing of innocents during a holy war. Their theory is that "true innocents" will go directly to heaven when killed in a jihad. (According to bin Laden, Americans can never be true innocents since our tax dollars pay for the war against al Qaeda.) Some of these affiliates receive training and even limited funding from al Qaeda, while others operate independently except for moral support and religious guidance.

The struggle against al Qaeda is just one aspect of homeland security. If we killed or captured every member, we could declare victory in the war against al Qaeda, but we would continue to face threats to our homeland due to twenty-first-century technology and hatred that is driven by territorial disputes, economic inequalities, oil, water, politics, and religion.

Once we have covered the fundamentals in the first five chapters, the remainder of the book will synthesize the many aspects of homeland security into discussions of:

- this new security environment, and the resulting need for new thinking, new rules, and new organizations
- the responsibilities of corporate America
- preparing your local community
- preparing your family

We must change the way we think about security, and this means learning to ask the right questions. Unfortunately, just like that Secret Service agent at the White House, many of our leaders in government and industry, and citizens in our local communities, continue to ask the wrong questions, to the detriment of our national security. Let me provide a few examples.

Since 9/11, many in Congress and the administration have

asked the question: "What can we do to ensure that al Qaeda does not smuggle a nuclear weapon into the U.S. through one of our ports?"

Wrong Question

It is highly improbable that a terrorist organization would attempt to deliver a nuclear weapon to the U.S. in a shipping container, and even if it did, it is highly unlikely that we would detect it—no matter how much we spend on radiological scanning devices. Furthermore, even if we did detect it in a U.S. or foreign port, the terrorists would still have achieved success. Once al Qaeda or any other terrorist organization demonstrates the capability to acquire nuclear weapons, the entire international security equation changes. Life will never be the same for you, your children, or your grandchildren. Even if terrorists explode a device on a ship in mid-ocean, they will have made their point. The explosion will be followed shortly thereafter by the message: "Do what we say or the next three nuclear explosions will be in U.S. cities."

The correct question then is not how we can prevent a nuclear weapon from being smuggled into one of our ports, or how we can prevent a mushroom cloud over an American city. The correct question becomes, "How do we prevent a terrorist organization from becoming a nuclear power?" The answer to that question is far different from the answers that dominate the debate and the spending priorities of the Bush administration and Congress.

The aftermath of Hurricane Katrina is another prime example of asking the wrong questions. We all look to the federal government in times of disaster, and hope it will do a far better job than its response to Katrina. But the federal government should not shoulder all the blame; state and local government failed as well. According to Rich Cooper, the former business liaison director at the Department of Homeland Security, sixteen months before Katrina, the federal government gave $7 million (of your tax dollars) to New Orleans to build an emergency operations center (EOC). Government auditors and reporters haven't been able to find where the money was spent, but it was not used to build an emergency operations center. Had the operations center existed, officials at the federal, state, and local levels would have had a far better picture of what was going on in the hours and days immediately following the hurricane's landfall. This is called situational awareness, and without it, there is no way for leaders to make the right decisions.

During the congressional investigation into the poor response to Katrina by the Department of Homeland Security and the Federal Emergency Management Agency, this lack of situational awareness at the local, state, and federal levels became painfully clear. When the chief of the Homeland Security Operations Center, a retired Marine general, was asked why he didn't sound the alarm within the federal government that the levees had failed and New Orleans was flooding, he said, "I based my decision on what I assessed to be the most reliable information available." As it turns out, this information came from two sources: an Army Corps of Engineer colonel, new to the New Orleans area, who was in an underground bunker miles away from the critical levees; and a cable news TV report showing tipsy residents standing on a completely dry Bourbon Street (the highest area in New Orleans), smiling and saying, "We dodged a bullet."

Apparently, the Homeland Security command center was watching the wrong cable news network. One of America's top homeland security reporters, CNN's Jeanne Meserve, who arrived in New Orleans thirty-six hours before Katrina made landfall, left her makeshift shelter (a parking garage) near the

Superdome after the most severe weather subsided. She didn't go to Bourbon Street. Jeanne went with city officials directly to the low ground, the Ninth Ward, and reported massive flooding. Live on the air, she told anchor Wolf Blitzer, "This is Armageddon." Courageous and memorable reporting by Meserve, but situational awareness for federal, state, and local governments should not depend on which news network they are watching in their command centers.

There is plenty of blame to go around for the egregious response to Katrina, but a major share must rest with the state and local governments that failed to properly prepare. On the other hand, we must also expect that key federal leaders be properly prepared for their jobs. Can you imagine a president appointing an attorney general who is not a lawyer, a surgeon general who is not a doctor, or a chairman of the Joint Chiefs who is not a general or an admiral? Emergency management is a profession, and many schools offer graduate programs to prepare those individuals who are interested in making it their career. There are numerous people working at all levels of government with decades of experience in emergency management, and America deserved someone better qualified than Michael Brown. We must expect more from government.

The most frequently asked question about the failed response to Katrina is, "Who is to blame?" I won't qualify this as a *wrong question*, but I will say that looking for an answer is a wasted effort that quickly gets bogged down in partisan politics, cable news hysteria, and finger pointing among federal, state, and local officials. The answer is so simple that it deserves little attention. Leaders at all levels were not properly prepared. The most important question that citizens and taxpayers should be asking is, "What can we do to avoid such a disaster in the future?" The answer to that question is education at all levels—executive, graduate, undergraduate, high school, elementary school, and for ordinary citizens. (Reading this book is part of the solution.)

Several members of the national media, such as Pam Fessler from National Public Radio, who have studied homeland security and reported on it for several years do a great job of asking the right questions. Unfortunately, too many journalists and reporters cover homeland security as a part-time job, and their work clearly demonstrates their lack of knowledge. While writing this book I have had several calls from both print and broadcast reporters asking me to go on record discussing the fact that most cities are poorly prepared for a mass evacuation. They, and many elected officials ask, "Why aren't we better prepared for such a contingency?"

Wrong Question

When I get this question, I ask them to name a reason why we would have to conduct a mass evacuation, other than for an approaching hurricane. In that particular example, we would have several days to coordinate and execute the evacuation, and our focus should be on how we would evacuate those who require assistance. The American Red Cross estimates this figure to be around 20 percent in most communities. (FYI: The New Orleans Hurricane Plan estimated that one percent of the residents would require assistance, while the American Red Cross estimated the number to be slightly more than the national average—in this case, closer to 24 percent.) For the remainder of scenarios, whether we're talking about dirty bombs, suicide bombers, chemical attacks, pandemics, or another 9/11, rarely, if ever, is a mass evacuation the right solution. The correct questions should focus on creating plans for sheltering-in-place and ensuring that all families have appropriate transportation plans, communication plans, and readiness kits at work and at home.

Unfortunately, the majority of Americans fail to take even these three rudimentary steps to protect their families. I recall watching a TV report just thirty-six hours after Hurricane Wilma hit Florida in October 2005. The camera was showing a large group of angry Florida residents waiting in line for drinking water. Several of the citizens were complaining, "This is ridiculous!" "Where's FEMA?" "Why can't we get any water?"

Wrong Question

The crowd was correct about one thing: The situation was ridiculous. But the correct question that should have been asked was why residents who had four days' warning about the hurricane were already out of water a mere thirty-six hours after it passed through the area. Have we truly become a nanny-state where the government is responsible for all of our needs from cradle to grave? A month later I talked to the deputy mayor of that town. She told me that an even better question would have been, "Why don't you go down to the Wal-Mart (less than a half mile away) and buy some water? There's no electricity, but Wal-Mart is open and selling water for the normal price."

Finally, I recently heard a member of Congress acknowledge that bioweapons are one of the two most serious threats to our homeland (correct assessment), but then ask what system we needed to buy to ensure that no one smuggles a bioweapon into the U.S.

Wrong Question

Considering that just a couple of pounds of weaponized bio-agents are considered an enormous quantity, it's impossible to build an inspection system capable of preventing the importation of bioweapons. According to the Drug Enforcement Agency, drug runners brought 300 metric tons of cocaine into the United States in 2004. So what do you think our chances are of stopping determined terrorists from smuggling in a few pounds of dry-powdered anthrax? Inspecting shipping containers for bioweapons makes as much sense as building a wall along our southern border to prevent terrorists from entering our country, yet some prominent members of Congress, and pundits such as Bill O'Reilly and Pat Buchanan, want to spend your tax dollars building such a wall from Brownsville, Texas, to Imperial Beach, California. That wall might reduce the number of gardeners and house cleaners, but do you really think it would deter people who are willing to fly airplanes into buildings?

Both O'Reilly and Buchanan have told me that the U.S. should use military troops to secure our southern border. Apparently, neither was aware of a study submitted to Congress by the Department of Defense stating that it would require at least 350,000 troops to secure our two-thousand-mile-long southern border against drug smugglers. That's more than twice the number of troops we had in Iraq at the peak of the conflict in 2003. And even if we could secure our southern border, what would we do about our 5,500-mile border with Canada, or our 95,000 miles of shoreline? We don't have an adequate amount of troops available, couldn't afford the mission if we did, and more importantly, what rules of engagement would we have them follow? Would we order our soldiers to shoot sixteen-year-old girls coming to America wanting to be nannies? What about middle-aged housekeepers? Obviously, there are TV pundits who also practice the D.C. tradition of "Ready! Shoot! Aim!" It does make for entertaining TV and sells commercial time, but this approach does nothing to make your family more secure. These people would be far more valuable to the debate if they just asked the right questions.

I understand many Americans' frustration with our porous borders, but we need to spend our limited resources on solutions that will really work. There are ways to significantly reduce illegal immigration, but I guarantee you there is no way to prevent terrorists from smuggling a bioweapon into this country. Furthermore, al Qaeda training manuals available on the Internet state that it's better to build weapons inside the country one plans to attack, rather than transport them across international borders. In virtually every al Qaeda attack, this is precisely what the terrorists did, whether in Kenya and Tanzania in August 1998, Bali in October 2002, Morocco in May 2003, Turkey in December 2003, Spain in March 2004, or London in July 2005. That is why biodefense requires different solutions than those required to reduce illegal immigration. And defending America against nuclear terrorism demands a completely different approach than protecting our food supply, hazardous chemicals stockpile, and information networks. We must start asking the right questions. The good news is that some people already are, and they will be highlighted in this book. The first example is Sheriff Donald Sowell of Grimes County, Texas, and the genius and potential benefits of his questions and solutions are not limited to a rural county in Texas.

I first met Sheriff Sowell during an interview on *Homeland Security: Inside and Out*, a public radio show that I co-host. Each week we interview someone from inside the nation's capital and someone from outside. Last year we conducted an interview with Howard Safir, a former police commissioner and fire commissioner of New York City. As Mayor Rudolph Giuliani's first police commissioner, Safir had led the 41,000 officers in the nation's largest police force. Immediately following this taping, we interviewed Sheriff Sowell. This county is one third the size of Delaware in terms of square miles, and has fewer residents than New York City has police officers. Sheriff Sowell has a force of twenty-one deputies. Anyone who has ever run a 24/7 organization knows that an operation of this size will normally have two or three personnel on duty during an average twelve-hour shift. (Two thirds are always off-duty, some are on vacation or sick, and in the case of law enforcement, training days and court appearances have to be taken into account.) During a crisis, you could surge to eight to ten people per shift, but only for a short period. However, in a large-scale disaster like Katrina, you also need to consider that your first responders' priorities are going to be saving their own families and homes.

I asked Sheriff Grimes what he would do if there was a major disaster in Grimes County. He replied, "That's not just a rhetorical question; it happened last year. When Hurricane Rita was approaching the Texas coast, 3.2 million people evacuated. Several hundred thousand came through Grimes County."

I asked him, "Sheriff, how do you handle that type of law enforcement challenge?"

He replied, "Well . . . you just posse up."

He then went on to explain how he had developed emergency plans to use game wardens (who are sworn law enforcement officers in Texas) from other counties outside the evacuation zone. As the director of the Sheriffs' Association of Texas, he also had developed a program where sheriffs across the state could support the sheriff (or sheriffs) in a disaster zone. Finally, he has a reserve corps of deputies in Grimes County. Because of these proactive measures, Sowell was able to increase the size of his force by a factor of ten in a matter of hours. This was possible due to superior prior planning, and none of the plans required billions of your tax dollars.

Sheriff Sowell asked the right question before the crisis: "What can I do *on my own* to significantly improve my response capabilities?" The answer: "Posse up!" America needs more elected officials like Sheriff Sowell. *America needs more posses.*

Do not confuse posses with vigilantes. Vigilantes are people who take the law into their own hands. That is a bad idea, and I do not encourage it. When I refer to a posse, I am talking about two groups. The first is used to augment a law enforcement organization. They are properly trained, equipped, and under the direct command of a government law enforcement official. The second type of posse is a group of citizens or corporations who form a volunteer group that has no role in law enforcement. You will find examples of both types throughout this book.

Bioterrorism is one of the greatest threats we will face in the twenty-first century. One of the most notable successes of the federal government's biodefense preparedness efforts is something called a Push Pack. Today, if the federal government even suspected that a bio-attack had taken place in your community, one or more Push Packs, each containing 97,000 pounds of medical supplies, would be delivered to the affected area. The feds would get high marks for doing their job, but unfortunately, few communities today are properly prepared to distribute the life-saving antibiotics once they arrive. However, corporate America and local communities can solve this problem—all they have to do is *posse up*. Doing so can make the difference between a manageable crisis and a national catastrophe.

A Push Pack posse is a response effort, but we have also created posses for prevention. One of the most significant and successful examples of a prevention posse is the Highway Watch program created by the Transportation Security Administration. More than 300,000 transportation workers have been trained to look for and report suspicious behavior on our nation's highways. This posse includes a wide range of commercial drivers, from those in eighteen-wheel semis to small-package delivery personnel in step vans, to school bus drivers. Who better to spot something unusual or out of place than the people within the industry?

Other prevention posses also have no costs to taxpayers. The vast, heavily wooded perimeter of George Bush Intercontinental Airport in Houston, Texas (the nation's fourth largest), is patrolled, on horseback, by a part-time posse of eight hundred riders.

Since 9/11, some communities have created both prevention and response posses, but many Americans are failing to prepare and are hoping instead that the government will take care of them in the event of a crisis. Most individuals understand that hope is not a successful strategy for investing in the stock market, and likewise, you should understand that hope is not an effective strategy for protecting your family, your local community, and your economic well-being from man-made and natural disasters. The first step in developing an effective strategy is learning how to ask the right questions, a skill I used to teach at America's premier graduate school for military officers.

While serving as the chairman of the Department of Military Strategy and Operations at the National War College, I had the opportunity to assist in the graduate education of many of America's most promising military leaders. These students were Army, Air Force, and Marine colonels and Navy and Coast Guard captains. They had commanded battalions, squadrons, and ships in peace and war. We did not provide them a year of graduate education on national security studies to prepare them for their next assignment. Our mission was to prepare them for a decade down the road, when they would be serving in the most senior positions within the Department of Defense. It would have been impractical to provide them with the answers to national security problems, due to the limited shelf life of such solutions in this rapidly changing field. The mission of the National War College is to teach these officers *how* to think about national security—not *what*. (I wish I could say the same for my daughter's professors of government and international relations.) General Colin Powell and Lieutenant General Brent Scowcroft are graduates of the National War College, and both will tell you that this was where they learned to ask the right questions. That is my goal in writing this book—to help you ask the right questions about homeland security. Determining the correct questions is the first step in improving the security of your family, local community, business and economic well-being, and your country.

I will provide you with some of the answers, but only those that address the more practical issues of preparedness. This knowledge comes from my twelve years of experience in the field of homeland security, three decades of military service, and three years in the corporate world as the vice president and corporate officer of a high-visibility company. Whether you are a member of Congress, a federal, state, or local government official, a corporate executive, or a parent, it is critically important that you be prepared.

A young reporter once asked Albert Einstein what his theory of relativity had changed. He said, "Everything . . . everything except the way people think." We must change the way we think about securing our homeland. Throughout the Cold War, national security was the purview of those in Washington, D.C. Homeland security, on the other hand, while still involving Washington, extends all the way from the Oval Office to the front office to your kitchen table. When you finish this book, you will know what questions to ask, and you will have a far better understanding of the practical issues and the actions you must take. These actions will not require a large investment of your time or money, but the return on your investment will be substantial.

You could turn directly to the chapters concerning what to do for your business, local community, and family; however, you will be far more effective, and far better prepared, if you first learn the big picture. It will help you understand what must be done and why, because when it comes to homeland security, Americans tend to worry too much, and often about the wrong things.

If we continue down this road, refusing to see the whole chessboard and failing to formulate the right questions, then the greatest threat this nation could face will be realized: *We will have become our own worst enemy*. We must avoid this at all costs, and to that end, let us begin with perspective.

Chapter 2

Perceptions

*Wrong Questions Spring from Wrong
Perspectives*

ON THE MORNING OF FEBRUARY 26, 1993, RAMSEY YOUSEF AND HIS TEAM
parked a small truck in the basement parking garage of the World
Trade Center in New York City. The truck held a bomb comprised
of 1,300 pounds of urea pellets, nitroglycerin, and five other common chemicals. Yousef also added sodium cyanide to the mix so
the deadly vapors would go through the ventilation shafts and
elevators of the towers. The total cost of the materials was under
$400.

The bomb exploded at 12:17 P.M., blasting a 110-foot-wide
hole through four levels of the garage. Amazingly, only six people were killed, but more than 1,000 others were injured. The
explosion cut off the center's main electrical power line, much
of the telephone service for New York City, and caused smoke to
rise up to the ninety-third floor of both towers. Fortunately, the
explosion neutralized the cyanide.

Ramsey Yousef evaded capture for two years. He fled the U.S.
and initially went to the Philippines, where he built another
bomb factory and planned two operations: one to assassinate
the pope, and another to blow up eleven U.S. airliners over the

18

Pacific. Do you remember those two "dumb" questions at the airport that everyone used to complain about? "Did you pack your own bags? Did anyone give you anything?" Those were the "Ramsey Yousef questions," and they really weren't that dumb. Yousef planned to put his bombs inside large dolls. (Keep in mind, it was only fourteen ounces of plastic explosives packed inside a small tape recorder that brought down Pan American Flight 103 over Lockerbie, Scotland, in 1988.) This was back in the days when anyone could be in the departure lounge. Several members of Yousef's team, dressed as priests, were going to give these dolls to young girls, "to give them comfort on their long overseas flights." The bombs inside the dolls had timers made from electronic watches, set to go off several hours after departure.

Yousef tested his new device using only a very small amount of explosive material. He placed it in the life vest pouch under his seat, and set the timer to go off during the next flight. The bomb worked exactly as designed, but since it was a small explosive charge, it only killed the Japanese businessman who occupied the seat directly above it.

Fortunately, Yousef's Philippine bomb factory caught fire. He fled the country, inadvertently leaving behind his laptop computer, which was filled with a wealth of information for the intelligence and law enforcement communities. Yousef was eventually tracked down and arrested in Pakistan, and immediately extradited to the U.S. to stand trial for his role in the bombing of the World Trade Center. He told his interrogators that he thought his bomb would topple one of the towers into the other, causing several hundred thousand casualties. Yousef's team had known exactly where to place the truck to obtain maximum effect, but a Port Authority police car had been parked in that spot. One of the investigators on the case told me that had the bomb been placed where intended, Yousef might have achieved his goal.

Several days after his arrest, the FBI was transporting Yousef to Manhattan for arraignment in U.S. District Court. As they flew up the Hudson River on a Port Authority helicopter, an FBI agent removed the hood over Yousef's head, pointed toward the Twin Towers and said, "Ramsey, they are still standing."

Yousef replied, "We are not done yet."

As I travel around the U.S. talking with various audiences, the most frequent question I receive is, "They haven't hit us in a long time. Is this over?" If you only remember one thing from this book, remember this:

They are not done yet

We must understand that our enemy has a different perception of time than we do. We are Americans, and we're impatient. We want our pizzas in thirty minutes or less. I live in Alexandria, Virginia. We are very proud of Old Town Alexandria. We have 200-year-old townhouses, but in many parts of the world, a 200-year-old house is not a big deal. It's almost considered new. Oxford University has a dormitory that the students call the New Building. It was built in the seventeenth century. In 1970, at the height of the Cultural Revolution in China, a reporter asked the premier of the People's Republic, Chou En-lai, what he thought of the French Revolution. Chou thought for a moment and then said, "Too early to tell." When you have a 5,000-year recorded history, a couple of hundred years is a short period of time.

The enemies we face today, Islamic terrorists, have a long-term strategic vision—something we are not particularly good at these days in the U.S., whether we are talking about national security, Social Security, the environment, or most other important issues. Islamic terrorists envision a seventh-century caliphate that will extend from Spain to the southern tip of the Philippine Islands, funded by Persian Gulf oil and armed with Pakistani nuclear technology. They know this will not happen next week, next year, or maybe even in the next decade—but they know where they are headed, and they are not done yet. That is why I am disturbed when I hear politicians frequently ask, "How do we win the War on Terror?"

Wrong Question

This question demonstrates that there are two fundamental issues that are misunderstood. First, fighting a war against terrorism is like fighting a war against blitzkrieg. Blitzkrieg and terrorism are tactics, not an enemy. We can no more win a war against terrorism than we can stop burglary, prostitution, and bribes to politicians. We can develop strategies and plans to limit or contain such activities. We can focus our efforts to prevent the most horrific events. We can take action to mitigate the effects. But we cannot win the so-called War on Terror. Whenever you hear a politician say that we are going to win this war, be advised—this individual does not understand the situation.

Second, the idea of "winning the War on Terror" presupposes that we will be able one day to return to a pre-9/11 world. You need to understand that those days are gone forever. It is like wishing we lived in a world with no nuclear weapons. It's a nice dream, but despite the ultimate goal of the Nuclear Non-Proliferation Treaty (eliminating all nuclear weapons), it is not a possibility in your lifetime, or the lifetime of your children or grandchildren. This is a critically important concept.

When the president says he has authority to do whatever is necessary to defend America in time of war, what does that mean if the war has no end? When Congress spends vast sums of money for feel-good programs, does it understand that these new security measures must last for decades, if not longer? Does Congress really think we can afford them? Our misguided over-reactions to 9/11 might pose a far greater threat to the security of America than al Qaeda; most certainly they are a greater threat to our economy. Therefore we must keep the threat in perspective. Nearly 3,000 Americans died on 9/11. It was a human tragedy on a scale that was difficult for most of us to comprehend. However, during a four-year period from January 1, 2002, to December 31, 2005, not a single American died in our homeland from international terrorism. During that same period, 20,000 Americans died from food poisoning, 160,000 died in automobile accidents, and nearly 400,000 died from medical mistakes.

In August of 2001, a report was released stating that we could reduce automobile fatalities in the U.S. by 40 percent if every occupant of every vehicle would wear a NASCAR-quality helmet. That means we could save the lives of 16,000 Americans every year. Think about that—16,000 lives each year. More than five times the number of people who died in the 9/11 attacks. Do you want Congress to pass this legislation? Do you want the president to sign the bill? I pose this question in every speech I give, and ask for a show of hands. Less than one percent of my audiences is in favor of such a bill. When I first read the study, I asked my secretary what she thought about it. She replied, "I guess every day is going to be a bad hair day." Is a good hair day for America worth 16,000 lives? Amazingly, the answer is yes. According to a 2004 report from the U.S. Department of Transportation, 58 percent of motorcycle riders don't wear helmets. I know we won't convince these people to wear helmets in their sedans. Do you want to put on a hot, heavy helmet every time you get in the car? I didn't think so.

We are Americans, and we like our freedoms. We don't want the government or anyone else telling us what to do. I understand that. Personally, I wouldn't ride a motorcycle without wearing a helmet, but I certainly don't want to wear one in my car. So why is it that when a couple of bombs go off on a train in Madrid or a subway in London, members of Congress run in front of the cameras saying we need to spend hundreds of millions, even billions, of dollars on new security systems? Why would we spend hundreds of millions of dollars on security measures designed to prevent an attack on a train or subway that might kill a hundred people, when we won't take action that could save 16,000 lives each year? Could it be, "Ready! Shoot! Aim!"? Or is it that many do not understand the realities of this new world in which we live?

Jim Gilmore, the former governor of Virginia and the leader of a national commission on homeland security, calls this new security environment "the new normalcy." Terrorism and homeland security should not become the dominant theme in our lives or our national economy. We need to understand the threats and the requirements, and treat them like we do other risks in our lives. Determining probabilities for terrorist attacks is a significant challenge. The insurance industry is still struggling to adjust to the post-9/11 security environment. But for most of us, perspective is the first step in understanding homeland security. When we see for ourselves the statistical probability, it allays fears and provides opportunities to take the right actions.

The probability of an automobile accident is far easier to predict. We know that close to four hundred Americans will be killed on the roads each three-day weekend. That is a well-documented threat. But do we refuse to take our family to the beach on three-day weekends because of this increased risk? Of course not. Why? Because it is part of our normalcy. This risk didn't exist when my grandmother was a little girl because there were very few cars, but today it's a part of life. There are certain precautions we know to take: wear our seat belts, consider safety ratings when buying a car, don't drink and drive, and be on the lookout for those who do. We understand the risk, take proper precautions, and then go to the beach. That is the same attitude we must develop about terrorism.

On an evening in the spring of 2002, I was sitting in the Holiday Inn in Mount Vernon, Illinois, preparing for a speech I was giving the next morning to the Illinois Sheriffs' Association. CBS News called and said that the White House had put the nation on Orange Alert—the first time for a nationwide Orange Alert. CBS decided to send a satellite truck to Mount Vernon, so that I could do *The Early Show* live. As we were about to go on the air the next morning, Hanna Storm (the co-anchor back in New York City) said, "Randy, you always tell us the nation's capital is the number one terrorist target in the U.S." She then asked if I was worried about my nineteen-year-old daughter, who was in college back in D.C. I told her to ask me that question again when there were forty seconds left in the interview.

My answer that morning: "Hanna, I always worry about my daughter; that is part of the job description for being a father. However, let me tell you the priorities of my worries today. Number one, I worry about drunk drivers. Number two, I worry about violent criminals. Number three, I worry about nineteen-year-old boys—I was one once. And number four, I worry about terrorists."

We must keep these things in perspective. The press had a field day when a college student smuggled a few box cutters on an airliner in 2003, but do we really want a security system that is 100 percent effective? If so, it will take us hours to get through an airport. A system that is 80 percent effective is not an attractive target, even to a suicide bomber. A system that stops four out of five attackers is a strong deterrent, and if it is part of a layered defense (passenger and cargo screening system, augmented by hardened cockpit doors, thousands of armed sky marshals, armed pilots and passengers who have not forgotten Todd Beamer and his compatriots aboard United Flight 93) it will provide the security required.

What we cannot afford are shortsighted, wasteful programs. In 2005, the Transportation Security Administration initiated a program to fingerprint every person who has a permit to transport hazardous cargo and compare them to those of known terrorists. On the surface, it may sound like a reasonable idea—we certainly don't want terrorists driving large trucks full of dangerous chemicals through our communities. But the important question to ask is, If this program worked perfectly, would it make us significantly safer? Unfortunately, the answer is no. The fact is, even if this program had been in effect in 1993, and worked perfectly, it would not have prevented Ramsey Yousef from attacking the World Trade Center, or Timothy McVeigh from parking his truck in front of the day care center at the Murrah Building in Oklahoma City.

Today there are 2.7 million people with hazardous cargo permits. TSA estimates it will cost $100 per person to implement this program. In other words, this program is costing American taxpayers more than a quarter of a billion dollars, and that figure doesn't include the additional costs associated with drivers taking time off to go to special locations for electronic fingerprinting. When

> *Perhaps the most important thing you should understand about perspective is the fact that our enemies want to control it.*

the program began, there were only three offices in the entire state of California where drivers could be fingerprinted for this program. Does it sound like a waste of time and effort? Wait, it gets worse. By definition of the Department of Transportation, the following items are considered hazardous cargo: paint, Coke syrup, fingernail polish remover, Listerine. I guess we should all sleep better tonight knowing that TSA is preventing al Qaeda from attacking us with Coke syrup and Listerine bombs. (In fairness to the Transportation Department, there is a big difference between safety and security. The problem is that we have worked for decades to make America safer from accidents, but security against terrorism is entirely another matter. When we fail to understand these differences, we end up paying for programs such as this.)

But it is not just the executive branch that has been misguided in some of its actions. On some days, the hyperbole, hype, and hollow promises from Capitol Hill frighten me more than terrorists. Following the president's 2004 State of the Union address, the Democratic leader of the House, Nancy Pelosi, stated that less than five percent of cargo entering the U.S. is currently inspected. She demanded that 100 percent of the cargo that comes into this country by sea, and 100 percent of the cargo carried on domestic and international flights, be inspected. (Bad ideas are not a disease attributable to any specific political party. Prominent Republican leaders on the Hill also call for such wasteful, disruptive, and unrealistic programs.) The cost to the consumer of such an initiative would be mind-boggling, and a recipe for economic disaster. We must maintain our perspective, lest we become our own worst enemy. Our government's misguided reactions could cause far more damage to our economy than al Qaeda.

Okay, enough government bashing for now. That is not the purpose of this book. I could write several more chapters about government waste, fraud, and abuse, but you already know that exists. What can I tell you that you don't already know?

One of the primary goals of terrorism is to create fear and to cause people—leaders and citizens—to overreact. We must not help terrorists achieve their goals.

In June 2003, I designed and led an exercise for participants in the McGraw-Hill Homeland Security Summit and Exposition.

As the first general session of the conference began, a simulated breaking news story was shown on large-screen TV. A reporter at Chicago's O'Hare Airport stated that two shoulder-launched missiles were fired at a departing airliner, and that both had missed their target. Moments later, this report was interrupted by another fictitious breaking story from the airport at Dallas–Fort Worth, where the same type of attack had taken place, with identical results. The audience members, a mixture of federal, state, and local officials, plus defense and homeland security contractors, were then told they had the opportunity to provide advice and counsel to the president of the United States. Should the president ground the entire airline fleet? Should the president halt only operations at O'Hare and Dallas–Fort Worth? Should the president leave the decision to airline executives?

Attendees were also given a few short briefings about the realities of these decisions. They were informed that airlines fly 27,000 flights each day, and that the only means of providing protection would be to install airborne defensive systems on each airliner, an effort that would take years and cost billions of dollars. Therefore, if the president precipitously shut down the airlines, he would find it extremely difficult to tell the American people it was safe to fly again until these systems had been installed. Shutting down the airlines would cause enormous damage to the U.S. economy.

Each of the 300 participants had a handheld device to register his or her vote, which was then instantly displayed on large screens. In response to the question "Should the president immediately ground all airline operations in the U.S.?" *82 percent voted no.*

I always find these exercises interesting, because there is no way of determining what decisions the participants will make. I was pleased that in this instance, the audience did not overreact. The fact is that this type of incident or one similar will likely take place someday in the U.S. Thousands of shoulder-launched missiles worldwide are unaccounted for, and could easily end up on the black market. Terrorists can buy them for less than what you would pay for a used car. Fortunately, however, virtually all of these missiles were built with unsophisticated, 1960s technology, and have about as much chance of hitting an airliner as a Roman candle would. Several decades ago Libyan strongman Colonel Muammar Qaddafi gave a dozen to the Irish Republican Army. The IRA launched them at airplanes taking off from Heathrow Airport just outside London, and not one came close to hitting a plane.

I also asked the audience a follow-up question. I said, "Your mother just called. She is about to board a plane in San Francisco to fly to New York City. The airline says the flight will depart as scheduled. Your mother is looking for advice. Would you tell her it is safe to fly?" *91 percent voted no.*

In other words, the decisions made by airline executives, and even the president of the United States, may be irrelevant if the American people overreact.

Those who have studied this issue would be quick to agree that the 1960s generation shoulder-launched missiles that are readily available on the black market today (such as the Soviet-built SA-7) are probably not capable of hitting an airliner. However, proponents of missile defense systems (particularly those who stand to make a profit) ask, "Isn't it just a matter of time before the terrorists get their hands on a state-of-the-art missile with a super-cooled seeker head that will have a high probability of hitting a passenger jet?"

Wrong Question

I agree that someday terrorists could acquire such a missile; however, hitting an airliner is not the critical issue. The warheads on shoulder-launched missiles are small—not much larger than the fist of a grown man. These missiles were primarily designed for use on the battlefield to shoot down single-engine jet fighters, or jet fighters with two engines mounted side by side in the fuselage. (They have also proven effective against helicopters.) The missiles seek the hottest part of the airplane, which is the exhaust section. Because military fighter jets have variable exhaust nozzles that can be easily damaged with a small explosive, a shoulder-fired missile with a small warhead is capable of destroying one, or at least damaging it in such a manner that it becomes noneffective on the battlefield.

The same is not true for a modern commercial airliner. These planes have either two or four engines (today the vast majority have two) mounted on opposite sides of large fuselages. These engines do not have the vulnerable variable exhaust nozzles of a fighter jet, and have known to eat small flocks of large birds and continue to operate. Even more importantly, the planes are designed to be able to lose an engine and continue to fly. To be certified as a commercial airliner, a plane must demonstrate that under the worst conditions (maximum-gross-weight takeoff, hot day, high-altitude airport), it can lose an engine at the most critical point on a takeoff and then continue to climb to a safe altitude (most could climb up to 15,000 feet) before safely returning for a landing. In a worst-case scenario, where a direct hit by a missile caused an "uncontained failure" (the engine explodes and throws shrapnel in all directions), the fuselage would protect the engine on the opposite side of the airplane. In the case of a fighter jet with engines sitting side by side in the fuselage, an uncontained failure of one would likely destroy the other.

Defense contractors who would make billions by installing defensive systems on airliners will respond by saying, "What if the terrorists fire multiple missiles at a single plane? You could lose both engines."

Wrong Question

If terrorists fired half a dozen missiles at an airliner, no defensive system would protect it. The right questions are: What are the real threats from shoulder-launched missiles? What are the costs of defensive systems? Yes, there is a risk that terrorists may one day shoot at a U.S. airliner with a shoulder-launched missile. In fact, in 2005 a missile struck the engine of a DHL Airbus 300 departing from Baghdad International Airport, causing an uncontained failure of the engine. As it was designed to do, the Airbus safely returned for landing. There is risk involved every time an airliner takes off, and the challenge is managing that risk in a manner that meets our criteria of what is safe and affordable.

Shortly after 9/11, several defense contractors lobbied for funding to put "battle-tested" military defensive systems on commercial airliners, and some prominent members of Congress, including Senators Charles Schumer (D-NY) and Barbara Boxer (D-CA), supported the idea. However, systems that protect an Air Force fighter-bomber over a high-threat battlefield are impractical for commercial airline operations. There are many reasons why such a system would not be feasible, but one of the best is what is known as "mean time between failures" (MTBF). Essentially, MTBF is the amount of time it takes for an electronic or mechanical component to fail, and is used as a benchmark for reliability. The mean time between failure of the components that comprise the missile defense system on Air Force fighters is around four hundred hours, which is an acceptable amount of time for a plane that may fly an hour or two per day. In contrast, due to the extensive flight hours required of most commercial aircraft, equipment on these planes have mean time between failure rates of 20,000 hours. Thus, if one were to put equipment with an MTBF of 400 hours on a commercial jet, the equipment would fail once per month on average. Complicating matters further, replacement of such equipment is not simple or expedient. If a radio on an airliner needs to be replaced, mechanics can accomplish this while passengers are being loaded and offloaded. This is not possible when performing repairs on missile defense systems, where the plane has to be moved away from the terminals.

Another particularly thorny issue that advocates of missile defense systems often avoid in public debate is the "minimum equipment list" (MEL). There are systems on airplanes that must be operational prior to takeoff, and they are listed on the MEL. Other systems that have redundant backups (such as a VHF radio), or are considered nonessential (such as a coffeemaker), can be inoperative and have no effect on safety. Should a missile defense system be on the MEL? If the answer is yes, the military system that defense contractors wanted to install would have caused a precipitous drop in on-time departure rates for the airlines. If the answer is no, then there would have been little incentive for the airlines to properly maintain them.

Finally, there is the issue of secrecy. There is a wide range of defensive systems for use against shoulder-launched missiles, but the most capable are highly classified. If these systems were installed on a fleet of commercial airliners it would be difficult and prohibitively expensive to prevent foreign intelligence services from stealing the technology. If they gained access to our superior technology, the information could be used to increase their probability of shooting down our military airplanes, and decrease our probability of shooting down theirs. Senior State Department officials have made it clear that they would not allow our best technology to be compromised by installing it on commercial aircraft, so the American taxpayer would have to pay billions of dollars for a system that was second-rate at best.

Bottom line: The missile defense systems for fighter planes have been proven effective in combat. However, the systems that would be available to civilian airlines would be an enormous waste of money, and the potential benefit would be minimal at best (except for the defense contractors and their lobbyists). Thankfully, the Department of Homeland Security dug in its heels and convinced Congress that spending money only for research and development on defense systems for airliners is a wise expenditure of tax dollars—looking for new technologies and new concepts that may provide an effective defensive system that we can afford. One of the new concepts being examined is a ground-based defensive system.

There will be no missile defense systems on our airliners in the near future, so what would happen if a terrorist fires a missile at one of our planes? Chances are it won't hit anything (other than the ground, or perhaps a terrorist if we were really lucky). My concern is that our overreaction to this threat could enable the terrorists to succeed in causing severe and unwarranted disruptions to our economy.

Terrorism is a type of warfare that preys on our fears and anxieties, and that is why it is so important that we understand the probabilities and maintain control of our perceptions. I am often asked, "What is the probability that we will see a major attack in the next year?" or "What is the probability we will experience an attack with a weapon of mass destruction?" I tell people that probability is hard science and that there are far too many variables in that equation to make an accurate prediction. However, I do provide them with the following assessment:

I can't tell you what the probability of an attack is in your local community, but I can tell you that during the next five years, the probability that you, someone in your family, or someone you know will be killed or seriously injured in a terrorist attack is quite remote. On the other hand, during the next five years, the probability that you, someone in your family, or someone you know will suffer economic distress from a terrorist attack occurring somewhere in the U.S. is considerably higher.

What's the worst terrorism scenario you can imagine? For me it is a nuclear weapon. If a nuclear bomb went off in Los Angeles, hundreds of thousands would be killed, but virtually all of the deaths would occur in Los Angeles County. If you lived in Montana, Texas, Indiana, or New York City, the detonation would be of no physical threat to you or your family.

On the other hand, it would have a devastating impact on your economic well-being. We need to understand this issue. Remember, bin Laden has made it clear that one of his primary targets is the American economy:

It is important to concentrate on the destruction of the American economy.

—Osama bin Laden, December 26, 2001

By God, the youths of God are preparing for you things that would fill your hearts with terror and target your economic lifeline.

—Osama bin Laden, October 6, 2002

America's financial elite certainly understand the threat. According to a June 2006 U.S. Trust Survey of Affluent Americans, 77 percent of Americans with assets in excess of $5 million placed terrorism at the top of their list of financial concerns. But it wouldn't take a nuclear weapon to threaten the U.S. economy or your own economic well-being. What if a terrorist launched a shoulder-fired missile (one of those 1960s vintage models) at an airliner tomorrow? There is a very high probability that it would not even hit the plane, let alone cause it to crash. But what would *your* reaction be? Would you stop flying? Would you tell your family or your employees to stop flying? If we all did that, then we would all be guilty of assisting the terrorists in attacking our economy. Our overreaction would cause far more damage than the terrorists could ever hope to inflict. We would be accessories after the fact—our own worst enemy. That is why we must understand the probabilities and control our perceptions. Our enemies are betting that we won't.

We can learn to avoid overreactions. It's a skill that I developed as a young pilot and taught to many Air Force pilots who were learning to fly the supersonic T-38 (the plane that astronauts have flown since the days of the Apollo program). Most of these pilots had logged between 100 and 200 hours of flight time, but none in high-performance aircraft. These student pilots had spent most of their flight time in planes that generally flew at speeds under 200 miles per hour, but the T-38, a "white rocket" that comfortably cruised at nine miles per minute, required them to think ten miles in front of the airplane instead of two. They tended to overreact when something went wrong, but there are actually very few situations that require immediate and dramatic action—even at the speed of sound.

If you are just 100 feet off the ground after takeoff and hit a flock of birds, causing both engines to fail, then the situation does require dramatic and immediate action. The critical emergency checklist (called BOLDFACE) that pilots would follow in this type of situation has just two steps—"handgrips raise, triggers squeeze." (Pilots, with their infinite sense of black humor, often refer to this as "jettisoning the airplane.") In less than a second, the canopy departs the aircraft, a rocket motor attached to the bottom of your seat fires you several hundred feet straight up, your seat belt releases automatically, a device throws you away from your seat, and your parachute opens automatically. You then have just a couple of seconds before you hit the ground. This scenario certainly requires immediate and dramatic action, but it accounts for fewer than one hundredth of one percent of emergencies in the T-38.

For the remainder of emergencies, we used to tell the young student pilots that the first thing they should probably do is wind their watches. (I guess I'm dating myself; how long has it been since you've seen a watch that actually requires winding?) Of course we didn't really expect them to wind their watches, but we wanted them to avoid overreacting. Every pilot, civilian and military, learns three fundamental steps for responding to an in-flight emergency: maintain aircraft control, analyze the situation and take proper action, and land as soon as conditions permit.

Following the next attack on our homeland, I hope that our leaders in both government and industry will consider winding their watches while they maintain control, analyze the situation, and take appropriate action to ensure a soft landing of our economy, rather than a pilot-induced crash in what should have been a manageable crisis.

As for the citizens of this nation, we can learn a lesson from the Israelis, who have been dealing with terrorism for several decades. Terrorists have been putting bombs on buses in Israel since the late 1940s. These attacks are horrific tragedies, but amazingly, Israelis get back on the buses the next morning and go to work. There are 600,000 miles of bus lines in Israel. Buses are the way most Israelis get to work and school, and the way most Israeli soldiers ride to work. The Israeli nation and economy cannot function without people riding buses. The same can be said of airlines in the United States. In the next chapter you will learn that attacks against our economy, although the most likely of scenarios, would only be successful if we allow ourselves to become accessories after the fact.

Terrorists alone cannot take away our freedoms. Terrorists alone cannot corrupt our political system. For the most part, terrorists alone cannot severely disrupt our economy. They can only achieve these goals if we help them. One of the best things you can do to fight terrorism and defend the American homeland and your family is to keep terrorism in perspective. *Be prepared to get back on the bus.* If we overreact to the next attack, it will only encourage more.

Chapter 3

Dangers

Understanding the Weapons of Terrorism

To UNDERSTAND THE TYPES OF WEAPONS THAT MAY BE USED AGAINST OUR homeland in the twenty-first century, we must first appreciate what has changed and what has not. Some have said that everything changed on 9/11, but that is not true.

When Americans went to bed on September 10, 2001, the majority assumed that the two vast oceans and two friendly neighbors that had protected America during the nineteenth and twentieth centuries would continue to do so in the twenty-first. This assumption was wrong. The reality had already changed, and that change had nothing to do with hatred, Muslim fanatics, or bin Laden.

Hatred was not invented on 9/11. It has been around since the beginning of man. However, fifty years ago bin Laden would have just been another angry guy with a rifle in the desert—not a threat to your family. Technology is what has changed the international security equation. The first two threats discussed in this chapter, nuclear and biological, are the two greatest threats America will face in the twenty-first century, and they are both the result of exponential changes in technology.

I am not alone in my assessment of these two specific threats.

37

Senior government leaders, both Republican and Democrat, have reached the same conclusion. In fact, it is one of the few issues in homeland security that has near universal agreement. When the chairman of the House Homeland Security Committee, Chris Cox (R-CA), reorganized his subcommittees in January 2005, the first one created was solely focused on nuclear and biological issues. Chemical, radiological, cyber, and other types of weapons will pose serious threats, but none of these is in the same class as nuclear and biological.

This does not mean nuclear and biological are the most likely scenarios; they most certainly are not. But a nuclear- or biological-armed al Qaeda could threaten national survival. I often say, "Nuclear and sophisticated biological attacks are the only two types of attacks that could bring a superpower to its knees." Some of my more analytical friends have asked for a bit more specificity. That is a fair request.

When I use the term "nuclear weapon," I am referring to a device at least as powerful as the bomb dropped on Hiroshima. When I refer to a sophisticated biological weapon, I am talking about a weapon similar to the one described in the 1993 *Report on Weapons of Mass Destruction* issued by the U.S. Congress Office of Technology Assessment. This report stated that 220 pounds of high-quality, dry-powdered anthrax, properly dispensed over Washington, D.C., under ideal conditions, could kill between 1.4 and 1.9 million people. It also concluded that this type of scenario would kill more people than a one-megaton hydrogen bomb, which is the equivalent of approximately fifty-seven Hiroshima bombs.

When I speak of bringing a superpower to its knees, I am talking about three factors: deaths that would be counted in the tens and hundreds of thousands, with a far greater number of injuries or serious illnesses, significant and long-term economic disruptions throughout the nation, and responses by the government that would change the nature of our rights, judicial procedures, civil liberties, and concepts of privacy. Some ask if America would actually take such drastic actions. I remind them of our response to the bombing of Pearl Harbor, when 110,000 Japanese-Americans, 75,000 of whom were U.S. citizens, were placed in detention camps. Since there are very few people alive today old enough to have memories of World War I, and since our education system totally fails to teach high school and college students about infringements on freedom of the press and speech during World War I, most are shocked to learn what took place during the administration of Woodrow Wilson. The Sedition Act of 1918 made it a crime to "use disloyal, profane, scurrilous, or abusive language" about the United States government during time of war. People received prison sentences of up to ten years for protesting the war and the draft.

A few truck bombs or a handful of suicide bombers in shopping malls would not bring about the extraordinary infringements on civil rights and civil liberties that occurred during World Wars I and II. However, an attack on our homeland with nuclear or sophisticated biological weapons would likely cause extraordinary government actions that would infringe upon our civil rights and liberties, in addition to nationwide public health, economic, and social consequences.

The fact that only nuclear and sophisticated biological weapons have the capability to bring our nation to its knees is not an area for significant debate. What people disagree upon is how to defend America from these weapons. In this chapter I will discuss the facts concerning these two threats, along with other serious, but less draconian, types of potential attacks. If we ask the right questions, and remove the fog and disinformation of partisan politics and the distractions of the homeland security industrial complex, it will be relatively easy to understand the actions required to defend America and your family against these two types of weapons.

The bad news is that the threat is real. The good news is that there is much we can do.

Warning: This chapter is a bit frightening. Nevertheless, it is important that you read and understand this material. Why? The reason is simple. In order for you, as an individual citizen, to take action to help protect your family, local community, economic well-being, and nation, you need to understand the nature of the weapons we face in the twenty-first century.

To aid you in your understanding of these weapons, and more importantly, to educate you as to the actions we must take to reduce the danger, I will use the following formula:

Intention x Capability x Vulnerability x Consequence = Danger

The first thing you should understand about this formula, which in military circles can also be referred to as a model for analysis, is summed up by an old military saying: "All models are wrong, but some are useful." This one is useful for two reasons. First, it allows us to place the dangers in their proper perspective. Second, it assists us in deciding where to focus spending and actions to reduce the danger.

To demonstrate this model, let's assess the danger to the United States of British nuclear weapons. The British certainly score a 10 for *capability.* They have a large stockpile of nuclear weapons. And we get two 10s for *vulnerability* and *consequence.* However, the British *intention* for conducting a nuclear attack on a U.S. city is 0; therefore the *danger* is 0.

When using this model to assess the danger of al Qaeda and other radical Islamic terrorists, the intention factor in this equation does not require considerable analysis. Bin Laden and many of his followers accuse Americans of causing the deaths of four million Muslims, half of whom were children. Therefore, bin Laden reasons that it is not only justifiable, but a religious duty to kill four million Americans, and has said as much on numerous occasions since 1998. In a 2006 presentation at the Aspen Institute in Washington, D.C., Michael Scheuer, the former chief of the CIA's bin Laden unit, stated that a Saudi cleric gave al Qaeda permission to kill ten million Americans.

There are only two means of bringing such destruction to America: nuclear and biological weapons. If one had several nuclear weapons, they would provide the simplest solution. However, going back to the second element of our formula—*capability*—you will learn that it is far easier to achieve the capability to produce biological weapons than nuclear weapons. One cannot make a nuclear weapon with a limited budget and equipment purchased on the Internet, but thanks to the biotechnical revolution, our enemies can make sophisticated biological weapons in this manner.

As you read about each type of weapon, think about the danger in terms of our enemies' capability to build and use each weapon, our vulnerability, and the consequences from a national perspective. Timothy McVeigh had the intention and capability to attack the Murrah Federal Building, and it was vulnerable to a truck bomb attack, but the physical consequences were limited to Oklahoma City. On the other hand, attacking five major cities with a highly lethal bio-agent would have national consequences. Later in this chapter we will use this formula to compare the various dangers.

Remember ninth-grade algebra? What's important to understand about this formula is that if any factor in the equation becomes 0, the product (*danger*) becomes 0. In the late 1950s, polio was a serious public health threat that frightened most families in America. Viewing Mother Nature as the terrorist in that case, she certainly had the intention and capability to spread the disease. The American population was vulnerable and the consequences were substantial, both from a public health and a psychological perspective. (For those of you who were not around or do not remember, mothers across the country refused to let their children go to public places during peak polio seasons.) When the Salk and Sabin vaccines became mandatory, the vulnerability was virtually reduced to 0 and the danger, as a result, became nil.

Obviously, this formula is not a sophisticated analytical tool, but it can help you understand the rough order of magnitude of the dangers we face. More importantly, it can help us understand which factors of the equation will provide the best actions for reducing a particular danger. But before assigning numbers to this formula, let's look at some background information on the various chemical, biological, radiological, nuclear, and enhanced conventional explosive (CBRNE) dangers, so you can better understand why I ended up choosing the numbers I did.

BIOLOGICAL WEAPONS

That test tube of weaponized *Bacillus globigii* that I carried into Vice President Cheney's office was once a weapon that required superpower technology to build. Today, a biological weapon can be made with equipment bought off the Internet for less than what many people pay for a luxury sedan.

One of the greatest challenges of preparing America for biodefense is that so few leaders understand the true nature of this threat. For one thing, they often compare it to chemical weapons. When many people refer to biological weapons, they use the term "chem-bio," even though chemical and biological weapons are completely different. There is virtually no similarity between the two with regard to how one makes, uses, responds to, and cleans up after them.

A biological attack is an epidemic that is brought into your community. It is not a scenario that will be the typical flash-bang explosion, or anything like a chemical attack or industrial accident. It is terrorism in slow motion, and it is our lack of understanding that causes great problems in preparing for this most serious danger.

Unfortunately, most civilian government entities are still decades behind in understanding the nature of this threat. There are others who do not believe that bioterrorism is a realistic threat. They say, "It is just too hard to do and it has not been used before, so why worry about it now?" This certainly fits into that category of *wrong question*. Those who ask this question have neither an understanding of the history of biowarfare, nor knowledge of modern technology. Let's take a quick look at both.

Offensive and defensive biological operations have been around since before this nation was formed. The first well-documented case of biowarfare in America occurred in 1763. Colonel Henry Bouquet was the commander of British forces on the Pennsylvania frontier. In a letter to Sir Jeffrey Amherst, the British commander-in-chief of North America, Bouquet reported that he faced two serious problems at Fort Pitt: an outbreak of smallpox among his troops, and Indian raiding parties that were "laying waste to the settlements, destroying the harvest and butchering men, women and children." Amherst wrote back and suggested that Bouquet use one problem to solve the other. Bouquet decided to make a "peace offering" to the local tribes, giving them blankets and kerchiefs that came from the smallpox hospital he had established a few miles away from the main fort.

Medical historians have documented the fact that smallpox

decimated several Ohio and Shawnee tribes in western Pennsylvania that spring. Some would ask, "Since we know that smallpox was already in the Pittsburgh area (the soldiers had it), how can we know for sure that the smallpox came from the blankets and kerchiefs?"

It is not possible to prove that the smallpox epidemic in the Indian tribes was caused by the actions of Colonel Bouquet, but that is irrelevant. The important fact in this story—a fact that is indisputable—is that more than 240 years ago, a military field commander attempted to use biological weapons. Biowarfare is not a new idea. The enabling technology has just greatly improved.

During World War I, FBI agents raided a house in Silver Spring, Maryland, where they discovered German agents brewing anthrax and glanders. These German agents had traveled up and down the East Coast exposing horses and mules (primary battlefield transportation assets) that were in holding pens awaiting transportation to France. There is no reliable data on the effectiveness of this terror plot, but there is no question of its existence.

During World War II, every major combatant had an offensive biological warfare program. In the United States, the War Research Office coordinated the work of biologists in twenty-eight universities including Harvard, Columbia, Cornell, Notre Dame, and Stanford. The United States and Great Britain collaborated on research and development efforts. Extensive testing of anthrax weapons was conducted on Gruinard Island, a remote island off the coast of Scotland, which became so contaminated with anthrax that for decades it was not safe to visit without the use of protective gear.

Japan, however, was the only nation that actually used biological weapons during World War II. Most of the information about the Japanese bioweapons program was highly classified until the early 1990s. However, extensive information on the Japanese biowarfare program is now widely available in various

U.S. government publications and scholarly articles. A museum has been built by the Chinese in Manchuria on the site of a former Japanese biowarfare facility.

In 1940, plague-infected fleas and grain were dropped from Japanese aircraft on eleven Chinese cities. (The grain was used to attract rats, which helped move the fleas around the city.) The Japanese also attacked Chinese villages with tainted food. In one case they distributed typhoid-laced dumplings to 3,000 Chinese prisoners and then freed them to return to their villages.

Between 1932 and 1945, Unit 731, commanded by General Shiro Ishii, and Unit 100, commanded by General Kitano Masaji, conducted biological warfare research in Manchuria and China. During laboratory tests, human subjects, including Allied prisoners of war, were infected with plague, typhus, smallpox, yellow fever, tularemia, hepatitis, gas gangrene, tetanus, cholera, dysentery, glanders, anthrax, undulant fever, tick encephalitis, epidemic hemorrhagic fever, and other diseases that resulted in the deaths of more than 10,000 individuals.

By 1945, Unit 731 had stockpiled nearly 1,000 pounds of anthrax to be used in specially designed fragmentation bombs, delivered by balloons. General Ishii's plans to attack U.S. forces were canceled by the Japanese army chief of staff and surgeon general. However, in May, General Ishii received approval to drop plague-infected fleas on the American airfield on Saipan. The operation was foiled when an American submarine sank the ship that was carrying the Unit 731 technicians toward Saipan.

General Ishii then received approval for an attack on San Diego, California. Three submarines carrying disassembled airplanes were to cross the Pacific and surface at night off the coast of California. After assembling these amphibious airplanes, they would be launched to drop plague-infested fleas on the city. This operation was scheduled for September 1945. Fortunately for the residents of southern California, the Japanese surrendered in August.

While the Japanese efforts were extensive, there is little data available on their effectiveness. Their weaponization efforts and delivery systems were primitive at best. They exposed people to pathogens through vectors (fleas and ticks) and through the gastrointestinal tract by contaminating food and water. In 1945, Japan began experimenting with what would become the basis for modern biological warfare—inhalation exposure. Weaponization for inhalation exposure requires three to five micron-sized particles (a human hair is 100 microns in width) that move through the lungs directly into the bloodstream.

This became the standard for all modern biowarfare programs. Many nations, including the United States, Great Britain, France, the Soviet Union, and China developed sophisticated biowarfare programs following World War II employing bio-agents that could be released into the air and inhaled by the victims. The science, technology, and operational considerations were challenging, but by the late 1960s, sophisticated bioweapons were part of the arsenals and war plans of the major powers.

In the 1960s, real bioweapons, not simulants, were tested in the South Pacific. Several thousand miles southwest of the Hawaiian Islands, U.S. Navy airplanes released weaponized bio-agents. Forty miles downwind from the release, 50 percent of the nonhuman primates (monkeys) were infected by the aerosol release. No one is sure how much further the deadly microbes were carried by the wind—the most distant barge was forty miles from the release point. This series of tests, called Shady Grove, proved once and for all the reality and lethality of modern bioweapons.

In 1969, President Richard Nixon ordered a unilateral disarmament of all bioweapons in the U.S. inventory. America then led the effort to ratify the Biological and Toxin Weapons

Convention (BWC). By 1975, 151 nations had signed this treaty, including the Soviet Union. Unfortunately, the Soviets violated this treaty for more than twenty years. This is neither speculation nor an intelligence estimate. Several top Soviet scientists eventually defected to the United States and provided detailed information on their programs, and in a 1992 speech to a joint session of Congress, President Boris Yeltsin finally admitted to the deception.

The Soviet bioweapons program employed 40,000 scientists, doctors, engineers, and technicians. They developed a wide array of weapons, including anthrax, plague, and smallpox, and also developed strains that were reportedly resistant to our vaccines and treatments. According to Dr. Sergi Popov, a chief scientist in the genetic engineering program, the Soviets were working on the use of HIV, Legionnaires' disease, and several forms of neuromuscular diseases as weapons.

Supposedly the Russians have discontinued their biowarfare programs, even though one of the principal defectors believes it is still ongoing, and that thousands of scientists, engineers, and technicians once engaged in these massive programs remain a potential threat to the U.S. We know for a fact that nations such as Iran have attempted to recruit some of these top scientists.

Today it is not necessary to have been a member of a nation's bioweapons program to have the know-how needed to build a biological weapon. The widespread availability of such knowledge among scientists around the world is why it is impossible to prevent a bio-attack on America. This is a frightening thought, but one that needs to be understood if we are to build a successful defense. Dr. Richard Danzig, the former secretary of the navy and one of America's top biodefense strategists, estimates that there are more than one million people in the world today capable of building a sophisticated biological weapon.

I will not go into the technical details of developing bioweapons with twenty-first-century technology, but suffice it to say that the processes and equipment required that were available only to rich and powerful nations in the 1960s are now available to small nations and terrorist organizations.

The technology routinely used in pharmaceutical delivery systems such an inhalers means that anyone with the capability to brew beer and produce pharmaceuticals can also produce bioweapons. The test tube of weaponized *Bacillus globigii* that I carried into Vice President Cheney's office was produced a few years ago in a government program called Bachus.

Bachus was a program designed to see if a terrorist-style bioweapons lab would produce any type of "signature" for the intelligence community to detect. If you build a nuclear weapons program or a large-scale chemical weapons program, you create a signature that can be detected by various elements of what we euphemistically refer to as our "national technical means." Unfortunately, the Defense Threat Reduction Agency (DTRA) learned that there would be virtually no detectable signature from a terrorist-style bioweapons lab. It could be constructed in a facility no larger than a two-car garage and all the equipment is of a dual-use nature; that is, it can be used for legitimate research and commercial purposes. What DTRA also learned was that producing bioweapons was no longer difficult to accomplish.

Since some would have considered it a violation of the Biological and Toxin Weapons Convention to actually produce *Bacillus anthracis* (anthrax) in weaponized form, the Bachus team decided to make *Bacillus globigii*, which is nearly identical to *Bacillus anthracis*, but harmless. Many nations, including the United States and the Soviet Union, used *Bacillus globigii* to test their production and dispersal equipment. If you can weaponize *Bacillus globigii*, you can weaponize *Bacillus anthracis*.

A small team of scientists, with no experience in the production of bioweapons or access to classified information on the process, demonstrated how easy it is to weaponize *Bacillus globigii* using open source information and equipment bought over the Internet. The experiment demonstrated that the funding required to weaponize *Bacillus globigii* and other pathogens is less than the price of a luxury car. (Had the team bought used lab equipment instead of new equipment, it would have cost only $50,000.)

The al Qaeda bioweapons laboratory that U.S. forces discovered in Afghanistan had all the necessary equipment required to produce a modern bioweapon. If one had access to any of the former Soviet scientists, the process would go quickly. Without experienced bioweaponeers, it would likely take longer. It might even take a terrorist organization a year or two to fine-tune the processes, but this we know for sure—the documentation we discovered in Afghanistan demonstrated that al Qaeda knows the process. Do not forget that several known al Qaeda members are trained in biology, and bin Laden's deputy, Ayman al-Zawahiri, is a medical doctor. (There are unconfirmed reports that a small quantity of "extremely virulent" anthrax was successfully produced in the al Qaeda laboratory.)

Once a terrorist organization has developed a biological weapon, delivery will not be difficult. In October 2001, we witnessed the efficacy of using the U.S. Postal Service to deliver anthrax, an incident now referred to as "Amerithrax." Amerithrax was an excellent example of one unique feature of biological warfare—the ability of the perpetrator to remain anonymous. Conventional weapons often provide experts with significant clues as to their origin. Although many aspects of forensic investigation are exaggerated by Hollywood and TV series such as *CSI*, the considerable capabilities of the FBI, the Treasury Department's Bureau of Alcohol, Tobacco and Firearms, and some major cities' bomb squads had enabled authorities to quickly identify those responsible for the attack on the World Trade Center in 1993, the Murrah Federal Building in Oklahoma City, the

U.S. embassies in Kenya and Tanzania, and numerous other terrorist attacks and criminal activities. I am continually impressed
with the forensic capabilities of these law enforcement agencies. There is, however, one glaring exception—Amerithrax.

As of this writing, the FBI has been unable to identify the perpetrators of these attacks. It has very publicly pointed a finger at
one individual, whom I will not name because the FBI has failed
to produce any credible evidence of his guilt. More importantly,
I am convinced there is a reasonable probability that the attack
was orchestrated and carried out by al Qaeda.

I will not go into all of the details, since they would fill an entire book, but here, in chronological order, are a few key points
to consider:

- In September 2001, when federal agents found a prescription bottle for Keflex (a common antibiotic) in Mohamed
  Atta's apartment, they traced it back to Dr. Cristos Tsonas,
  an emergency room physician at Holy Cross Hospital in
  Fort Lauderdale, Florida. When questioned, Dr. Tsonas
  informed the FBI that in June 2001, he had treated Atta's
  roommate, Ahmed Alhaznawi, for a lesion on his leg. Alhaznawi claimed that he had sustained the ugly wound,
  which resembled a dark carbuncle, from "bumping into a
  suitcase." Dr. Tsonas thought this was an odd explanation,
  but he cleaned the wound and prescribed antibiotics (see
  New York Times March 23, 2002, story by William Broad
  and David Johnston).
- After several cases of anthrax had been reported by the
  press in October 2001, Dr. Tsonas began researching
  the symptoms (U.S. doctors rarely, if ever, see cases of
  anthrax), and quickly discovered that the lesion on Alhaznawi's leg looked just like the photographs in the medical reference books (interview with Dr. Tom Inglesby,

who currently serves as the deputy director of the Center for Biosecurity—University of Pittsburgh Medical Center).

- Dr. Tsonas contacted the FBI to report that the lesion he had treated on Alhaznawi was "consistent with anthrax." Virtually all lesions of the type described by Dr. Tsonas, with the exception of an anthrax lesion, are painful and sensitive to pressure. According to Dr. Tsonas, Alhaznawi's was not sensitive to touch (interview with Dr. Inglesby).

- An individual who worked as a biodefense expert in the White House during the Amerithrax investigation (and asked to remain anonymous) told me, "Since the first week of the investigation, the FBI was solely focused on looking for a domestic perpetrator." He said this decision was based on two pieces of "evidence":

  1. An analyst at the CIA told the FBI, "It is highly unlikely that a foreign nation would provide al Qaeda with a biological weapon, because of the high probability of retaliation by the targeted country."

  2. The FBI profilers believed that the handwriting and word choice indicated that the anthrax letters were not written by a foreigner.

- Based on the lack of response and follow-up, it appears the FBI team in charge of the investigation did not consider the information from Dr. Tsonas to be a serious lead. After several months of inaction, an individual on the team who had become frustrated with this lack of response called Dr. Inglesby, an infectious disease and biowarfare specialist.

- Immediately following that call, Dr. Inglesby spoke with Dr. Tsonas. After discussion and review of the case, Dr. Inglesby and the director of the Center for Biosecurity, Dr. Tara O'Toole, concluded that Dr. Tsonas's judgments and recollections about Alhaznawi's medical condition were entirely consistent with cutaneous anthrax. (Cutaneous anthrax is the type one acquires when the bacteria only come in contact with the skin. The far more serious form, inhalation anthrax, requires that the bacteria enter the lungs.) If the skin lesion and Alhaznawi's overall medical condition were as Dr. Tsonas reported, there are very few medical illnesses other than cutaneous anthrax that would explain Alhaznawi's condition. Drs. Inglesby and O'Toole notified U.S. government officials of their concerns.

- According to numerous press reports and FBI statements, the FBI seemed to be convinced that the anthrax had been produced in a U.S. Army lab. It was weaponized, meaning that the concentration was at the trillion-spore level; however, it had none of the telltale attributes (additives) associated with the anthrax produced by the U.S. Army in the 1960s (before the U.S. shut down its offensive bioweapons program). A trillion-spore concentration is more difficult to obtain in a large-scale production effort than when produced in very limited quantities, such as the amount used in the Amerithrax attacks.

- Some officials inside the government and the press reports were focused on the fact that this was the Ames strain of anthrax, a particularly virulent strain that was used in the former U.S. offensive program. However, this strain was also considered the gold standard for testing anthrax vaccine (commonly used by veterinarians) and available in numerous civilian laboratories in the U.S. and overseas.

- Some government officials stated that Mohamed Atta's team (the nineteen hijackers) could not have mailed the anthrax letters, since they were all postmarked after 9/11 (September 18 and October 9). However, several al Qaeda members were later discovered to have been in the U.S. before and after 9/11, including Aafia Siddiqui, an MIT-trained microbiologist. A White House counterterrorism expert confirmed that the interrogations of Khalid Shaikh Mohammed (mastermind of the 9/11 attacks) revealed that Siddiqui and her husband had provided logistical support to the 9/11 hijackers.

- A June 16, 2004, report released by the 9/11 Commission stated, "Al Qaeda had an ambitious biological weapons program and was making advances in its ability to produce anthrax prior to 9/11."

- The Commission on the Intelligence Capabilities of the United States Regarding Weapons of Mass Destruction (known as the Robb-Silberman Commission) concluded that al Qaeda's "biological program was further along, particularly with regard to agent X, than pre-war intelligence indicated." (Numerous press reports state that the "agent X" mentioned in the unclassified version of this report is identified as anthrax in the classified version.) This report also stated, "The program was extensive, well-organized, and operated for two years before September 11, but intelligence insights into the program were limited. The program involved several sites around Afghanistan. Two of these sites contained commercial equipment and were operated by individuals with special training." According to a military biodefense expert, traces of a virulent strain of anthrax were detected in one of these camps.

- The individuals and offices that received anthrax letters fit the profile of likely targets—political leaders (Senator Daschle as well as Senator Patrick Leahy) and major print and broadcast news outlets. They were chosen because their high visibility made it possible to obtain maximum psychological impact from a small amount of anthrax. The only anomaly was Robert Stevens, a photojournalist for the *Sun*, an AMI tabloid. While not a major piece of evidence, it is interesting to note that several AMI tabloids had published unflattering articles in the summer of 2001 regarding bin Laden's alleged deviant sexual practices. It is also an interesting coincidence that Gloria Irish, a real estate agent and wife of *Sun* editor Michael Irish, had rented property to Hamza Alghamdi and Marwan al-Shehhi. (FBI spokeswoman Judy Orihuela confirmed this information on October 15, 2001.) Both of these men were on United Airlines Flight 175, the second jet to strike the World Trade Center. In fact, fifteen of the nineteen hijackers had either lived within a few miles of AMI headquarters, or had visited those who did. Mohamed Atta drove past AMI whenever he traveled to the local airport for his flying lessons, as his apartment was a mere three miles away.

- According to a United States Department of Agriculture loan officer, Johnelle Bryant, Atta attempted to apply for a loan from the USDA in order to purchase a six-passenger airplane. He said he wanted to remove all the passenger seats and install a tank to use for crop dusting, and sought $650,000 to start his business. A six-passenger airplane would be virtually useless for traditional crop spraying, as it could not perform the near-acrobatic maneuvers required for low-level spraying. On the other hand, it would be more than adequate for releasing biological agents over a city. While three to five micron-sized dry-powder is the preferred type of anthrax weapon, this powder could also be suspended in water and sprayed from any type of moving vehicle.

- The FBI was not qualified to conduct the investigation. However, I must also state that there were, in fact, no organizations within the U.S. capable of conducting a proper forensic investigation of a bio-attack in 2001. Unfortunately, the very nature of bioweapons is such that attribution will remain difficult, even with properly trained and equipped personnel.

- The FBI is a law enforcement agency. Its primary (if not exclusive) focus in 2001 was building a case that could be proven in a court of law. Such a case requires a very high standard of proof—beyond reasonable doubt—and while the aforementioned facts might not be the type that would stand up in a court of law, they do cause me to seriously question the FBI's sole focus on a domestic perpetrator.

Nevertheless, for several years the FBI was convinced that the Amerithrax attacks were domestic terrorism, not al Qaeda. The FBI now says, "Nothing is off the table" regarding whether it was a domestic or foreign perpetrator. Whether you believe my suspicions or the FBI's original conclusion, the most important lesson to understand is the difficulty of attribution of bio-attacks—another reason they appeal to terrorist organizations.

I hope this short tutorial on bioweapons has provided enough information to convince you of the seriousness of the threat. Believe me, I haven't divulged any secrets to the enemy—the bad guys already know the information in this section of the book. It has been available in any good library since I first began my studies of bioterrorism in 1994.

Last year I attended a conference on bioterrorism. A skeptic in the audience asked one of the presenters, "Do you really expect me to believe that some terrorist living in a cave in Afghanistan will suddenly become a bioterrorist?" Gerald Epstein, from the Center for Strategic and International Studies replied, "No, that is not what I worry about. I worry about a biologist becoming a terrorist."

Assuming a terrorist organization has the intent and capability, are we *vulnerable* to a bio-attack? Yes. Viruses and bacteria, not just from terrorists, but primarily from Mother Nature, are still the two greatest threats to the human race. This has been true since man first walked the earth. Today the biotechnical revolution means that we must be concerned about more than just Mother Nature. An accidental release from a Bio-Safety Level IV laboratory (where research on the most deadly viruses and bacteria is conducted) could pose a serious threat, and an intentional release could unleash the most devastating attack this nation, or the world, has ever seen. We know what Mother Nature did with a flu pandemic during the winter of 1918–19. As many as 100 million people died worldwide (estimates range from 20 to 100 million, including 600,000 in America). More U.S. Army soldiers died of influenza that winter than died on the battlefields. In October 1918, 12,000 people died of influenza in Philadelphia alone. Human beings are highly *vulnerable* to biological attacks, both naturally occurring and man-made.

We cannot control the *intent* of the fanatics who wish to kill four million Americans, and we cannot control their *capability* to make bioweapons. We can, however, control the *consequences* by limiting our *vulnerability*. By investing in research and development for vaccines and treatments, and building a public health and medical care delivery system that can rapidly detect and treat an epidemic, we could contain an attack and its effects.

We cannot prevent an attack, but we can control the decimal point—we can move it to the left. Instead of 100,000 dying in an attack, a properly prepared nation could reduce that number to 10,000, or 1,000, or perhaps only 100. The only question is, will we take the necessary actions, or will we continue to waste money on programs that don't make our families any more secure?

After two decades of study in the field of national security, and more than a decade focused on homeland security, it is the biological threat that keeps me awake at night. If you are still a skeptic, you don't have to take my word for it. Here are a few quotes I use when briefing senior military officers.

The one that scares me to death, perhaps even more so than tactical nuclear weapons, and the one we have the least capability against, is biological weapons.

General Colin Powell
Chairman, Joint Chiefs of Staff, 1989–1993

Bioterrorism is the single most dangerous threat to U.S. national security in the foreseeable future.

R. James Woolsey
Director of the Central Intelligence Agency, 1993–1995

Today one man can make war. A lucky bio-buffoon could kill 400,000 people.

Dr. Joshua Lederberg
Nobel Laureate in Microbiology

There are no actions that the president, Congress, or anyone else can take to prevent terrorists from obtaining and weaponizing these pathogens. It is only a matter of time until a significant bioterrorism event occurs. And when it does, it will not be an isolated event. Because of something called the "reload factor," the moment we detect a bio-attack in one city, we will need to assume it could quickly occur in many cities. Reload factor is a term coined by Richard Danzig. Once a terrorist organization decides to produce and use a bioweapon, it won't be like hijacking airplanes or obtaining a few nuclear weapons. It requires only slightly more effort to produce a sufficient quantity of bio-agents to attack several cities than it does to produce enough to attack just one. It is unlikely that we will see a single isolated event—even though that assumption seems to be the standard for the majority of government bioterrorism exercises.

NUCLEAR WEAPONS

One Hiroshima-sized bomb in an American city would forever change the course of our history. A second nuclear weapon in a second city would threaten the foundations of our political, economic, and social structures. A nuclear-armed al Qaeda could bring the United States of America to its knees. This is neither hyperbole nor fear mongering. It is simply a fact.

Fortunately, no terrorist organization today, or at any time in the foreseeable future, will have the capability to build a nuclear weapon from scratch. Numerous independent studies have concluded that it would cost more than a billion dollars to do so. This is just not within the capabilities of even the most well-funded terrorist organization. Unfortunately, there is more bad news than good. Even though terrorists cannot produce fissile material, it would not be difficult for them to build a nuclear weapon if they bought or stole the highly enriched uranium or plutonium (particularly uranium)—and a nuclear weapon does not require a lot of it.

It only requires as little as thirty-five pounds of highly enriched uranium (HEU) or nine pounds of plutonium to produce a bomb. In other words, a large briefcase could contain enough weapons-grade material to build a bomb. Additionally, building a crude nuclear device, similar to the one that destroyed Hiroshima, is far easier than most understand. By August 1945, the scientists at Los Alamos had constructed three bombs: two of plutonium, and one from highly enriched uranium. The construction of a plutonium bomb is far more complex, because it must be imploded. This requires building a conventional bomb around a volley-ball-sized amount of plutonium. It must be designed to explode in a perfectly symmetrical manner so that it compresses the plutonium. This complexity was the reason that the bomb makers elected to test one of the plutonium devices in the New Mexico desert. The second plutonium bomb, Fat Man, was dropped on Nagasaki, Japan, causing an estimated 45,000 immediate deaths.

On the other hand, there was only one uranium bomb, and therefore no way to test it. However, the scientists who constructed the uranium bomb were positive that no test would be required. The scientists understood that if they placed a sub-critical piece of HEU on the floor, climbed a fifteen-foot step-ladder and dropped another sub-critical piece of HEU onto the first one, they would create a nuclear explosion. The physics of HEU makes the design of a gun-type bomb quite simple. The crude device (Little Boy) that exploded 10,000 feet above Hiroshima and killed an estimated 70,000 to 130,000 people was not considerably more sophisticated. The scientists placed two pieces of HEU in opposite ends of a Navy gun barrel. Then they constructed a device that slammed these two pieces of sub-critical material together, creating a critical mass and a nuclear explosion. Some might find it odd to refer to a bomb that killed 70,000 to 130,000 people as crude. However, this is a term that is commonly used when describing an HEU, gun-type bomb—also called an atom bomb. Little Boy was nearly 1,000 times more powerful than the largest bombs used in World War II. Nevertheless, by today's standards, it was quite crude. In the Cold War, both the United States and the Soviet Union built incredibly complex fission-fusion bombs (often called hydrogen bombs) that were 1,000 times more powerful than Little Boy.

There is no chance terrorists could build a hydrogen bomb. Even if they bought or stole one from the former Soviet arsenal, because of the extraordinary complexity and built-in safety systems, it is highly unlikely they could make it work. Therefore, you don't need to lose sleep worrying about a terrorist attack with a hydrogen bomb. However, terrorists who obtained highly enriched uranium could build a crude bomb—one that would completely destroy a one-mile radius in a city, and make a much larger area uninhabitable. (If you wonder why Hiroshima and Nagasaki are inhabited today, it is because both Little Boy and Fat Man exploded well above the cities, so the fireball did not touch the ground. Most likely, a terrorist bomb would be detonated on the ground, creating an enormous amount of radioactive material.)

The nuclear danger is relatively easy to understand, but sometimes it is difficult to comprehend the level of destruction. A nuclear bomb produces five types of damaging effects: blast, heat, immediate and intense radiation, fallout (long-term radiation), and electromagnetic pulse.

The blast of a 17-kiloton bomb will flatten all wooden and un-reinforced masonry structures within one mile. While there is no test data on the blast effect in the concrete canyons of a modern city, it will most certainly be less than if detonated in an area other than a city center.

Heat may cause temperatures at the blast site to exceed 100 million degrees Centigrade. This is about ten times the surface temperature of the sun. At these temperatures, matter cannot exist in its regular solid, liquid, or gaseous form. In Hiroshima, the firestorm incinerated virtually everything within 1.2 miles from ground zero.

People within 1.5 miles of ground zero will be exposed to 500 rems, meaning they would have a 50 percent chance of dying from radiation sickness, radiation burns, and other illnesses within a few days to two weeks. Shielding, such as that provided by dense buildings, will reduce these effects.

Fallout consists of small particles of radioactive dust that eventually fall back to earth. An airburst, such as the one over Hiroshima, produces a minimum of radioactive dust. However, most terrorist scenarios will be ground bursts that generate large amounts of fallout. Depending on the size of the blast and the winds, this fallout would contaminate areas downwind from the blast creating enormous cleanup challenges.

Electromagnetic pulse (EMP) can cause considerable damage to electronic components. One recent study concluded that a Hiroshima-sized bomb detonated 400 kilometers over Omaha, Nebraska, would have EMP effects over the entire United States. Given that most terrorist nuclear attacks would occur at ground level, the EMP effects would be limited to the immediate area, but would still cause major disruptions in disaster response efforts.

These are scary facts. I provide them to help you understand why I, and many others, see nuclear weapons as one of the two most significant dangers we will face during the next several decades. But could a terrorist organization really threaten us with a nuclear weapon? Unfortunately, the answer is yes—if it obtained about thirty-five pounds of highly enriched uranium.

Where could a terrorist find enough highly enriched uranium to build a crude bomb? It is not as difficult as you might think. There is enough HEU sitting in research reactors to build scores of Hiroshima-sized bombs. There are more than 100 such reactors in forty countries that use HEU as fuel.

What about nuclear power plants? Actually, security at these facilities is quite high. More importantly, the fuel rods in a nuclear power plant are composed of low-enriched uranium (LEU)—not the type of material that can be used in an atomic or hydrogen bomb. It is very radioactive, but not capable of producing an explosion. Ironically, the highly radioactive nature of the fuel rods in a nuclear power plant makes them difficult to steal. At best, the thieves would be on a very short suicide mission.

On the other hand, the HEU in the research reactors is generally not highly radioactive. This HEU would not require massive shielding to protect the individuals who would transport it, and a significant quantity could be safely carried in an ordinary suitcase. A 1977 unclassified report from the Argonne National Laboratory, one of the Department of Energy's largest research centers, stated that the process required to convert this HEU into weapons-grade material could be accomplished with commercial, off-the-shelf equipment. Details on the chemical processes required are also available in open literature.

Amazingly, we have far better security for protecting low-enriched uranium that cannot be used to make a bomb than we do for the highly enriched uranium used in the Hiroshima-type bomb. Go figure.

I am certainly not saying that we have too much security at our nuclear power plants. They require the highest levels of protection. The material cannot be made to explode, but the massive quantity of highly radioactive, low-enriched uranium could create an enormous environmental disaster, such as at the Soviet Chernobyl plant in what is now Ukraine. However, the top priority should be more security at the research reactors and other sources of highly enriched uranium.

By far, the largest source of weapons-grade nuclear material that could fall into the hands of terrorists is in the former Soviet Union. This material is not measured in pounds, but hundreds of tons. In 1991, Senators Richard Lugar (R-IN) and Sam Nunn (D-GA) authored the Nunn-Lugar Act, which created the Cooperative Threat Reduction program. Its goal is "locating, locking down, and eliminating" this nuclear material. Considerable progress has been made on the first goal, locating, but much work remains to be completed on locking down and eliminating. Most estimates, including those from Senator Lugar, the Nuclear Threat Initiative (a not-for-profit organization funded by Ted Turner and led by former Senator Sam Nunn; www.nti.org), and Thomas Kean and Lee Hamilton, co-chairs of the 9/11 Commission, state the task of properly securing this weapons-grade nuclear material is only 50 percent completed.

This program provides one of the best returns on investment of any national security initiative. In addition to the obvious security benefits, the United States buys the highly enriched uranium from Russia, brings it to the U.S., and steps it down to low-enriched uranium for use in nuclear power plants. Former Senator Sam Nunn likes to point out that one out of every ten light bulbs in America is powered by a former Soviet nuclear weapon. Today, nuclear power plants provide 20 percent of the electricity in the U.S. Half of the fuel currently used in these power plants is the fuel that has been reprocessed from former Soviet nuclear weapons. I know of no other national security program that provides such extensive benefits.

CHEMICAL WEAPONS

Chemical weapons can create havoc, but in comparison to nuclear and biological attacks, their effects would be limited in scale. They could not be used by terrorists to bring a nation to its knees. The psychological effects, however, could be substantial. An attack on a subway system could kill a few hundred people, or perhaps a few thousand, and would be similar to a hazardous material incident, not unlike a large chemical spill.

Military-style chemical weapons, including nerve, blister, and blood agents, are incredibly lethal. However, they are difficult to produce and store, and transporting significant quantities into the U.S. would be an enormous challenge for the terrorists. Why would terrorists go to the expense and risk of detection to bring chemical weapons into the U.S. when vast quantities of highly lethal industrial chemicals are already conveniently positioned in most of our major urban areas?

We saw the effects of what an industrial accident could do in Bhopal, India, on December 3, 1984. While there is still controversy as to whether this disaster was the result of a disgruntled employee or lack of proper safety procedures, and there are widely varied estimates on injuries and deaths, it is safe to say that the deaths were counted in the thousands and the serious injuries in the tens of thousands.

Industrial chemicals that are stored and transported in major metropolitan areas throughout the U.S. are the most likely type of chemicals terrorists would use. In fact, one of the most common chemical weapons used in World War I is the same chemical agent used in many water treatment facilities in the U.S. today. The first use of chemical weapons during World War I occurred on April 22, 1915, in Ypres, Belgium, when the Germans released 160 tons of chlorine gas.

One major difference between nuclear, biological, and chemical attacks is that a nuclear weapon capable of destroying a mid-sized city, and a sufficient quantity of biological agents to attack a dozen large cities, would both fit in a minivan. To transport quantities of chemical agents (either military-style or industrial) sufficient to cause a similar number of deaths would require a freight train. However, there are certain areas within the U.S. where large quantities of hazardous chemicals are stored in or near major population centers.

The chemical threat is not just from fixed sites. A Google image search for "chlorine rail tanker car U.S. Capitol" produces a famous Sierra Club photo of a rail tanker car crossing a bridge over South Capitol Street, just one quarter mile from the U.S. Capitol Building and Supreme Court. The tanker car is clearly labeled "Chlorine." Several years ago a newly appointed senior official at the Defense Threat Reduction Agency asked his staff how terrorists would be able to attack a train loaded with hazardous chemicals. While on his way to work the next morning, a Marine colonel at DTRA stopped his pickup truck in the middle of a rail crossing as a slow-moving freight train pulling tanker cars approached. The engineer stopped the train. Later that morning the Marine colonel shared this story with his boss (the senior DTRA official) and added, "I guess that would be when the bad guys would go place the explosive charges on the rail tanker cars."

Is a chemical attack possible? Yes. Is it one of the more likely terrorist scenarios? Yes. Have we done all that is necessary to prevent such an attack? No. America's chemical industry has a great safety track record. Safety was the primary focus in the twentieth century, and it will remain important in the twenty-first, but we must now consider security as an equally high priority. This will be neither easy nor inexpensive. While the effects of these chemicals will be limited to a relatively small area, from the perspective of the terrorists, the capability and vulnerability factors in our equation are high.

RADIOLOGICAL WEAPONS

Radiological weapons, referred to as radiological dispersal devices (RDD) or dirty bombs, would cause significant psychological effects, and in some cases, considerable economic impact in the immediate area of release. However, in terms of lives, more people would likely die from stress-induced heart attacks than from radiation sickness. There would be no immediate deaths from exposure to radiation from a dirty bomb. The long-term threat would be increased probability of certain cancers, but only for those people who remained in the area for twenty years (and that is assuming the radiation was not properly cleaned up), and for those who may have inhaled certain radioactive particles, such as plutonium.

Cleanup is possible, but would be very expensive. In 1966 a B-52 crashed in Spain. It was carrying nuclear weapons, and one of the bombs released radioactive material. This was an H-bomb, one of the fission-fusion devices. The conventional explosive materials detonated during the crash and spread radioactive material across a 450-acre field. Cleanup required a major effort. More than three million pounds of topsoil was removed, but ultimately the operation was a success. Today, tomatoes are grown on this acreage. (No, they don't glow in the dark. They are completely safe to eat.) However, a cleanup in a major city would be far more difficult and costly.

Dirty bombs are more of an economic weapon than a threat to human life, but they are easy to construct, and are therefore the most likely type of CBRN weapon terrorists will use. It would not have been beyond the technical capability of Timothy McVeigh, the Oklahoma City bomber, or Ted Kaczynski, the Unabomber.

The cleanup issue would present problems, particularly for corporate America. Radioactive particles would enter ventilation systems and might become embedded in structures, and would tend to adhere to asphalt materials commonly used on rooftops and streets. There are no EPA cleanup standards. Rather than require the destruction of a building to achieve cleanup (in effect doing what terrorists were unable to do), it is more likely that the government would attempt to declare low levels of radiation acceptable or safe. Any government declaration, at any level, may not convince health insurers. There are many unanswered questions about radiological dispersal devices. These types of weapons, however, do not threaten the lives of large numbers of people, and the direct economic impact would not be nationwide, but limited to the local area. (However, the indirect economic impacts could be quite large if the government overreacts—"Close all ports!")

ENHANCED CONVENTIONAL EXPLOSIVES

Large conventional explosives, also called enhanced conventional explosives, have become increasingly popular with terrorist organizations. The attacks on the United States Air Force Headquarters Europe, Ramstein Air Base, Germany, on August 31, 1981, and the attack on the Marine barracks in Beirut, Lebanon, on October 23, 1983, were carried out using conventional explosives that were enhanced through the use of propane gas bottles.

Timothy McVeigh's attack on the Murrah Federal Building in Oklahoma City was technically classified as a conventional explosive device; his 5,000-pound bomb, made from diesel fuel and fertilizer, created a major explosion that destroyed the nine-story building. Al Qaeda demonstrated a new style of enhanced conventional explosive when it used fuel-laden wide-body aircraft to deliver thousands of gallons of jet fuel to the top floors of the Twin Towers. These weapons have proven highly effective, but as with other so-called weapons of mass destruction, other than nuclear and biological weapons, they only have local effects.

One of the major concerns about enhanced conventional explosives is if they are used to attack critical infrastructures. In certain cases, a properly placed explosive device could produce effects felt over a large geographic area, such as taking out electrical power or petroleum pipelines over a three- to four-state area.

Last year the press had a field day with the headline "DHS Identifies 77,000 Critical Infrastructures Including an Ice Cream Parlor and Popcorn Factory in Indiana." This dominated the print and broadcast media for a day or two, and gave certain members of Congress something to talk about. Unfortunately, few took the time to discover the truth. This critical infrastructure database was built with information provided by state and local governments. If the press wanted to blame someone for including popcorn factories, it should have identified the state and local officials who submitted these items. An expert panel at the Department of Homeland Security reviewed this master list and pared it down to approximately 2,000 key facilities in the United States that, if attacked with properly placed enhanced conventional explosives, could result in large-scale effects across a multi-state area.

Enhanced conventional explosives do have the potential for large-scale destruction. When Ramsey Yousef drove his truck into the underground parking garage at the World Trade Center on the morning of February 26, 1993, his goal was to bring down both of the Twin Towers. In this scenario, there would not have been time for the majority of occupants to evacuate. If he had succeeded, the casualty figures for the 1993 attack would have been far greater than those on 9/11.

CALCULATIONS AND CONCLUSIONS

Using the formula mentioned earlier, we can now assign numbers to these factors to obtain a rough order of magnitude of the danger.

Intention x Capability x Vulnerability x Consequence = Danger

Let me be right up front here and tell you that the policy wonks, defense contractors, and scientists in the national labs will look at this formula and scratch their heads. They will wonder why I chose the word "Danger," instead of "Risk" or "Threat." My reasoning is that there are dozens of different definitions of risk and threat that are tossed around in the literature. Danger is a word suggested by Dr. Dave McIntyre, the director of the Integrative Center for Homeland Security at Texas A&M University. He said, "Use a term no one else is using; then it can't be confused with someone else's definition."

One could certainly build a far more complex model, but I wanted a formula that is easy to understand, yet provides a mechanism to compare the relationship between the different factors. The goal is to reduce the danger. When we use this formula to assess the danger of the threats discussed above, it will provide us the information required to prioritize spending and actions.

I use a scale of 1 to 10 for each factor (10 being the worst case). The consequence is based on the effects on the nation as a whole. The Murrah Building bombing in Oklahoma City had terrible consequences for the residents of that city, but had little effect outside the local area. I rate it as a 1, or perhaps a 2, due to the psychological shock we all felt.

Since we know al Qaeda has the stated intention of killing four million Americans, all assessments will use 10 for intention. Since intention is high, probability is included within the capability factor. You may not agree with the numbers I use. That's okay. Do your own analysis—that is part of your learning process.

Biological

While it is unlikely al Qaeda or any other terrorist organization presently has the capability for the most sophisticated types of bio-attacks, such as with a genetically engineered pathogen, the capability for building the type of weapons developed by the U.S. and U.S.S.R. in the late 1960s is quite high. Based on what is possible and what we discovered in the al Qaeda laboratory in Afghanistan, I rate their capability as a 7. Is the U.S. vulnerable? Yes. Discussions with a wide range of biodefense experts lead me to rate vulnerability as an 8. While some would rate the consequence of a contagious pathogen higher, I do not. The reload factor makes a noncontagious pathogen a danger to the entire nation. (For this model, I am only assessing lethal pathogens.)

Intention x Capability x Vulnerability x Consequence = Danger
10   x   7   x   8   x   10   = 5,600

Nuclear

The most likely nuclear weapon, made of fissile material (also called special nuclear material or explosive nuclear material), would be a gun-type bomb made from highly enriched uranium (HEU).

Since we cannot harden the entire nation against a nuclear attack, vulnerability is rated as a 10. Likewise, a single nuclear weapon in an American city will produce consequences for all Americans as demonstrated in numerous studies, the most recent in the summer of 2006 by RAND (available at www.rand.org). Capability is more difficult to rate. Based on discussions with a wide range of nuclear and security experts, I rate capability as a 5.

Intention x Capability x Vulnerability x Consequence = Danger
10   x   5   x   10   x   10   = 5,000

Chemical

The availability of industrial chemicals already located in our major urban areas makes them easy targets, but there will be some degree of difficulty in properly attacking a chemical storage facility. I rate capability as a 6. As the Bhopal disaster demonstrated, we are highly vulnerable to these chemicals.

I rate the consequence as a 6 because coordinated attacks on chemical facilities would not affect the entire nation, but could have a substantial impact on metropolitan areas. Chemical attacks could certainly kill more people than most conventional and enhanced conventional attacks, but they nevertheless only threaten a local area, not the entire nation, as do nuclear and biological attacks. A terrorist organization would have even less capability to produce and transport large quantities of military-quality chemical weapons, such as nerve gas and blister agents. Therefore, I rate chemical weapons as follows:

Industrial Chemicals

Intention x Capability x Vulnerability x Consequence = Danger

10 x 6 x 10 x 6 = 3,600

Military-Style Chemical Weapons

Intention x Capability x Vulnerability x Consequence = Danger

10 x 3 x 10 x 6 = 1,800

Radiological

The ubiquitous availability of radiological material is why many experts believe that a dirty bomb is the most likely CBRN (chemical, biological, radiological, nuclear) scenario. I agree. Capability is a 10. Vulnerability is more difficult to rate. It is a bit of an apples and oranges issue. All other weapons in this comparison are dangers to human life. A dirty bomb is an economic and psychological weapon. Virtually no one would face immediate death, and in most cases a dirty bomb would only be a danger to those who refuse to evacuate the area and continue to live in a hot zone for more than a decade (assuming it was not cleaned up). There are some exceptions. A dirty bomb constructed from plutonium would be a serious health hazard if the plutonium were inhaled. Therefore, I rate vulnerability as a 3, but I rate consequence slightly lower than chemical, because the radiation will cause no immediate deaths.

Intention x Capability x Vulnerability x Consequence = Danger
   10   x   10   x   3   x   5   = 1,500

Conventional and Enhanced Conventional Explosives

I rate capability as a 10, due to the ease in acquiring the materials required, as has been demonstrated on numerous occasions. I rate vulnerability as a 4 based on statistics from various terrorist bombings such as the 1993 attack on the World Trade Center, the Murrah Federal Building, and the attacks on the trains in Spain and the subways in London. Only a small percentage of those people in the immediate area were killed or injured. Consequence is also minimal except in an extreme case, such as 9/11. That event most certainly affected the entire nation, but the impact was primarily due to the psychological aspects and short-term economic disruptions. New security measures make it highly unlikely that a 9/11 event (turning a fuel-laden airplane into a weapon of mass destruction by flying it into a large building) could be repeated. Nevertheless, I will divide this into two categories:

Conventional Explosives

Intention x Capability x Vulnerability x Consequence = Danger
   10   x   10   x   4   x   2   = 800

Enhanced Conventional Explosives

Intention x Capability x Vulnerability x Consequence = Danger

$$10 \quad x \quad 6 \quad x \quad 6 \quad x \quad 4 \quad = 1,440$$

A Comparison of Dangers from Different Weapons

Weapon	Danger
Biological	5,600
Nuclear	5,000
Industrial Chemicals	3,600
Military-Style Chemical Weapons	1,800
Radiological	1,500
Enhanced Conventional Explosives	1,440
Conventional Explosives	800

CYBER WARFARE

According to David Keyes, former commissioner on the President's Commission on Critical Infrastructure Protection (PCCIP), the one aspect of the cyber threat that sets it apart from all other weapons discussed in this chapter is that "every computer connected to the Internet most likely experiences daily probes to identify exploitable vulnerabilities. Each day brings new stories of automated virus tools, denial-of-service attacks, IP spoofing, trojans, keystroke capture, password crackers, logic bombs, and other attack tools that are readily available on the Internet."

A few years ago, a team of computer hackers from the National Security Agency were selected as a "red team" to break into the Department of Defense computer systems. They were not allowed to use NSA hacker programs, such as the technologies NSA uses to break into al Qaeda systems, but could only use hacker programs available for free on the Internet.

This NSA red team was successful in thirty-five out of thirty-five attempts to break into various Pentagon computer systems. Even more worrisome is the fact that they were detected in only two instances. During an exercise named "Eligible Receiver," another NSA red team was able to disrupt a major military exercise in the Pacific.

Our information systems are far better protected today than they were a decade ago. When the President's Commission on Critical Infrastructure Protection released its report in 1997, it was a shocking assessment of our vulnerability. Thanks to this wake-up call and the work done in preparation for Y2K, major improvements have been realized.

On the other hand, new and more sophisticated dangers emerge nearly every day, and you don't have to be a cyber geek to become a hacker. Thousands of downloadable malicious programs are available on the Internet, free of charge, that require no skill more sophisticated than pointing and clicking. It is also interesting that two of the most challenging aspects of biowarfare are also present in cyber warfare: Attribution is problematic, and both types of attacks can be contagious. Both biological and cyber attacks can self-propagate.

Attribution was a major challenge during "Solar Sunrise." This was the name given to an attack on the Defense Department's unclassified logistics, administration, and accounting systems that control our ability to manage and deploy military forces. The attack occurred at a time of heightened tension because of Iraq's noncompliance with United Nations inspectors.

Many assumed a successful investigation would lead to a Middle Eastern source, and in fact, a major response and investigation by more than a half dozen federal agencies first traced the attack back to computer systems in the United Arab Emirates. However, it turned out the attack was conducted by two California university students who were working with a teenager in Israel.

We also witnessed what two junior college dropouts from the Philippines did with the "I Love You" virus in May 2000. This simple virus disrupted many businesses in the U.S. for an eighteen-hour period. I worry about what 1,000 computer engineers in the Chinese military, trained in the top universities in the United States and Europe, could do to our military command and control systems and to our economy.

There is no question that many nations, including the U.S., have major offensive capabilities to attack opponents' information systems. At an unclassified Air Force conference in the summer of 2006, John Thompson, chairman and chief executive officer of Symantec Corporation of Cupertino, California (a global leader in information security, best known for Norton Systems), stated: "There are at least twenty nations that have their own cyber attack programs."

David Keyes, now a private consultant, but who previously served as the FBI inspector in charge of the Office of Computer Investigations, talks of a "digital divide." He says, "True cyber security protections are only available to the very large or particularly well-financed companies. Mid-sized, and particularly small companies and individual users are hard pressed to keep up with the security challenges, much less security solutions." Keyes sees a requirement for an increased role of the federal government in providing security for small and mid-sized business and individual users. He calls this "a common defense of the electronic lanes of interstate and foreign commerce." He also calls for expanded public and private sector partnerships for cyber security.

In addition to the enormous challenges of cyber security and homeland security, the cronyism of modern American politics is a major reason why we have become our own worst enemy. Nowhere has this been better demonstrated than with the fact that the position of chief of cyber security for the Department of Homeland Security (and America) was left unfilled for a year. The main reason it went unfilled is that it is extremely difficult to find a qualified individual who is willing to work for a small fraction of what the private sector will pay for such skills and experience. It is also difficult to find highly qualified people who are willing to put up with the petty partisan politics of Washington, D.C.

An eminently qualified and patriotic candidate was finally identified, and received the endorsement of the Secretary of Homeland Security, Michael Chertoff; his deputy, Michael Jackson; and the Homeland Security Advisor to the President, Frances Townsend. Unfortunately, the candidate was rejected by the president's chief political advisor, Karl Rove. The reason: He had served in the Clinton White House. What is most disturbing about this episode is that this world-class cyber security expert had served as a Coast Guard officer, not as a political appointee. The cronyism that permeates personnel decisions within the federal government, in both Republican and Democratic camps, is a cancer that threatens our ability to defend our homeland against a determined and thinking enemy.

A THINKING ENEMY

Finally, there is one other element we must consider when analyzing the various weapons terrorists may use to attack our homeland—the human element. We are dealing with a thinking enemy. When Hurricane Andrew struck Florida in 1992 it was incredibly powerful, but it was no smarter than Hurricane Hugo, which struck South Carolina in 1989. The same is not true of terrorists. If we take appropriate actions, we can reduce the threats of hurricane force winds and storm surges, and Mother Nature will not respond with a new type of hurricane. However, a thinking enemy will adapt to our defensive efforts and continually seek out new vulnerabilities. This is why we cannot afford to put three dead bolt locks on our front door and leave the windows and back door open.

When people talk about defending our ports, they are generally talking about two issues: defending the port itself, and defending the nation from what can enter the U.S. through the port. The problem with their analysis and calls to action is that they are solely focused on inspecting the ships that enter the ports, and do not consider that a terrorist would quickly determine that the best way to attack a port would be to bring the weapons in on trucks or trains.

We have seen that conventional, enhanced conventional, radiological, and chemical weapons (at least the ones made from industrial chemicals) can be easily acquired or constructed in the U.S. Whenever you hear the politicians and pundits calling for billions of dollars to scan and inspect the cargo coming off ships, just remember that we would need to double that effort to also scan and inspect everything entering these ports from the land side.

Albert Einstein said, "The one thing more important than intelligence is imagination." The 9/11 Commission concluded that one of the major factors in our failure to prevent 9/11 was a "lack of imagination." Imagination may be the most effective weapon in the terrorists' arsenal, and the lack of it may be our greatest vulnerability. It will certainly make us our own worst enemy.

Chapter 4

Strategy

The Long View

A successful strategy is a concept of cause and effect that will produce what you are willing to accept, at a price you are willing to pay.

        —Dr. David McIntyre, Director of Integrative Center
               for Homeland Security, Texas A&M University

ON THE EVENING OF MARCH 19, 1995, MEMBERS OF THE AUM SHINRIKYO cult received a tip that Tokyo police planned to raid the cult's headquarters the next morning. During the previous two years, members of Aum had done considerable testing of chemical and crude biological weapons. They purchased a large ranch in Australia to conduct some of their experiments. However, on the evening of March 19, when the decision was made to launch a preemptive chemical attack the following morning, no chemical weapons were available.

With precursor chemicals on hand, several Aum members hastily produced a crude type of chemical weapon. Most press reports identified it as sarin. It was close, but not the high-quality sarin produced by nation-states for use in combat. Aum also lacked a sophisticated delivery system.

Early Monday morning, plastic bags filled with this poisonous liquid were placed on five trains headed to central Tokyo. The bags were wrapped in newspapers and placed on the floor. Just prior to departing the final station before central Tokyo, Aum members, some wearing masks, used the sharpened tips of umbrellas to puncture the bags, and then stepped off the train. The liquid ran onto the floor and began to evaporate, releasing toxic vapors.

Due to the poor quality of the chemical agent and primitive dispensing system, only twelve commuters died that morning. Close to 1,000 were hospitalized for more than three hours, but up to 5,000 "worried well" patients were sent or reported to hospitals. Less than one month later, terrorism returned to America.

Shortly before 9:00 A.M. on April 19, 1995, Timothy McVeigh parked a Ryder truck in front of the Murrah Federal Building in Oklahoma City. From his previous visits, he knew he was positioning his 5,000-pound diesel fuel and fertilizer bomb directly in front of and just below the child care center. He set the timing device and casually walked away. At 9:02 A.M., a thunderous explosion destroyed the front third of the building. Upper floors gave way, pancaking those below. The blast killed 168 people, including nineteen children.

In response to these two acts of terrorism, plus the lingering memory of the 1993 attack on the World Trade Center, the U.S. government was forced to take action driven by a new post–Cold War reality: The "peace dividend" was short-lived. The two oceans and two friendly neighbors that had protected the United States for more than two centuries were no longer an adequate defense against America's enemies.

Action in Washington, D.C., means spending money—lots

of money—your money. I have nothing against the government spending money. Sometimes it is even beneficial for those not writing or cashing the government checks.

But I do not want to sound too pessimistic or cynical. The National Defense Highway System, later called the Interstate Highway System, was one of the greatest returns on investment the American taxpayer has ever received, along with the G.I. Bill, which educated an entire generation of returning soldiers and played a key role in the incredible economic boom we have seen since the end of World War II. The Rural Electrification Program, various programs that helped families buy their first house, Pell Grants, Medicare, and the defense spending that protected us during the Cold War were all programs that had their fair share of waste, fraud, and abuse, but were nevertheless important to Americans. The litmus test is conducted by asking just one question: Is America better today because of these programs? The answer is yes.

Unfortunately, I cannot say the same for all the spending that has taken place since 1995 on homeland security. An appalling amount has been wasted. Shareholders in a corporation expect corporate leaders to produce a positive return, and taxpayers should expect the same from government leaders. In the corporate world, that return is measured in terms of dollars; in government, it is in terms of services, infrastructure, and security. The folks here in Washington certainly know how to get small returns on investment. They are at their worst when they are in a hurry and ask the wrong questions—or in some cases, when they don't even take the time to ask any questions at all before they just start spending.

This is precisely what happened in the late spring of 1995. "Ready! Shoot! Aim!" To an extent, this reaction is understandable. A crisis calls for immediate action—some of which will be misguided. What is not acceptable is the fact that we have seen this pattern of behavior endlessly repeated during the past decade. After the 1993 attack on the World Trade Center, and the 1995 attacks on the Murrah Federal Building in Oklahoma City and the subway in Tokyo, America began spending substantial sums of money on homeland security. Following the events of 9/11, Congress vastly increased this rate of spending, but it was not until the summer of 2002 that the White House actually published a national strategy for securing the homeland. And even then, the term "strategy" was a misnomer. The principal author of the document agreed it was not a strategy so much as it was a "good plan." Well, at least we finally had a plan—better than the "Ready! Shoot! Aim!" of the previous six years, but still not the longer-range holistic strategy that we need.

Unfortunately, as of this writing, America still does not have a long-range, comprehensive strategy for defending the American homeland. This is why it frequently appears that the right hand is not communicating with the left hand. It's also why we are spending enormous sums of money and enacting legislation that damages our economy, and fails to provide the security we require.

In preparation for a congressional hearing in 2004, I was asked to examine six strategies published by the Bush administration since the summer of 2002: the National Security Strategy of the United States of America, the National Strategy for Homeland Security, the National Strategy for Combating Terrorism, the National Strategy to Combat Weapons of Mass Destruction, the National Strategy to Secure Cyberspace, and the National Strategy for the Physical Protection of Critical Infrastructures and Key Assets. These are all useful documents. Some provide strategies for certain sectors, and most provide good plans. However, not a single one provides a national strategy for defending the American homeland that is all-encompassing in terms of missions and participants.

That is what is missing: a single, unifying strategy that

integrates *all missions*—from deterrence, prevention and preemption, to incident management and recovery—and *all participants*—from the president to the police officer, from members of Congress to mayors, from a cabinet secretary to a soldier, and from a county public health officer to a corporate CEO. It is also vital that we develop a strategy that all American citizens can understand. Some would question whether it is possible to develop a concise yet broad strategy such as "Europe first" in World War II and "containment" in the Cold War. I believe it is not only possible, but essential to our success, and there is certainly precedent.

In 1947, George Kennan provided America with a strategy that guided eight presidents and twenty Congresses, and ultimately led to victory in the Cold War. It was a strategy that could be boiled down to a single word: *containment*. Kennan stated that if we and our allies contained Soviet expansion, their empire would eventually collapse from its own inefficiencies. That strategic concept guided us through the Berlin Crisis of 1948, the creation of NATO, the Korean War, the Cuban Missile Crisis, the Vietnam War, our efforts in Latin America to replace totalitarian regimes with democracies, and perhaps most importantly, the collapse of the Soviet empire, and along with it the threat of global thermonuclear war. That single concept, and the philosophy behind it, guided policy and spending programs for more than three decades. In 2006, the Bush administration published several updated strategies (including National Security and Combating Terrorism), but no one has yet to offer a single unifying strategy for the challenges ahead.

Here is a good question: How many leaders in this nation have read the six strategy documents? Not many, I suspect. But if leaders have not read these documents, how can they successfully develop and implement plans and programs to defend our homeland? If you were a football coach, would you take your team to the Super Bowl without a game plan? In essence, that is exactly what our leaders are doing.

It is always easy to complain and criticize; such behavior is a blood sport in partisan politics and punditry. Therefore, following my criticism, I offered the congressional committee my proposal for a strategy. I was fortunate to have learned how to think about strategy from the best teachers in the nation, perhaps the world—the faculty of the National War College.

To design a single strategy for homeland security, one must begin with assumptions, and these assumptions are far different from those during the Cold War, or perhaps any other time in our history. Strategists talk of *ends, ways,* and *means.*

> Ends—what is it that we are trying to achieve?
> Ways—how are we going to do it?
> Means—what resources will we use?

Most agree that the *ways* and *means* have changed dramatically.

During the Cold War, preemption and preventive war were considered taboo, because they were euphemisms for first use of nuclear weapons. Whether or not you agreed with President George W. Bush's decision to oust Saddam Hussein from power in Iraq, preemption and preventive war are clearly options for American security policy in the twenty-first century. In Afghanistan, the U.S. Army, which for decades had prepared for large tank battles in Central Europe and the deserts of Southwest Asia, found its soldiers riding into battle on horseback and using laser designators to guide 500-pound bombs that were being dropped from 1960s-era airplanes built to fight a nuclear war. The *ways* and *means* have definitely changed. I am not confident, however, that most understand the change in the *end state.*

When America entered World War II, we believed that Nazi

Germany and Imperial Japan could be defeated. When the Cold War began, we believed that a containment of Soviet expansion would eventually lead to the collapse of the Soviet empire. But who today truly believes we can defeat terrorism?

First of all, the concept of a War on Terror is foolishness. We can no more conduct a war against terrorism than we can against blitzkrieg. Blitzkrieg was a *type* of warfare used by Nazi Germany in World War II. We can and did win a war against Nazi Germany, but we can't win a war against blitzkrieg or terrorism. I understand why we initially used this term after 9/11. We didn't want to sound like we were planning a "crusade against the Muslim world." But the fact remains (and President Bush finally got around to admitting it three years after 9/11) that this is a war against al Qaeda.

Is it possible to win the war against al Qaeda? Good question. The answer is maybe, but it will take a long time and will require a lot more than just military power. We must understand that even a total victory in the war against al Qaeda does not secure the American homeland. Technology is what has changed the international security environment, not hatred. Hatred has always existed, but never before could a small group of individuals on the far side of the globe threaten a superpower. Therefore, our strategy must be more encompassing than just a war against al Qaeda, even though this has become the focus of today's war.

So the fundamental question is whether we can win the war against all those who would threaten our homeland. The answer is quite simple, yet very difficult for elected and appointed officials to say in public: "No." But until we are ready to admit the obvious, we will continue to flounder. We must build our strategy on reality, not fantasy and political rhetoric. A perfect analogy can be found in the world of medicine.

In 1967, the president of the American Medical Association stated that the end of infectious disease was at hand through the use of vaccination and antibiotics. Obviously he was mistaken. While it may be possible to eradicate some infectious diseases, just as it may be possible to eliminate al Qaeda, winning the war against terror is as likely as winning the war against all infectious diseases.

A ten-year World Health Organization program successfully eradicated smallpox in 1977. This was a disease that killed 300 million people in the first three quarters of the twentieth century. Earlier attempts by WHO to eradicate malaria had failed, because malaria was carried by mosquitoes. Smallpox has no animal host, and can only be passed from human to human. There had been a continuous human chain from as early as the Egyptian pharaoh Ramses V to Ali Mallin in 1977, the last human to suffer from naturally occurring smallpox. Once that 3,000-plus-years chain had been broken for just a few months, the disease was eradicated. On the other hand, it is not possible to eradicate polio. The polio virus can live in human intestines for up to fifteen years. We can successfully contain polio with vaccination, but we can't stop giving the polio vaccine like we did for smallpox. Likewise, when talking about attacks on our homeland, the best we can do is limit their frequency and severity.

Therefore, a strategy to defend the homeland is far more complex than winning the war against al Qaeda. We must understand this is about a permanent change in the international security environment. We must think long-term, and we must seek an end state that is realistic. Small actors can now threaten a superpower, and this fact will not change.

Therefore, a single unifying strategy for defending the American homeland must look beyond a single group, tactic, or weapons technology. Rather, it must include the following elements:

- Relentless pursuit, on a multilateral basis when possible, of individuals and organizations who threaten our homeland, including those who support them.

- Renewed and aggressive programs to prevent the proliferation of weapons of mass destruction, particularly nuclear and biological weapons—such as the Nunn-Lugar Cooperative Threat Reduction program.
- Concerted effort to win the war of ideas, particularly important in the information age—an excellent, yet the least-publicized, recommendation from the 9/11 Commission.
- Development of standards for prevention, mitigation, and incident management programs that are fiscally sustainable for the long haul.
- Understanding that overreactions by Congress and the administration could cause more long-term damage to the American economy than terrorists.

The word I use to describe this strategy is not new. I borrowed it from George Kennan. In 1947 he coined the term *containment*. However, the philosophy behind the strategy of containment in the twenty-first century is far different from Kennan's strategy for containing the Soviet empire. It is unrealistic and even naive to believe that we can permanently end terrorism or terrorist threats to our homeland. In early 2004, General Wesley Clark stated (in a television advertisement) that if elected president, he could prevent attacks on the American homeland—a preposterous idea that he quickly withdrew, shortly before he withdrew from the race. Nevertheless, in the case of defending our homeland, we all hate to admit the truth, but the reality is that we cannot defeat terrorism. Not only can we not win the War on Terror, we likely will not win the war against al Qaeda in the short term either.

Unconditional surrender by Germany and Japan ended the threat that caused us to enter World War II. Unconditional surrender by all terrorist individuals and organizations is not a realistic goal, and former Homeland Security Secretary Tom

Ridge knew this when he stated, "There will be no victory parades." He is absolutely correct. Therefore, let us make our strategy reflect this reality. We should seek to control certain factors, or better yet, *contain* the threat from terrorism. We must *contain* the capabilities, global reach, and financial resources of terrorists and terrorist organizations. We must *contain* the proliferation of weapons of mass destruction, particularly those weapons that most threaten our survival, nuclear and biological. We must *contain* the spread of hatred with our own proactive campaign in the war of ideas. We must *contain* the vulnerabilities of our nation. And we must seek to *contain* our response to the new threats. We must not overreact.

Some will respond that this is a defeatist strategy. I say it is realistic. We cannot stop every determined suicide bomber, but we must prevent a terrorist organization from obtaining nuclear arms, and we must be prepared to quickly detect, respond to, and recover from a biological attack. We can't kill, capture, or deter every terrorist, but must *contain* them by limiting their capabilities, their global reach, and their financial resources. We cannot prevent the proliferation of all weapons of mass destruction. Chemical agents, including industrial chemicals, are far too easy to produce or buy. Radiological material for use in a dirty bomb has already proliferated beyond control. It exists in most hospitals, laboratories, and even at many large construction sites around the world. However, we must *contain* the proliferation of nuclear weapons and we must take actions to *contain* a biological attack on our homeland. Because of the biotech revolution, it is no longer possible to prevent terrorists from getting their hands on bioweapons. We must therefore prepare to *contain* such an attack on our homeland. We must prevent a biocrisis from becoming a biocatastrophe.

We must also work to *contain* the terrorists' capability to conduct fund-raising and recruiting operations inside U.S. borders. Radical Islamists support schools, organizations, and special programs around the world, some in our own country. Registered with the IRS as 501(c)3 charitable institutions, members preach hatred and violence against America and Americans. One such organization raised millions in "charitable donations" from a two-person office in a northern Virginia strip mall.

Terrorists have learned how to use our freedom of speech and religion guarantees to hide their recruiting and fund-raising activities. A University of South Florida professor, Dr. Ramadan Abdullah Shallah, also served as the director of the World Islamic Studies Enterprise (WISE) where he raised money and recruited followers. On two occasions he was invited to speak at U.S. Central Command at MacDill Air Force Base, Florida. When Fathi Shikaki, the leader of Islamic Jihad, was assassinated, Shallah quickly departed Florida. He was next seen in news clips from Damascus in his new role as the newly elected leader of Islamic Jihad, a terrorist organization based in Syria that primarily operates in the West Bank and Gaza.

We cannot end all coordinated information campaigns against the United States, but we must retaliate with our own offensive campaign to *contain* this contagion of hatred, disinformation, and instigation. During a 2006 Aspen Institute conference, former President Bill Clinton talked about the value of being seen as "the good guys."

There are two Muslim countries where our standing is better than it was a couple of years ago, and they are both important: one of the largest, Indonesia, and the other, the most troublesome, Pakistan, because it's home to so many Taliban and al-Qaeda sympathizers—the reasons are the tsunami and the earthquake. When President [George H. W.] Bush and I took our first trip over the tsu-

nami and earthquake area, we visited these little kids.
Part of their therapy was to draw pictures of what they
saw. Picture after picture after picture . . . American
military helicopters dropping food, not bombs.

Increased funding for humanitarian, information, and educational programs targeted at key areas and audiences will provide far more than just humanitarian assistance. They are high-priority initiatives for securing the American homeland.

Another critical element in our effort to contain the spread of hatred is a concerted effort to convince Islamic clerics and other Islamic leaders to unconditionally condemn acts of terror directed at innocent civilians. All too often, we hear Islamic leaders respond to an attack, such as the 2005 subway attack in London, by saying, "We do not condone these actions, but we do understand the grievances of these young men." They must stop using these qualifiers. The correct response must always be, "There are no circumstances that justify the killing of innocent civilians."

One of the most effective information initiatives in the war against Islamic terrorists comes from the world of rock and roll. Last year I interviewed Ahmad Dhani, the lead singer of a rock group called Dewa, who is often referred to as "Indonesia's John Lennon" (interview available at www.hlsinsideandout.org). Dhani was raised by a fundamentalist father who sent him to a Wahhabi school where he was taught a radical, violent form of Islam that included hate for all infidels. However, as a teenager, he rejected this cult of hatred and embraced rock and roll. Dhani maintains that "rock and roll is about love and peace, not war and hatred." Watching videos of his performances in Indonesia brings back memories of the Beatles in Yankee Stadium—for those of you under forty, ask your parents. Tens of thousands of screaming teenagers drowned out the music of the Beatles. When Dhani begins singing "Warriors of Love," tens of thousands of young Indonesians go into the same frenzy that captured millions of American teenagers in the mid-1960s. Information, education, communication, and perhaps even rock and roll and popular culture are some of our most effective weapons in this war.

Finally, we must *contain* our impulse to overreact. We are a free and open nation. That makes us a target-rich environment for terrorists. We must take prudent and fiscally responsible actions to reduce these vulnerabilities, and implement realistic and measurable prevention and incident management programs. The measurement aspect is critically important. If we do not set standards and goals, how can we measure progress?

One distinguished group of Americans released an often quoted report in late 2003. Despite the fact that the task force members had incredibly impressive résumés (three Nobel Laureates, two retired four-star generals and one retired four-star admiral, a former U.S. senator, a former director of the FBI and CIA, several CEOs of major defense contractors, and the commissioner of the National Football League), the majority had no particular qualifications in either homeland security or first responder issues. In fact, only one of the task force members had any experience in state and local government, and that was as a lawyer and state attorney general.

Nevertheless, the members called for an *increase* in spending for first responders that would approach $100 billion over five years. But in 2003, no one had yet established standards and measurable goals for such programs. (For the most part, we still have not.) How did they determine this number? Actually, they went to all the first responder associations and asked what resources they would like to have at their disposal. (My three daughters would have loved for me to have established their school clothing allowance in much the same manner—"Just tell me what you want.") As you might have guessed, I would call this asking the wrong question. How did this task force expect Congress to allocate and prioritize spending? ("Ready! Shoot! Aim!"?) The proposal would certainly be great for pork and sending money to every congressional district. Unfortunately, it also had a partisan political agenda.

Despite the fact that the distinguished task force members represented a wide swath of political loyalties, the project director, who can often have enormous influence, was nowhere close to nonpartisan. In fact, when the task force was first announced, he asked me to work with him. He said, "We are really going to stick it to the Republicans. We are going to prove that they aren't doing anything to help first responders." His focus was the 2004 election—not first responders, and not the American people. (I declined the offer to work on this effort.) Neither partisan politics nor pork barrel projects will make us more secure. Furthermore, emotionally driven, massive spending programs after the next attack, either in our homeland or in the homeland of our allies, will not make our families more secure. (Members of Congress, please wind your watches.)

We must *contain* our impulse for overreaction. This tendency for impulse spending and overregulation will most likely occur during election years and immediately following terrorist attacks. In the first sixty days following 9/11, the House of Representatives saw 132 bills introduced that had the term "Homeland Security" in the titles. What will make us more secure is a single unifying strategy that all Americans can understand—a strategy that provides a vision, realistic and measurable goals, and clear priorities for how to best allocate our limited resources. *Containment* is the single, unifying strategy that provides the common thread to all other strategies and plans associated with defending the American homeland. It is a strategy that provides guidance for actions and spending. It is attainable, and it is affordable. Containment is both the strategy and the end state we seek.

Chapter 5

Priorities

Where Do We Focus the Spending?

To defend America from the Soviet Union, Congress provided funds to the Department of Defense and the intelligence community. The dangers of the twenty-first century require funding programs in the Departments of Homeland Security, Health and Human Services, Justice, Agriculture, Defense, Treasury, the Environmental Protection Agency, the intelligence community, and state and local governments.

One estimate stated that there are as many as 87,000 government jurisdictions in the United States—most, or perhaps all of which look to Washington, D.C., for homeland security funding. How can the federal government possibly establish priorities within all these stovepipes?

My recommendation is that we focus our efforts on dangers, not organizations.

Some will say that the range of these dangers is nearly as diverse as the government organizations involved. That may be true, but remember that there are only two dangers capable of bringing this nation to its knees—*nuclear* and *biological weapons*. These two dangers must receive top priority for spending. Additionally, education programs and information systems can provide substantial security benefits for a broad range of dangers—from weapons of mass destruction to suicide bombers in shopping malls.

I rated the danger of bioterrorism higher than nuclear terrorism, mostly due to the fact that the technology required to build and deliver biological weapons is easier for terrorists to obtain. Nevertheless, I will begin this chapter with nuclear weapons. Why? Because defending this nation against nuclear terrorism is far simpler than defending it against bioterrorism. Let me clarify: I didn't say easier, I said simpler.

NUCLEAR WEAPONS

Since 9/11, Congress has held many hearings on the subject of preventing nuclear weapons from being smuggled into the United States, but the first such hearing was in 1947. Dr. Robert Oppenheimer, often referred to as the father of the atomic bomb, was called as a witness. He was asked what America needed to do to prevent atomic weapons from being smuggled through U.S. ports. He advised Congress to "buy lots of screwdrivers." This was long before steel containers and container ships. The majority of cargo was transported in wooden crates. Oppenheimer said we would need to purchase large numbers of screwdrivers to open each and every wooden crate and look inside. His tongue-in-cheek response made as much sense as inspecting 100 percent of containers today. Unfortunately, Congress still doesn't seem to get the joke. For that matter, neither do many editorialists, columnists, and security "experts."

At times it appears as if many of our leaders have not learned much since the "screwdriver hearings" of 1947. On the other hand, most of the decision makers in Washington do understand that prevention is the only viable strategy. There are no means to mitigate the effects of a nuclear detonation. Once the Soviets improved the accuracy of their missiles, we learned that even a reinforced facility buried under tons of solid granite in the Rocky Mountains was vulnerable. It is physically and economically impossible to harden America against a nuclear attack, and in contrast to a biological attack, there is no effective response. Therefore, virtually all are in agreement—the only effective strategy is prevention. The question is, how do we do it?

The most common strategy calls for a multilayered defense. I have no problem with multiple layers, but I do question the assignment of priority given to these different layers.

Whether we are talking about nuclear weapons, bombs carried on airliners, or a chemical attack in a subway, our focus should not be on preventing such events two minutes and ten meters prior, but two months and 10,000 miles in advance.

In other words, I have no problem with the multilayered defense of passenger screening at airports, hardened cockpit doors, armed sky marshals, and armed pilots, but the priority for spending and action should be on intelligence and law enforcement operations, both at home and overseas. One only has to look at the terrorist plot to blow up airliners over the Atlantic in August 2006 to recognize the value of these communities and the work they do. This is particularly true in the case of nuclear weapons. Unfortunately, that is not what we are doing. Why? First of all, it is very difficult to establish priorities when no one is in charge of defending America against nuclear terrorism. Hard to believe, but true. *There is no single person in charge of defending America against a nuclear attack.*

During the first presidential debate of the 2004 campaign, both candidates stated that if elected, their number one goal would be to halt the proliferation of nuclear weapons. Unfortunately, neither the Bush administration nor Congress is placing the proper priority on locating, locking down, and eliminating weapons-grade nuclear material. This is not just my opinion. On

March 31, 2005, the Commission on the Intelligence Capabilities of the United States Regarding Weapons of Mass Destruction, also known as the Robb-Silberman Commission, released its final report. Its assessment of the intelligence community's lack of focus on nuclear weapons was frightening:

We would like to emphasize that the United States has not made [intelligence] collection on loose nukes a high priority.

In a hearing before the House of Representatives Homeland Security Committee on April 19, 2005, I read this and asked, "What could possibly be a higher priority?" None of the fifteen Members of Congress attending this hearing volunteered an answer to my question.

The current Bush administration plan for replacing the highly enriched uranium in those 100-plus research reactors around the world with low-enriched uranium (which allows for research but cannot be used to build a bomb) is totally unacceptable. The current program does not call for the completion of the process until after 2014. Here is a good question: Why is it taking so long? The U.S. government has been moving at such a glacial pace that a privately funded organization, the Nuclear Threat Initiative, funded the removal of HEU from the research reactor in Belgrade in the former Yugoslavia. This facility contained 100 pounds of HEU (enough to build at least two bombs). During the air campaign in 1999, this facility was clearly marked as off-limits to air strikes. Three years after the war ended, the State and Energy Departments were still debating whether they should pay the $5 million demanded by the then Yugoslav government. Frustrated with government inaction, Ted Turner, the founder of NTI, wrote the $5 million check to make sure this material did not fall into the hands of another bidder, or well-armed terrorists. It is inexplicable that such an important program for U.S. security must be accomplished by a not-for-profit organization. For more details on the great work currently performed by NTI, see www.nti.org.

Compounding the problem that no one in the federal government has overall responsibility for preventing a nuclear attack on the American homeland is the fact that it seems to be part of our culture, with some strong support from the homeland security industrial complex, to look for technological "silver bullets." Therefore, we end up with a policy that favors high-tech screening devices in our seaports, effectively narrowing our focus to that last two minutes and ten meters.

The president's budget for fiscal year 2006 proposed the creation of a new organization to help protect America against nuclear terrorism: the Domestic Nuclear Detection Office (DNDO) in the Department of Homeland Security. When I was asked to advise Congress on this proposal in the spring of 2005, many details regarding the roles and responsibilities had yet to be determined. However, the word "domestic" led me to believe its focus would be inside U.S. borders. That's all well and good, except for one tiny, overlooked fact: The vast majority of the nuclear material that could fall into terrorists' hands is *outside* the U.S. Additionally, the ability to detect nuclear material inside our borders should be our last line of defense, not our first. Detection certainly falls under the category of the last two minutes and ten meters, and in the case of a nuclear weapon, that's two minutes and ten meters too late. A goal-line defense doesn't work against nuclear weapons. (Many individuals in DNDO agree with this assessment.)

As I walked into the Capitol that day, I noticed a gamma detector just outside the building. During the hearing I asked the chairman of the committee, "Why are you spending my tax dollars putting gamma detectors outside this building? Don't you understand that when a nuclear weapon gets that close, it's already too late?" Once again, none of the fifteen members of Congress attending this hearing volunteered an answer to my question. Wouldn't it also be too late when a nuke gets inside the harbor in New York, Baltimore, Los Angeles, or San Francisco?

One other problem that stands in the way of a more rational approach to the nuclear threat is the homeland security industrial complex. President Dwight Eisenhower warned us about the military-industrial complex as he was leaving office. Today, we have a problem with its cousin. I have been involved in national security for four decades, and at no previous time have I witnessed such problems as we currently have in the Department of Homeland Security. When Ike talked about the military-industrial complex, they were two separate and distinct entities—the military and corporate America. Today, they are commingled.

Here are three examples of the incestuous relationships that exist within the homeland security industrial complex since the summer of 2006. My sources will remain unnamed, but they are three senior leaders inside the Department of Homeland Security who are as frustrated about this issue as I am.

- A directorate with 122 people has only three government employees; the rest are civilian contractors.
- A highly paid contractor who holds a position in DHS in the summer of 2006 did his work from a boat in the Caribbean. This is not some highly dedicated individual checking e-mail while on vacation; this is where he routinely "went to work" in the morning.
- According to a June 29, 2006, *Washington Post* article ("U.S. Cybersecurity Chief May Have Conflict of Interest"), a division director, four levels below the secretary, was receiving an annual salary of $100,000 more than Homeland Security Secretary Michael Chertoff. According to a September

22, 2006, AP story, this individual received $245,481 from the U.S. government, and an additional $43,320 each year from Carnegie Mellon University. This individual was hired under a program called the Intergovernmental Personnel Act. This program allows for assignments from or to state and local governments, universities, and not-for-profit organizations through temporary assignment of highly skilled personnel. (I'm not criticizing the IPA program, which generally offers a valuable service by providing highly skilled individuals from the private sector to augment the government workforce.) However, in three decades of government service I had never heard of an IPA or government employee receiving such a large salary. Frankly, I didn't believe the press report, so I asked a senior leader at DHS to confirm. To my shock and dismay, he did. Additionally, the *Washington Post* reported that Carnegie Mellon University received $19 million in contracts from DHS in 2005. (Carnegie Mellon University denied any link between this individual's work in cyber security at DHS, and the cyber security contract they had with DHS.)

We used to worry about the revolving door, where senior officials resign their government position on Friday and show up for work the following Monday as a corporate vice president of a prime government contractor. Today we seem to have made it possible to make the big bucks while still inside the government.

Since a large number of government jobs go unfilled, and those who do take them tend to leave after a year or two, contractors have quickly become the corporate memory and have significant power within DHS. Add to this the fact that defense and homeland security contractors will make a lot more money by building radiological detectors for our ports than they would by supporting programs such as the Nunn-Lugar Cooperative

Threat Reduction program, and you will understand why we are headed down the wrong road.

In addition to the civilian contractors in the Department of Homeland Security, there are many other people who are not DHS employees. The Science and Technology Directorate is filled with people "on loan" from Department of Energy national laboratories. (Providing "on-loan" personnel is a common practice in the federal government. The parent organization pays the salary and benefits, but the on-loan personnel work in a host agency.) Sometimes the parent agencies farm out their problem children to on-loan programs, but often these on-loan people are brilliant scientists and engineers. Yet world-class credentials in physics and engineering do not necessarily make one a strategic planner or competent project manager. Nevertheless, the science and technology cabal control the largest pots of available funds, which gives them major influence over policy. This is exactly the opposite of what should be happening. When I was a military pilot, I wanted the best aeronautical engineers in the world designing my airplanes, but those same scientists were not necessarily the best people to develop the air-tasking orders for fighting an airwar. Here is just one example of why I say this.

Several years ago I received a proposal from two nuclear physicists at one of America's major defense laboratories. They had heard my objections to major funding for screening devices in seaports, and they sent a proposal that they believed would change my mind. But before I get to the proposal, let me explain why I object to this type of spending.

First, I assume that anyone smart enough to obtain a nuclear device will be smart enough to put half an inch of lead around it. Highly enriched uranium is a very low emitter of radiation. Even this limited amount of shielding will allow the nuclear material to move undetected through our most capable radiological detectors.

Second, if you and I were standing in a country on the far side of the globe, and I gave you $500 million in cash with the promise that if you could get the money into the U.S., it would be yours, tax-free, would you rent a forty-foot steel container and put it on a ship? I surely wouldn't. I would never take my hands off that money. Most likely, I would rent a corporate jet, file a flight plan, and fly into the U.S. (Remember, I do not need to get it through Customs or any kind of inspection. The only requirement is to get the money to the U.S.) If I chose to transport the money by sea, I would bring it across the ocean on a private ship, and then transfer to a high-speed boat for the last 50 to 100 miles. There are 95,000 miles of unguarded coastline in the U.S. Or, as former Ambassador Robert Gallucci, now of Georgetown University, likes to say (referring to nukes), "Why not just hide it inside a bale of marijuana? People have no problem getting *that* into the U.S."

Third, if I was going to use a large ship to bring it into a port, I would not put it on a container ship. I would put it inside a large bulk carrier, such as a grain ship or oil tanker, which would make it impossible to detect with current or even planned technologies.

Why do I use $500 million as my example? Because you and I would like to have $500 million, but bin Laden and other terrorists would place far more value on a nuclear weapon they could use to attack a U.S. city. We would never take our hands off the money, and they would never take their hands off a nuke. If a nuke ever comes to America, it will not be inside a forty-foot container, but that is where the majority of "experts" want to look. They are asking the wrong question. Do you remember the old story about the guy standing on a street corner looking down at the sidewalk? A police officer says, "What are you doing?"

The man says, "I lost my wallet. I am looking for it."

The police officer responds, "Did you lose it right here?"

"No," says the gentleman, "I dropped it in that alley over there."

The police officer asks, "Then why are you looking here?"

The gentleman replies, "Because the light is better over here."

This is an old story my grandfather told me fifty years ago, yet many have not learned the simple lesson it conveys.

Now back to the two physicists from one of our most prestigious national labs who were convinced that technology was the answer. Their proposal acknowledged the fact that HEU is a low emitter of radiation. However, they concluded that if a nuclear weapon, even one that was shielded, could be scanned for a long period of time, enough radiation would reach the detector. Since it would not be practical to significantly delay containers in ports, their proposal was to put detectors in all vehicles in the U.S. capable of containing a nuclear weapon. They knew it would make it through the port, but at least we could detect and locate it prior to reaching a target. (I can only assume they never visited the ports in cities such as New York, Baltimore, Philadelphia, or San Francisco, or they would have realized that these major metropolitan areas are within the nuclear blast radius of their ports.)

After reading the first few pages of the proposal, I became convinced that one of my friends was pulling my chain, and started looking around the room for the hidden TV camera. But I was wrong; this was a real proposal from two physicists at a national laboratory. They wanted to put radiological detectors with satellite communication devices in every vehicle in the U.S. capable of carrying a nuclear weapon—in other words, virtually every vehicle larger than a small sedan. I am not going to waste any more ink, paper, or your time further explaining their proposal, but this is an example of what happens when the wrong people become involved in developing strategy and policy. Policy should drive the requirements for science and technology, but that is not always the case in a culture enamored with technology—always in search of a technological silver bullet.

Five years after 9/11, there is still no undersecretary for policy in the Department of Homeland Security, but there has been an undersecretary for science and technology, one with a huge budget. DHS S&T is directly linked to the Department of Energy national laboratories and is a full partner in the homeland security–industrial complex, which means that science and technology are driving policy and strategy—exactly the opposite of what should be happening. So what can we do? Simple: Develop a strategy, organization, and funding priorities to prevent al Qaeda or any other terrorist organization from getting its hands on weapons-grade nuclear materials. There should be no higher priority for the defense, homeland security, law enforcement, and intelligence communities than "locating, locking down, and eliminating weapons-grade nuclear materials." That is where we should focus our spending.

I have no objections whatsoever to research and development funding for a new generation of radiological detectors, but we need to do this with our eyes wide open. During a hearing, a member of Congress began his question by stating, "Colonel, I know you do not have much faith in our current detectors, but technology doubles every eighteen months. We will soon have the capability to effectively screen all containers coming into our ports." I politely replied, "Sir, I think you are confusing Moore's Law, which states that the power of computers will double every eighteen months, with the law of physics. Physics does not change. HEU is a low emitter."

There are proposals for "active interrogation" rather than the current "passive scanning," but that technology is as of yet unproven. (Passive scanning is similar to the radio receiver in your car; it only receives signals. Active interrogation is like radar; a device sends out a signal and then interprets what bounces back.) If it does prove useful, I would recommend the first devices be placed around facilities in the former Soviet Union to detect anyone attempting to move weapons-grade nuclear material out of those facilities. I would also recommend sharing these devices with other nuclear powers so they could better secure their facilities. But until we have a single person or single office in charge of nuclear security, the uncoordinated funding that now runs through the Department of Homeland Security, the Department of Defense, the Department of Energy, and the Department of State will never be used in the most effective manner.

The Department of Defense should maintain the mission of nuclear deterrence. Our strategic missile force, both land-based and submarine-based, provides us with a superb deterrence against nation-states. Any nation that fires a 10-kiloton warhead at the U.S. (about half of a Hiroshima bomb) should expect to receive 10 megatons in return (about 500 Hiroshima bombs). Nuclear deterrence will continue to work against nation-states in the twenty-first century, but has virtually no effect on nonstate actors. Therefore, the first step must be to put a single person in charge of protecting this nation from nuclear terrorism. It should not be a part-time job for the secretary of defense, or Energy, State, or Homeland Security. The second step is to develop spending priorities to support our strategy of containment. I recommend the following. These are not exact figures, but representative of the spending priorities that will provide the best return on investment. Unfortunately, they are not representative of the current priorities of Congress and this administration. (My recommendations first appeared in a *Wall Street Journal* op-ed article on May 25, 2006.)

- Seventy percent of funding should be spent on preventing terrorists from obtaining weapons-grade nuclear material. This includes involving multiple disciplines, agencies, and programs. These actions would be funded and coordinated by a single cabinet-level official. This individual would be responsible for strategy, policy, and control of funding for all nuclear defense programs other than the Defense Department's deterrent force. Furthermore, we must ensure that this goal is the top priority for the intelligence community. Hopefully, we will have learned the lessons from the creation of the Department of Homeland Security and not make any foolish promises, such as "the creation of this new organization will be revenue-neutral" (Washington-speak for doing it on the cheap—which is how you end up with an office in DHS comprised of 3 government employees and 119 contractors). Of course it will cost money. It will be one of the most important functions of the U.S. government. This will not merely be drawing a new wiring diagram for the organizational chart.

- Twenty percent of funding should be allocated to the pursuit and recapture of material and devices should weapons-grade nuclear materials fall into terrorists' hands. One requirement is the need for a comprehensive, operational concept on pursuing and recapturing weapons-grade nuclear material. In close cooperation with friends and allies, host nation counterterrorism capabilities must be improved. The U.S. must also maintain the capability to unilaterally pursue and recapture weapons-grade nuclear material overseas. Supporting this operational concept should be research and development funds for new detection technology. A new generation of active detectors could offer far better capabilities than the current passive technology. Regardless, detectors, both current and next-generation, should not be placed at fixed sites in ports, and the ports with detectors should not be listed on the Internet, as they are now. One aspect of the operational concept would be to employ highly mobile detectors, not only to keep the terrorists guessing as to their location, but also to allow for the flexibility of rapid deployment in response to intelligence information.

- Ten percent should be spent on response and mitigation capabilities should a nuclear detonation occur. Developing prepositioned equipment for responders and the American population is required.

Bottom Line on Nuclear Defense

The deterrence strategy that defended America against nuclear attack during the Cold War will continue to defend America from a nuclear attack by a nation-state in the twenty-first century. The 70 percent figure above does not include the cost of these nuclear deterrent forces.

Defending our homeland from nuclear terrorism requires more than just money. Serious political and diplomatic roadblocks have hindered certain aspects of the Nunn-Lugar Cooperative Threat Reduction program. Strong bipartisan and multinational support is required. Locating, locking down, and eventually eliminating the massive quantities of weapons-grade material from the former Soviet Union must be one of our top three priorities. Another top priority is the funding, and political and diplomatic support, for the exchange of low-enriched uranium for the highly enriched uranium in those 100-plus research reactors around the world. We cannot wait until 2014 to complete this job. Finally, the intelligence community must be directed to ensure that collection activities on the nuclear threat are given the absolute top priority. It was a great success when the A. Q. Khan operation in Pakistan was shut down. Unfortunately, before this happened, he had provided technical assistance and equipment to our enemies around the world. Why did it take us so long? The Robb-Silberman Commission has answered that question. I find its assessment so disturbing that I repeat it here to end this section. If you have the opportunity to talk to your elected representatives in Washington, remember this quote:

We would like to emphasize that the United States has not made [intelligence] collection on loose nukes a high priority.

Ask them, "Why not?"

BIOLOGICAL WEAPONS

Protecting America against nuclear terrorism is a daunting challenge, but the solution is straightforward—we need to prevent the terrorists from obtaining weapons-grade nuclear material. Unfortunately, protecting America against bioterrorism is far more complex, and therefore, a far greater challenge. Equally troubling is the fact that the revolution in biotechnology means that the likelihood of a sophisticated biological attack during the next decade is far greater than a nuclear attack.

Going back to the strategy of *containment,* we must understand that it is not possible to prevent bio-attacks. Therefore, the major emphasis in biodefense must be investments in response and mitigation of consequences. Until our senior leaders will admit to this in public, we will not make significant progress.

There are no actions that the president, Congress, or anyone else can take to prevent terrorists from obtaining and weaponizing these pathogens. It is only a matter of time until a significant bioterrorism event occurs. And when it does happen, because of the reload factor, it may not be a single event. Someday, terrorists may be able to obtain a nuclear weapon, but it is not likely that they would be able to buy or steal many. On the other hand, once a terrorist organization learns how to make a few ounces of a weaponized pathogen, making pounds will be cheap and easy. A pound of high-quality, weaponized *Bacillus anthracis* (anthrax) properly dispensed on a U.S. city would constitute a major biological attack.

Biodefense efforts require a broad range of initiatives by federal, state, and local governments, plus the private sector. Such initiatives include research and development for vaccines and medicines, improvements in early detection, rapid diagnosis and situational awareness, significant expansion of medical care surge capacity, and public engagement. This will be a very expensive endeavor, but so was our victory in the Cold War. The stakes are the same: national survival. The good news is that there will be significant dual benefits from this activity. The vast majority of these efforts will likely result in major breakthroughs in the prevention and treatment of a wide range of naturally occurring infectious diseases such as pandemic flu, and perhaps even some chronic diseases.

Even though I firmly believe that knee-jerk reaction and feel-good spending programs, "Ready! Shoot! Aim!" activities, and pork barrel spending in the name of homeland security are major threats to the long-term security of your family and financial well-being, I am not against all major spending programs. During the next decade, America will need to spend a huge sum of money on biodefense. But I am concerned that certain key segments of our biodefense system are neither properly organized nor prepared for such a massive spending program.

From my perspective, not as a public health expert (which I am not), but as a national security strategist, I can tell you that a national public health system in the twenty-first century will be as important to national security as the Department of Defense was in the twentieth century. Unfortunately, America's public health system is in very poor shape.

This is not just my opinion. Dr. D. A. Henderson, who spent eighteen years as the dean of the School of Public Health at Johns

Hopkins University, agrees with my assessment. So does Dr. Elin Gursky, one of the nation's top authorities on public health. Dr. Gursky has spent almost two decades in public health practice in local and state government and in the private sector, and today advises both the legislative and executive branches of the federal government on public health issues.

I am not criticizing the half million people who work in federal, state, and local public health offices. Most are highly dedicated, overworked, and underappreciated. The problem, however, is four-fold: No one is in charge, there are serious deficiencies in the federal funding process, the current organization for response to large-scale disasters is dysfunctional, and finally, the majority of people working in state and local public health offices don't see preparedness for bio-attacks as their primary mission.

First, no one is in charge of biodefense in America. According to a 2005 report from the Center for Biosecurity–UPMC, we currently have twenty-six presidentially appointed and Senate-confirmed individuals working in a dozen different agencies, managing an annual biodefense budget of approximately $5.5 billion. But not one of them has this mission as a full-time job, and no one is in charge. (I first wrote about this problem in a *Washington Post* op-ed piece, "Years After 9/11 . . . No One Is in Charge of Fighting Our Two Biggest Threats," May 20, 2005.) However, not all national security programs have this problem.

One person, appointed by the secretary of defense, leads the missile defense program, and a presidentially appointed, Senate-confirmed undersecretary controls the $7.7 billion annual budget. We seem to be far better organized for defense against a delivery system than for the weapons themselves. By the way, the most likely delivery system for biological (or nuclear) weapons is not an intercontinental ballistic missile (ICBM), because missiles come with return addresses—bad news for the sender. The last time America suffered a biological attack, the U.S. Postal Service provided the delivery vehicles, and we still don't have a return address for the sender.

Second, there is insufficient control of federal funding that goes to state and local public health offices. Dr. Gursky has documented numerous examples of supplantation when the first large ($1 billion) allocation of federal preparedness dollars was awarded shortly after the anthrax attacks of 2001. When the federal money came in the front door of public health offices, state comptrollers pulled an equal amount of state funds out the back door to use in other programs that were often not even related to public health. In other words, a significant portion of that $1 billion was not spent on improving response capabilities at the state and local level.

Supplantation is not unique to public health. Governments have frequently used supplantation as a strategy to expand their ability to fund numerous programs. For example, many states have implemented lotteries to increase the amount of funds going to their educational systems. However, as lottery revenue poured into education, legislative earmarks and tax revenue for education diminished. The net result was little or no increase in funding for education.

Third, the organizational structure for biodefense is a disaster. To paraphrase General Eisenhower, "The right system will not guarantee success, but the wrong system will guarantee failure." Today, we are not properly organized to defend this nation against a biological attack. I often use the following analogy to describe this egregious situation:

Many people have submitted plans to transform the Department of Defense for the twenty-first century. Here is my plan. Instead of having it centrally organized, I suggest that we do away with the Pentagon and give each

of the 3066 counties in the U.S. the following: one tank,
one fighter plane, and one infantry platoon. Each state
will be provided with a few Navy ships. There will be no
standards for credentialing the officers or NCOs. Some
will be political appointees. Funding will come from var-
ious sources, and money that is sent from Washington
can be easily moved to other programs outside defense.

Sound like a good idea? Well, that's a reasonable description of the current public health system in this country. In fact, it is not a system. In some states, like Maryland, all of the county public health offices are under the centralized control of the state public health officer. In other states, such as New Jersey and Massachusetts, city and county public health offices are decentralized—marching to their own drummers. And in South Carolina, there is no state official whose primary responsibility is public health. There are no nationally recognized standards for credentialing of state and local public health officers. (The people who cut hair and toenails in most states have lengthy training programs and must be certified to practice. Not so for public health officers in most states.) The funding for these offices comes from a hodgepodge of uncoordinated sources. Furthermore, it has not been uncommon for federal bioterrorism funds to be diverted to programs that have no connection to bioresponse efforts.

In the report *Epidemic Proportions*, Dr. Gursky's seminal work on public health preparedness, reference is made to a September 2005 report to the Senate Health, Education, Labor, and Pensions Subcommittee on Bioterrorism and Public Health. This report outlined the inherent flaws in our public health infrastructure and concluded that the system was ill-suited for today's challenges:

The country's public health agencies were built almost two centuries ago to meet the relatively straightforward needs of communities: collect vital statistics, provide preventive services such as well-baby care, detect and mitigate local disease outbreaks, and promote health education and healthy lifestyles. Public health was never envisioned to fill the national security role associated with health consequences of deliberate acts of terrorism, and it is ill-equipped and untrained for pandemics and natural disasters that result in overwhelming numbers of casualties or patients with highly infectious diseases. Public health is organized to serve the health of individual communities with populations in the thousands, not coordinated health security of a nation of 280 million.

Many Americans mistakenly assume that the Centers for Disease Control and Prevention will be in charge during a biocrisis. While CDC is a world-class research organization, it is not organized, trained, or equipped to serve in an operational leadership role to the 50 states and 3066 counties during a biocrisis, either man-made or naturally occurring. To prepare for the biological threats of the twenty-first century, we must have a fundamental reorganization of public health at the federal, state, and local levels.

Prior to the 1960s, environmental issues were primarily seen as state and local responsibilities. We have since learned that the only effective way to approach the issue is with a national strategy, a national plan, and a national organization. Recommending the same approach to public health will not be well received by most state and local public health officers who don't want to give up their autonomy to Washington. I do not blame them, and I understand their concerns. Much of what state and local public health offices do on a daily basis is unique to their locations. But during a crisis, we must have a national response capability. Building such a national system will require the long-term commitment of significant funds, although it would likely be less than what we spend each year on national missile defense.

The fourth issue is that the majority of public health professionals do not see biodefense preparedness as a top priority. According to Dr. Gursky, as more Americans have lost access to health care and insurance, the delivery of medical care has become the top priority for public health departments. This all-encompassing responsibility allows little excess in terms of time and human resources to address preparedness and response to catastrophic events.

One bit of good news regarding medical response capabilities—some improvements can be made that will not require enormous amounts of taxpayers' money. For instance, Texas has more than 40,000 nurses who no longer work in health care. Creating a reserve corps of health care workers would require only a few weekends per year for training, but could provide some improvements in surge capability during a crisis. The Reserve component of the Department of Defense played a major role in winning the Cold War, and continues to play an important role today. Why not develop a Homeland Security Reserve Corps? Retirees, former health care workers, and corporations could play a major role in this volunteer effort.

Many government organizations measure medical surge capability in terms of the number of empty hospital beds, but this figure provides little insight into actual capabilities. An empty bed is meaningless; only one that is staffed is of any value. One useful barometer of capability is the number of staffed intensive care beds. During the 2004 presidential inauguration, Washington had a total of two ICU-staffed beds available—not a significant or reassuring number. However, how can we realistically expect hospitals to maintain surge capability? According to the American Hospital Association, one third of the nation's hospitals are currently operating in the red. In the 1990s, 1,000 hospitals and emergency rooms in the U.S. were closed. If you were the CEO of a hospital, struggling just to keep the doors open to serve your local community, would you maintain a significant excess capacity?

One potential solution to this dilemma can be modeled after the U.S. military. Andrews Air Force Base, best known as the home of Air Force One, has received some unfavorable press over the years from young reporters who didn't do their homework. When covering the issue of military waste (about which there is plenty to report), they would sometimes mention the covered tennis courts at Andrews. Yes, colonels' wives (as well as enlisted personnel) could play tennis in the winter, but that was not why tax dollars were spent. This facility was constructed and maintained because in just seventy-two hours these tennis courts can be converted into a 250-bed hospital. The beds could be staffed with Reserve doctors, nurses, and medical technicians, there is a sufficient amount of medical supplies on hand, and it is next to a major medical center where more extensive capabilities (laboratories, MRI/CAT scans, and surgery suites) are available.

But do not learn the wrong lesson from this example. It is not uncommon for some of our leaders to assume the military can provide surge medical capacity for the civilian community. We saw this during an exercise that Dr. O'Toole, Dr. Inglesby, and I designed and ran in June 2001 called Dark Winter. The effort was led by Dr. John Hamre, the former deputy secretary of defense. Senator Sam Nunn played the role of the president, David Gergen served as his national security adviser, and Frank Keating played the role of the governor of Oklahoma (a job he held at that time). A former FBI director, a former CIA director, a former deputy attorney general, and others participated. The scenario revolved around a smallpox attack by al Qaeda on three U.S. cities. The exercise lasted for two days.

During Dark Winter, "President" Sam Nunn considered activating Reserve medical units to assist civilian hospitals. John White, a former deputy secretary of defense, reminded "President" Nunn that this would not be additive, because almost all of those Reserve doctors, nurses, and technicians were already working in civilian hospitals in their civilian jobs.

To provide additional medical personnel, we must look for new and creative solutions, such as those 40,000 nurses in Texas not currently working in health care. How about retired doctors? I know a recently retired orthopedic surgeon in Illinois who still plays full-court basketball. I think he would agree to be part of a medical Reserve posse. What about veterinarians and retired nurses? (I guarantee that having a veterinarian and retired nurse care for your sick family would be preferable to having me do so.) During the Katrina and Rita evacuations, the large animal hospital at Texas A&M University was converted to a human facility. As the director said, "If we have room to do surgery on an elephant, we should be able to fit quite a few people into our surgery suite."

Increasing surge capacity will be a major challenge. In a traditional sense, it is probably not possible to increase the surge capacity of a hospital by more than 20 percent. However, Dr. Tara O'Toole of the Center for Biosecurity–UPMC says that a 20 percent increase could make a significant difference. It would most certainly help to push the decimal point to the left; however, in a large-scale disaster, traditional solutions just will not be able to provide sufficient capacity. We must learn to accept the concept of "graceful degradation of care." This is a concept long practiced in battlefield medicine, but it requires extensive planning and practice. It is a system that will ensure the best possible use of limited resources during a major crisis—far short of an ideal solution, but far better than the chaos that would occur in most civilian medical facilities today.

With proper planning and sufficient funding, nontraditional solutions are available. For instance, if (actually I should say "when," since it's only a matter of time) we have to deploy a Push Pack, creative solutions could save thousands of lives. You'll recall, a Push Pack is about 97,000 pounds of antibiotics and other medical supplies needed to respond to a bio-attack. It is packaged to fit inside a 747 air freighter or seventeen large trucks. The Push Pack program is one of the few biodefense success stories for the federal government. It was created in 1999 by a senior official in the Department of Health and Human Services, Dr. Peggy Hamburg. I say it was a success for the federal government, but it won't be a success for the nation until state and local governments develop and test plans to distribute the drugs.

The primary problem with Push Packs is that most state and local governments are not prepared to distribute the supplies once they are delivered to local communities by the feds. According to a 2005 study by the Trust for America's Health, only two cities in America meet the federal government's criteria for dispensing a Push Pack. Fifty tons of antibiotics and medical supplies sitting in containers at the airport will be of no value to your family. Federal officials have studied various proposals for distribution, ranging from first responders, the U.S. Postal Service, or the National Guard delivering them door-to-door. However, none of these proposals provided the answer the government was looking for. First responders might be needed for other duties, the American Postal Workers Union was against the idea, and assigning the task to the National Guard was considered a poor use of resources (in addition to the fact that the Guard lacks an adequate number of personnel). The solution to this challenge is a combination of two twenty-first-century posses: one corporate, and one of trained volunteers.

A 2006 study by the Center for Biosecurity–UPMC, *Getting Medicines to Millions: New Strategies for Mass Distribution*, recommended that we use the private sector: pharmacies, grocery stores, and wholesale clubs. Many of these retail businesses organize influenza vaccinations in their communities. According to the Centers for Disease Control and Prevention, one third of annual flu vaccinations take place in retail stores and other nonclinical settings. Many people also obtain their prescription medication from these large-capacity retail facilities, which have parking lots and electronic inventory control systems, and are highly experienced in receiving and managing large volumes of goods. The ubiquitous nature of such facilities is also a huge benefit. According to the National Association of Chain Drug Stores, 95 percent of the U.S. population lives within five miles of a retail pharmacy.

The retail executives who were interviewed in this study expressed an overwhelming willingness to participate in such a nationwide program as long as two key issues were resolved: liability and standardization of policies. Shortly after completion of the study, many of the liability challenges were resolved with the 2006 Department of Defense Appropriations Act, which mandated protection of corporations and persons as long as the secretary of health and human services declares a public health emergency. Some further refinements to policies and procedures will likely be required, but Congress clearly demonstrated its willingness to provide indemnification for participants in such programs.

Corporate executives also requested national standards rather than dealing with the potential of negotiating with 3066 separate county governments. This is a reasonable request that not only makes sense for corporations, but also for the public health community.

A second posse of trained volunteers could be used to augment the corporate effort. Community service organizations such as Rotary, Kiwanis, and religious groups could play a major role in providing extra personnel and delivering medicines to those unable to travel to retail outlets. College students would also be valuable members of such a posse, because in most cases they are young, healthy, and single—meaning that during a crisis, they would not be distracted by the need to care for their own families.

Lacking the means to distribute Push Packs is like having a high-speed Internet cable on your street, but no connection to your house; it's that last short distance that is critical. Corporate and volunteer Push Pack posses could make the difference between success and failure, but these efforts cannot be coordinated during a crisis—planning and practice must begin now.

Goals and Dual Benefits of Biodefense

The short-term (less than three years) focus for biodefense should be on information technology that will provide improvements in mitigation and response capabilities, primarily in the area of situational awareness. This situational awareness extends from the Oval Office to your kitchen table. The president, as well as the governors, county executives, and mayors need to know what is going on in their communities during a biodisaster. In every bio-exercise I have run or observed, the senior leaders complained that they were not provided with the information they needed to make proper decisions. The leaders wanted to know, "How many people are sick?" "How many are being admitted to hospitals?" "Is it contagious?" "How fast and far will it spread?" However, the exercise controllers were providing the participants with more information than they would receive in a real-world event, because the current real-world information would not provide sufficient information to even run an exercise.

This situational information is also critically important all the way down to the individual level. This deficiency can and must be corrected with electronic medical information. People who evacuated from New Orleans, virtually all without their health care records, had great difficulty obtaining their necessary prescription medications. Modern health care, particularly for those over fifty, often includes numerous prescriptions for daily medications. Imagine what it is like for both the patients with serious chronic diseases who are taking a dozen different medications each day, and the physicians who must try to reconstruct their health care records during a crisis.

The midterm goal (three to five years) should be the creation of a national public health system that can detect, respond to, and mitigate catastrophic health crises, either man-made or naturally occurring. We must also develop rapid clinical diagnostic capabilities. Today, it requires more than twenty-four hours to provide a positive diagnosis for most infectious diseases. A properly funded research and development effort may be able to reduce this by a factor of 10. Such rapid diagnostic capability would not only be invaluable in defense against bioterrorism, but also for naturally occurring diseases, such as pandemic influenza.

The long-term goal should be focused on research and development programs that will best use our technological advantage to create revolutionary capabilities, such as "bug-to-drug in 24 hours" (as recommended by a 2002 Defense Science Board study), and something called preclinical detection. "Bug-to-drug in 24 hours" means the capability to identify a new disease, and with genetic engineering techniques, create a successful treatment within twenty-four hours. I know it sounds like science fiction, and today it is. But just remember, in 1950, when airplanes had propellers, someone who claimed that within twenty years we could put people on the moon and safely return them to earth would have likely drawn some skeptical comments. "Bug-to-drug in 24 hours" is a realistic and obtainable long-term goal, but only if we make the investment. If we continue to waste money, we will not be able to invest in the programs that could make a difference.

The greatest challenge to "bug-to-drug in 24 hours" is that it only addresses half of the problem. Actually making the drug will provide no benefit if it is not licensed by the Federal Drug Administration. Since 2001, emergency provisions have been initiated that would allow for more rapid approval; however, the current emergency process still requires such a lengthy period that the drug would not be available in time to make a difference. This effort requires revolutionary ideas in science, technology, and policy, in both the public and private sectors.

Preclinical detection is another concept that could make an incredible difference. It could move the advantage from the attacker to the defender in both man-made and naturally occurring diseases. For instance, if you were exposed to the variola virus (smallpox) while at work today, you would not begin to show symptoms for at least seven days, and some people would take as long as seventeen days to become ill. In other words, you would be a walking time bomb. You would unknowingly be carrying a contagious and lethal disease to your families and friends. No currently available test could detect this disease in your body. Only when you became symptomatic and began to experience a high fever and rash would today's laboratory tests diagnose smallpox, and there is a 30 percent chance you would die. If you survived, you could be blind, you would have suffered extraordinary pain, and you would carry the scars of smallpox pustules for life. With preclinical detection, the variola virus could be detected soon after it entered your body, and the smallpox vaccine is effective if given within four days of exposure. Likewise, early antibiotic treatment against anthrax and plague would make the difference between a bio-incident and a biocatastrophe. Preclinical detection would not end the biothreat, but it would significantly *contain* the consequences. It could, over time, reduce the effects of these types of attacks to such a degree that it would serve as a deterrent. Preclinical detection can be achieved, but we must make the investment in research and development today.

The ability to detect disease before the onset of symptoms should be one of America's top funding priorities. This capability would also provide an incredible dual benefit to the health of all Americans. Early detection of any disease is critically important. This dual benefit is one of the greatest advantages of spending on biodefense. When you buy a new nuclear-powered aircraft carrier for national security, you get a powerful weapons system to defend America against its enemies, but in the end, it's just a weapons system. A properly designed biodefense system will reduce America's vulnerability to a bio-attack or a naturally occurring epidemic, and at the same time, significantly improve health care and food security.

EDUCATION

One of the primary reasons for the success of the U.S. military during the past quarter century has been an aggressive and unflagging commitment to executive education. This is far different from training. The Department of Defense spends billions of dollars each year on training: to drive tanks, fly airplanes, and shoot M-16s. A much smaller, but equally important investment is made in executive education: teaching leaders *how* to think (as opposed to *what* to think). This executive education takes place throughout an officer's career, and the final step in this program is called senior service school. During my final military assignment, I served as the chairman of the Department of Military Strategy and Operations at the National War College. Actually, the school is improperly named. At General Eisenhower's direction, it was going to be named the School of Strategic Studies. However, just prior to the press conference announcing the creation of the school, the secretary of the army said, "If it doesn't have the word *war* in the title, I'm not supporting it." The rest, as they say, is history.

I mention this story because the title of the school does not provide a proper description of the curriculum. War is certainly a major topic at the National War College; however, the education provided goes far beyond the ideas of Carl von Clausewitz. From the modern-day American perspective, the purpose of war is to build a better peace. Therefore, when the students at National War College look at World War II, it is from the perspective of how it changed the international structure: from the creation of the United Nations, to the Bretton-Woods Agreements that led to the International Monetary Fund, to the development of nuclear weapons that changed the entire international security equation. The students, a highly select group that is destined for senior leadership positions in the military, intelligence community, and other executive branch agencies, learn how to think about national security. Because of bureaucratic politics, it still says National War College on their diplomas, but in reality, they receive a master's degree in strategic thinking. This is certainly one of the reasons why the graduates go on to successful careers in government, and are also highly successful in the corporate world following retirement from the military. They have become strategic thinkers. A picture of General Colin Powell hangs outside my old office at the National War College. He signed it a few years ago with these words: "This is where it began for me."

This sort of executive education is what is missing in homeland security, both in the public and private sectors. I first witnessed this at the Dark Winter exercise. During the hot wash (a session where participants come out of their roles and discuss the events of the exercise), virtually all of these highly experienced national security leaders stated that not only did they not have answers to this challenge, they didn't even know what questions to ask. Since June of 2001, I have seen this repeated numerous times in other exercises with equally well-qualified current and former national security leaders—or at least I should say, national security leaders who were well qualified for the challenges of the Cold War.

This education is needed not only for leaders who will respond in a crisis, but also for leaders who will decide how America should prepare. What strategies should we adopt? Where should we be spending funds for homeland security, both in the public and private sectors? What should a CEO do to protect business processes and employees? How do leaders ensure they will produce a proper return on investment? How can we expect our leaders to make the right decisions if they are not properly educated for the task? This lack of education and understanding is the single greatest reason for America's misguided reactions to 9/11. There are two different requirements for homeland security education: long-term (traditional education in universities), and short-term, executive-level education. If we look back a few generations, we can identify two other times in history when national security interests initiated education programs that served not only our immediate security needs, but also played a major role in the economic development of this nation.

In 1862, President Lincoln signed the Morrill Act, which created the land grant schools. The legislation had failed to make it through Congress on previous occasions, but the addition of a requirement for military training (in response to the lack of qualified officers for the Union Army) guaranteed passage. The land grant schools were directed to focus their efforts on the two great engines of the American economy, agriculture and engineering, and they provided three services: teaching, research, and extension programs. These three key public services still serve as the core of land grant universities. What began as required classes on military subjects during the Civil War evolved into the Reserve Officer Training Corps (ROTC) in 1916. This program provided thousands of officers for service in World War I. The ROTC program was further expanded in 1920, and the investment paid great dividends when America's armed forces grew to 12 million during World War II.

In 1958, in response to the launch of the Sputnik satellite by the Soviet Union the previous year, the National Defense Education Program was created, and once again, education was a critical element of America's response to a national security challenge. With this program, if you could do math and science, you could go to college, no matter what your social-economic status. We trained an entire generation of scientists and engineers who took us to the moon, won the Cold War, and served as the foundation for America's economic growth in the technological era. It is not difficult to link America's leadership position in technology and dominance in the global marketplace back to the National Defense Education Program investment in education.

With these two programs as benchmarks, America must now look to its universities to prepare current and future leaders for the security challenges of the twenty-first century. Education must begin at the undergraduate level and continue through the graduate and postgraduate levels, but it must also include short courses for leaders who have already completed their formal education, and even shorter programs for busy executives. The vast majority of community colleges, colleges, and universities have developed "homeland security" programs.

However, few can be considered anything more than training programs for first responders. I am not suggesting that they have no value; undeniably, these are important programs, but they fall into the category of training, not education. Training programs teach people *how to do* things based on years of accumulated experience: fight fires, give first-aid, use a computer program or other piece of equipment. Education programs teach people *how to think*.

Here is one example. Law enforcement officers spend many hours each year in training programs. Several new training programs have been designed for homeland security, such as responding to chemical and radiological attacks. They are based on years of experience from military training programs ("if this event happens, here is a checklist of what you must do"). Education programs are quite different. I developed a one-day education program for the Washington Association of Sheriffs and Police Chiefs. During the morning session, the participants were directed to plan a terrorist attack on their own communities. They were given a political objective (cause serious economic, social, and psychological disruption), and told what resources they had at their disposal (numbers of terrorists, types of weapons, and other assets). The senior law enforcement officers were hesitant at first, but as they discovered how easy it was to plan and conduct such attacks, they began to develop a new perspective on the security of their communities.

After lunch, they were told to respond to coordinated suicide attacks on local shopping malls that had been conducted on the Friday after Thanksgiving. The officers suddenly found themselves at a loss. There were no checklists, and they had little experience in this type of scenario. Their entire careers had been focused on investigating crimes, pursuing and apprehending perpetrators, and moving them through the judicial system. In this case, the perpetrators were all dead. The mission of the law enforcement officials was to convince the citizens of their communities that it was safe to go back to the shopping malls. If the shoppers did not go back, it would cause enormous economic disruption—not only to the local business owners, but to local tax revenues. This new mission was uncharted territory for law enforcement officials. When it comes to first-aid, crime scene investigation, and weapons training, there are right and wrong answers. These right and wrong answers are based upon years of experience. The purpose of this one-day workshop was not to teach the answers, but to teach the senior officials what questions they should be asking. *This* is education. Today there is a significant amount of federal money being spent on homeland security training, but very little on homeland security education. That must change.

Several universities are working to develop undergraduate and graduate education programs in homeland security. Texas A&M (a land grant school) has a graduate program that provides the same type of education for homeland security leaders that the National War College has provided to national security leaders for several decades (see http://homelandsecurity.tamu.edu). Texas A&M is currently expanding its master's program to PhD-level studies. We need to leverage the successes of the past to develop this new academic discipline.

Finally, homeland security should not be viewed as just a course or a department in a university. It must be integrated throughout the various colleges and curriculum: science, economics, law, medicine and public health, engineering, and business. Homeland security is a fact of life in the twenty-first century. It will influence all that we do. A large-scale investment in homeland security education will allow America to control the high ground of security.

INFORMATION SYSTEMS

Information is the weapon that terrorists fear most. We must use it wisely, and in a manner consistent with the value we place on privacy and civil liberties, but we must understand that information is an area where we have a huge asymmetric advantage over the terrorists. Unfortunately, America has a poor track record in using this advantage. Here are just a few recent examples:

- Prior to 9/11, the Central Intelligence Agency discovered a way to identify forged passports used by al Qaeda, but did not share this information with the officials who examine the passports of people entering the United States. According to the 9/11 Commission, as many as fifteen of the nineteen hijackers carried this type of passport.

- Prior to 9/11, the chief of the al Qaeda analysis team at the CIA contacted the National Security Agency (which collects intelligence information through electronic intercepts of radios, telephones, the Internet, and so forth—known as SIGINT) and asked to receive the raw data from these intercepts, rather than just the NSA analysis. He was told, "We don't provide that information outside of this agency."

- In July 2001, a Florida state trooper stopped Mohamed Atta (operational leader of the 9/11 attacks) for a traffic violation. The officer queried the National Crime Information Center for information on Atta. No information was found, and he was released with just a citation for having an expired driver's license. At that time, Atta was listed in numerous federal government databases for suspicious behavior.

Information is a broad term, so let's first define the term within the context of this discussion. When talking about homeland security, information includes, but is not limited to: intelligence (from the most highly classified levels, to open-source, such as the Internet, newspapers, and radio broadcasts in foreign countries), knowledge about activities in other government agencies (left hand not knowing what the right hand is doing syndrome), and government and private sector databases other than those in the intelligence community.

Let us also agree on realistic expectations. Information is a highly useful tool for defending our homeland, but we should never believe that with enough investment in information, we could prevent all or even the majority of attacks on our homeland. Military intelligence officers like to point out that one's opponent in a chess game has an extraordinary amount of information: All pieces are in clear view, and the capabilities of each piece are well defined by the rules of the game. Nevertheless, there is an extraordinary amount of surprise and deception in chess. In the realm of homeland security, we can see only a small portion of the "chessboard," and the opponent often plays by different rules.

This is not meant to provide an excuse for the intelligence community's failure to predict or prevent 9/11. Actually, the intelligence community did predict 9/11. As early as 1998, the director of the Central Intelligence Agency, in open congressional hearings, stated that al Qaeda was targeting America. Nevertheless, there is considerable room for improvement. First, we must improve how we collect and analyze intelligence information. The Intelligence Reform and Terrorism Prevention Act, passed in 2005, is a great step forward, with the potential to significantly improve our collection and analysis efforts. The first director of national intelligence, John Negroponte, had the opportunity to eliminate obstacles, better coordinate efforts, and build an intelligence community to meet the challenges of the twenty-first century. His initial actions, which included initiatives to break bureaucratic logjams and cut red tape, were exactly what we need. Unfortunately, Negroponte left his post far earlier than most expected. The question is, Will his successor be able to maintain the initial momentum?

Second, the federal government needs twenty-first-century information systems. Today, many agencies "do not know what they know." The most egregious single example is the FBI. The previous director, Louis Freeh, did not like computers. In fact, on his first day in office in 1993, he told his staff to remove the computer from his desk. That became the corporate culture. While the rest of the world was rapidly moving into the information age, the FBI was continuing to handle information in much the same fashion as in the days of J. Edgar Hoover. According to the 9/11 Commission report, on September 12, 2001, the FBI did not have the means to securely e-mail photos of the nineteen hijackers to its field offices. Shortly thereafter, the FBI signed a contract to build an electronic case file system. With such a system, if a special agent in Arizona filed a report about Middle Eastern young men paying cash for flight training, an analyst at headquarters could search the database for reports of other such activity. Unfortunately, after spending $170 million trying to build the system, the project was shut down and declared a failure. It is incomprehensible that a nation that has been the world's leader in the technological revolution would allow the FBI to fail at such an important endeavor. Today, the FBI still doesn't know what it knows. It has an incredible amount of valuable information, but no means for electronic search and analysis. According to the current director, Robert Mueller, the next attempt to bring the FBI into the information age has an estimated completion date of 2009.

This same problem exists within the interagency community. I recently spoke to one of America's most experienced biodefense experts. He has worked for nearly two decades in the biodefense field, including assignments in the Department of Defense, the Central Intelligence Agency, the White House, and the U.S. Congress. I asked him if there was a database he could use to identify and track federally funded programs in biodefense. His answer was quick and direct: "No." In other words, the Departments of Defense, Health and Human Services, and even Homeland Security spend billions of dollars on research programs without coordinating their efforts. Scientists funded by one agency are completely unaware of similar work being conducted by colleagues funded by a different agency. This is a case of failing to use information technology to our best advantage.

The third area of information has to do with the linking of public and private sector databases. This is an area that causes great concern within the civil liberties and privacy communities, and I fully appreciate their reasoning. However, there are means to approach this issue that will provide the protection needed to meet our cultural and legal standards. Much work has been accomplished by think tanks and other not-for-profits on how we can use information technology without sacrificing our privacy. The Potomac Institute's commendable work on Project Guardian is just one example. It has designed a system that allows our incredible information technology to outwit the enemy, while at the same time involving all three branches of government to provide the oversight necessary to protect our privacy.

The technology exists today that would allow local, state, and federal law enforcement organizations, plus intelligence agencies, to pass information to a common data hub for national-level compilation and analysis. This hub would be the National Counterterrorism Center, which would also have the capability to convey processed intelligence information to all agencies and levels of law enforcement.

According to Newton Minow, the former chairman of the Federal Communications Commission (in a *Wall Street Journal* op-ed piece on June 3, 2004), if readily available intelligence and law enforcement information had been compared with information in commercial databases, here is what could have been discovered on the morning of 9/11:

- Nawaf Alhamzi and Khalid Almidhar, both on terrorist watch lists, purchased tickets on American Airlines Flight 77 using their real names, addresses, phone numbers, and frequent flier numbers.
- Salem Alhazmi and Mohamed Atta, who shared the same street address as Nawaf Alhamzi, checked in for American Flights 77 and 11, respectively. Additionally, Marwan Al-Shehhi, who shared an address with Almidhar, checked in for United Airlines Flight 175.
- A quick check of phone numbers (remember all the uproar about NSA phone number data mining in 2006?) would have identified five more men (Fayez Ahmed, Mohand Alshehri, Wali Alshehri, Waleed Alshehri, and Abdulaziz Alomari) who listed the same phone number as Mohamed Atta. These five were scheduled to fly on American Flights 11 and 77, and United Flight 175.
- A quick search of public records (we are talking milliseconds in computer time) would have revealed that Satam Al Suqami, booked on American Flight 11, shared a post office box with Waleed Alshehri. Another man, Hani Hanjour, a former roommate of Alhamzi and Almidhar, was booked on American Flight 77.
- An INS watch list would have revealed that Ahmed Alghamdi, booked on United 175, had an expired visa.

- Address information would have revealed that Alghamdi used the same mailing address as Hamza Alghamdi, Saeed Alghamdi, Ahmed Al Haznawi, and Ahmed Alnami. The first two men have tickets on United Flight 175, and the second two on United Flight 93. Al Haznawi once roomed with Ziad Jarrah, who was booked on United Flight 93.
- A quick check of frequent flier numbers would have revealed that Majed Moqed used Almidhar's number to purchase a ticket on American Flight 77.

In a matter of seconds, this technology could have connected all nineteen hijackers based on their links to the two who were on the terrorist watch list. Would it have happened? Hard to say, but imagine if it did. But what about the privacy issue? This leads to the fourth, and perhaps most controversial, subject under the banner of information—personal identification.

Today, fifteen European nations have a form of nationally standardized identification. The United Kingdom, after much debate, has recently decided to begin such a program. Some would say that we already have one in the United States—our state-issued driver's license. We all use it every time we transit an airport. The only problem is that it is not an effective anti-terrorism tool. We have all heard the stories about the 9/11 hijackers—that seven had Virginia driver's licenses, and none lived in Virginia. There are some states with laws that authorize the issuance of driver's licenses to people who are known to be illegal aliens. We all know that any reasonably intelligent college student understands how to use the Internet to get a photo ID card that "proves" he or she is twenty-one. During a congressional hearing in May 2005, I stated, "Any nineteen-year-old college student who can't figure out how to obtain a phony driver's license is probably not smart enough to be in college." I guarantee you that al Qaeda knows how.

We are in the process of spending billions of dollars on the US-VISIT program that was designed to deter or capture terrorists entering our country. If and when the system becomes effective, the terrorists will stop using our ports of entry and begin crossing our 7,500 miles of unguarded borders and 95,000 miles of shoreline. Remember, they are a thinking enemy. When we close and lock one door, they will move to another. We can spend ourselves into bankruptcy by staying just one step behind them.

I understand why many Americans worry about the creation of a national identity card, and I have serious concerns myself. Nevertheless, we have reached a point where the lack of national identity cards may be a greater threat to your family than the creation of such a system. Senator Lamar Alexander (R-TN) recently changed his mind on this subject. Twenty years ago, while serving as the governor of Tennessee, he vetoed a bill requiring photos on driver's licenses, believing it to be an unreasonable breach of privacy. Today, Senator Alexander is calling for national identity cards—with photos and biometrics (electronic fingerprints and iris scans). The reason he and many others have changed their minds is that the creation of national identity cards is something akin to medical procedures—they both have risks, but when the risk of inaction becomes greater than the risk of action, action becomes the better choice. However, if we experience several major attacks, larger and more deadly than 9/11, the American people may change their attitude on this subject. A poll taken shortly after 9/11 found that 70 percent of Americans favored a national identity system.

We need to take action now, before the next attack. Our analysis and decisions are likely to be far better than when we are in shock following a large-scale attack. First, we should conduct a comprehensive, nonpartisan study to examine the critical issues of a national identity system (ask the right questions). Second, we should consider quickly moving forward with a novel concept for identification—a privately issued, government-recognized, traveler ID card. This would be a voluntary program.

Congress should form a bipartisan commission to do a one-year study on a national identity system. The study should focus on four questions:

1. Does an organization and system exist that can ensure identification credentials are properly issued?
2. Does the technology exist to create a means of identification that cannot be altered or counterfeited?
3. Can we build a system that is affordable?
4. Do Americans feel secure that such a system would protect their privacy?

Today, the answers are: no, yes, yes, and no. The purpose of the study would be to determine if it is technologically and politically feasible to get four yeses, because until such time as we can do so, I do not think the American public will support a national identity system. Is this possible? Absolutely, but a lot of work is needed. The first question (ensuring credentials are properly issued) will be the most difficult to resolve. It will require that we answer other difficult questions, many of which involve immigration and illegal aliens. The last question (privacy) is the one that causes many to object, but in reality, getting this yes might not be as difficult as you think. Much work has been accomplished in this area, with technology allowing for the creation of a system that would make the threat of Big Brother far less than most would expect.

Perhaps we should include a fifth question: Would such a system make us more secure? The answer is yes. There is no way to effectively control 7,500 miles of borders and 95,000 miles of shorelines. If we spend billions making it virtually impossible for known terrorists to enter the United States through our sea, air, and land ports, they will begin crossing our borders in the same way the economic refugees and migrant workers from Mexico and Central America have for decades. And even though some members of Congress want to build impregnable borders with physical and electronic barriers, you must understand that such an initiative would be no more effective at protecting our homeland today than the Maginot Line was at protecting France in 1940. It would waste valuable resources and leave us no more secure.

On May 11, 2005, the president signed the REAL ID Act, which established national standards for state-issued driver's licenses. This is a step in the right direction; however, it will be 2008 until it takes effect, and even then, states are not required to comply. Nonetheless, the REAL ID Act is a step toward improving the reliability of identification, and it will focus efforts on the first question (ensuring credentials are properly issued). But 2008 may be too late. Perhaps we should look to the private sector for quicker solutions.

On June 9, 2005, the House Committee on Homeland Security held its first hearing to discuss the concept of privately issued, government-recognized, traveler IDs. If frequent travelers want to pay several hundred dollars for such a card, and don't mind being fingerprinted, iris-scanned, and background-checked, then the Transportation Security Administration would not have to treat their next trip through an airport as though it was their first. The card, similar to a pilot program run by TSA called "Registered Traveler," would allow TSA to focus its efforts on those who had not agreed to a background check and biometric scans. This strategy comes right out of the textbook on risk management. It would allow TSA personnel to spend more time focusing on those who might actually have nefarious plans. This is a winning strategy for all homeland security programs—focus resources where the threat is the highest. One thing I know for sure—when I get on an airplane with my family, I would like to know that the person sitting next to my daughter is not on a terrorist watch list. The system we have today does not provide me that assurance.

These are but a few examples of how information systems can serve as our most effective weapon in the war on terrorism. Corporate America can provide the technology—that is not the challenge. The challenge is breaking away from old paradigms, bureaucratic politics, and interagency squabbling. We must also develop an oversight system to ensure Americans that their privacy and civil liberties will be protected just as aggressively as we seek to detect, deter, and defeat the terrorists.

Preventing terrorists from getting their hands on weapons-grade nuclear material, significantly improving our capability to rapidly detect, respond, and recover from a biological attack, funding major expansions in our homeland security education system, and investing in new information systems are the first four priorities for ensuring major improvements in our security.

There are obviously many other areas that require funding and increased focus, but America's leaders, at the federal, state, and local levels, plus those within the private sector, need to understand these priorities. In the beginning of World War II, President Franklin Roosevelt made his priority clear: "Europe first." As we begin to prepare for the security challenges of the new century, we need to understand that our priorities must be nuclear and biological defense, plus education and information.

Chapter 6

Key Issues

New Thinking, New Rules, and New Organizations

ONE OF THE MOST COMMON ERRORS IN THE PRACTICE OF HOMELAND SECURITY is that people tend to examine (and in the case of politicians and the commentariat, pontificate on) issues before they have taken the time and effort to understand the fundamentals. This leads to "Ready! Shoot! Aim!"

The previous chapters of this book laid the foundation for understanding the fundamentals of securing our American homeland in the twenty-first century: learning to ask the right questions; understanding the threats, probabilities, and proper perspectives; and developing a realistic, effective strategy that incorporates the appropriate priorities for spending and action. The remaining chapters will examine issues from the federal government perspective, corporate responsibilities, state and local issues, and finally issues directly related to the security of your family.

Before considering these issues, however, we must understand that improving our nation's security is paramount, and if we are serious in this endeavor, the discussions and debates regarding these topics must be devoid of partisan politics, pork barrel interests, the lobbying power of the homeland security-industrial complex, and the emotions of hyperventilating cable TV shock jocks and radio talk show blabbermouths. Many security processes and procedures from the last century can be adapted to protect us from this century's threats, but those that cannot require a paradigm shift in our approach to homeland security. These challenges demand new thinking, new rules, and even new organizations. The only way to succeed in this vital mission is by putting our individual interests and agendas aside, and focusing exclusively on the decisions and actions that will benefit our nation as a whole.

The dogmas of the quiet past are inadequate to the stormy present. The occasion is piled high with difficulty, and we must rise with the occasion. As our case is new, so we must think anew and act anew.

Abraham Lincoln
December 1, 1862

NEW THINKING

Borders

In January 2000, I hosted a one-day workshop on homeland security at the National War College in Washington, D.C. It was the first time I had conducted such an event, and for most of the participants, their first time attending one. Those present included representatives from the military and intelligence communities, federal and local law enforcement, congressional staffers, a corporate CEO, two corporate security experts, several defense contractors, and vice presidents from several industries not normally associated with national security. I had developed an ambitious schedule of discussion topics, including thirty minutes for the first one, entitled "The Boundaries of the Homeland." I thought we would get through it quickly, but the eclectic group threw me some unexpected curveballs. The discussion on borders lasted three hours, and we didn't reach any conclusions, except that our conception of what constituted a border had changed more than most of us had realized.

The first vice president of a major bank based in New York City told us, "Our bank in Bonn, Germany, is as important to the U.S. economy as our bank in New York. Aren't our overseas corporate assets really part of our homeland? They are sure part of our economy."

The former director of the President's Commission on Critical Infrastructure Protection asked if we should include satellites as part of the homeland. He said, "We can't run our economy without our information systems, and they run through satellites."

Another participant asked, "Where are the boundaries of cyberspace?"

One of the private sector security experts noted, "Airplanes that enter U.S. airspace must pass through our Air Defense Identification Zone (ADIZ), people must pass through Immigration, and things must pass through Customs . . . what about the electrons flowing into the U.S. on the Internet? Should we have some sort of screening system for them? They can carry harmful computer viruses that could disrupt our economy, kiddie porn, or plans for terrorist attacks. Should they receive the same level of scrutiny that we apply to people and things?"

Others asked if the war on drugs and illegal immigration should be included in homeland security.

These were all good questions and observations that are still being debated today. In fact, the most frequent question I hear on the lecture circuit is, "How can we defend our homeland if we can't secure our borders?" I do not put this inquiry into the category of a wrong question, but I do note that when many people use the term "borders," they are thinking and speaking in eighteenth century concepts, not twenty-first-century realities.

There is no simple, all-conclusive answer to this challenge, but one thing is certain—it's time to rethink the concept of borders. The physical border of the United States consists of 95,000 miles of shoreline, 2,000 miles with Mexico, and 5,500 miles with Canada. Ours is one of the longest borders in the world, and for the most part, it is unguarded. Protecting 100,000 miles in the traditional sense is cost-prohibitive. Furthermore, threats such as cyber attacks and contagious diseases do not recognize physical borders, and issues such as illegal immigration may require enforcement in areas other than our physical borders, such as places of employment. For this discussion, we can divide border security into two primary issues: preventing unwanted *things* from entering the U.S., and preventing unwanted *people* from entering the U.S. The former is far easier to address than the latter, so we will begin with things.

Why is a discussion about things easier than one about people? Simple. There is considerable debate about allowing people into the country given the multitude of political, economic, social, and diplomatic considerations and ramifications. In contrast, all Americans can agree upon the fact that we don't want terrorists to smuggle nuclear weapons, or any other kind of weapon, into the U.S. But here's the most important question that needs to be posed in this debate: What is the likelihood that terrorists can and will transport weapons across our borders? To answer this question, we must ask and answer three more. Do terrorists have this capability? Yes. Are our borders vulnerable to penetration? Yes. Do they have the intent? In all cases of intent but one, the answer is no. Not what you expected? That is why proper analysis is so important. If we don't conduct an accurate assessment first, we end up with "Ready! Shoot! Aim!"

Using the same categories of weapons we discussed in Chapter 3, let's examine the probability that terrorists would want to transport such a weapon across our borders.

- *Conventional and enhanced conventional explosives:* The vast majority of explosive devices can be obtained or manufactured within the U.S. A few examples from recent history include Ramsey Yousef, who made his bomb in New Jersey from material purchased inside the U.S., Timothy McVeigh, who built his bomb in Kansas from diesel fuel and fertilizer, and the July 7, 2005, suicide bombers in London, who made their explosives in a bathtub in Leeds. Bombs made from acetone and peroxide, diesel fuel and fertilizer, and TNT can be made with material already located and readily obtainable within the U.S. And we must not overlook the 9/11 attacks. Delivering 30,000 gallons of jet fuel to the top floors of high-rise buildings is now the textbook example of an attack with enhanced conventional explosives. As noted previously, al Qaeda training manuals even state that it is safer to make these types of weapons in the target country, rather than trying to smuggle them across international borders.
- *Chemicals:* The 1984 disaster in Bhopal, India, demonstrated the type of damage that can be inflicted by industrial chemicals. No explosive devices were even required. Many experts, including Richard Falkenrath, the former deputy director of the White House Office of Homeland Security, place attacks on chemical facilities and chemical transportation systems at the top of their list for likely terrorist scenarios. While I don't consider a chemical attack to be in the same threat category as a nuclear or biological attack, I do

agree that it is one of the more likely scenarios, and that it could cause considerable loss of life, equal to or greater than 9/11. However, when considering the issue of border security in relation to this threat, I certainly find it hard to imagine why terrorists would attempt to import chemical weapons when we already have them conveniently located throughout our metropolitan areas in the form of industrial chemicals.

- *Radiological:* The material required to build a radiological dispersal device (RDD) or dirty bomb, is readily available inside U.S. borders at medical treatment facilities, research institutes, universities, and major construction sites. The ubiquitous availability of this type of material is the reason so many experts believe that a dirty bomb is the most likely CBRN (chemical, biological, radiological, nuclear) scenario.

- *Biological:* A terrorist would have no problem carrying a biological weapon across our border, just as I had no problem carrying my test tube into the White House and CIA Headquarters. However, even with an unlimited budget, there is nothing we could do to detect test tubes of pathogens coming across our borders. The most important aspect of biodefense to remember is that we cannot prevent an attack. Spending any amount of money on border security against bio-agents would be a total waste of money and effort.

- *Nuclear:* The most likely nuclear weapon would be a gun-type bomb made from highly enriched uranium. Without a doubt, this is the type of weapon that would be valuable enough to a terrorist to justify an attempt to bring it across our borders, which is why many argue in favor of buying and deploying more radiological detectors. But remember what we discussed in Chapter 5. First, a nuke built with

HEU is virtually undetectable if properly shielded. Second, with nearly 100,000 miles of borders, what is the probability that a terrorist would decide to bring it through a port where it might be detected or intercepted? Third, a terrorist organization does not need to bring its nukes to America; it can change the world by exploding a nuclear weapon anywhere. Spending large amounts of money on technology that can detect nuclear weapons at our borders would also be a waste of valuable resources. It would be far better if we used this money to prevent al Qaeda and any other terrorist organization from becoming a nuclear power, and to locate the weapons long before they came anywhere near our borders. A limited amount of money can be allocated to detection, as long as the primary expenditure is for highly mobile detectors that can be used for random, unpredictable checks and those based on intelligence information. This type of system might afford some amount of deterrence.

This analysis clearly demonstrates several key points about protecting our borders. First, due to the ubiquitous availability within our own country of the materials necessary to build conventional and enhanced conventional, chemical, and radiological weapons, very little would be gained by developing and deploying systems to prevent terrorists from attempting to bring such weapons across our borders. Second, although there might be some value in developing the capability to prevent biological weapons from being brought to America, such a system would be prohibitively expensive. More importantly, even a 100 percent effective system would make us no more secure, because terrorists could easily make biological weapons inside the U.S. Finally, spending billions of dollars on high-tech sensors for our ports in an effort to prevent terrorists from bringing in a nuclear weapon would only pay off if the terrorists were stupid—which they are not. Remember, we are dealing with a thinking enemy, one that will avoid our Maginot Line the same way Hitler avoided the French one—by going around it.

Therefore, when we talk about securing our borders, or more specifically, about preventing terrorists from bringing weapons into the U.S., the issue is not intuitively obvious. Undoubtedly, you have heard elected officials and TV pundits, neither of whom takes the time to seriously think through this issue, talk about preventing terrorists from bringing their weapons into the country. Encouraged by the homeland security–industrial complex that is eager to sell billions of dollars of equipment for deployment along our borders to detect these weapons, their focus is on that last two minutes and ten meters that will not provide us with the security we need.

That was the easy aspect regarding borders; now let's talk about the people. First of all, the politicians and pundits frequently make a very complex argument even more difficult to understand when they commingle the issue of illegal immigrants (those primarily looking for jobs and a better way of life) with terrorists and criminals who enter the U.S. to cause us harm. (According to the Department of Justice, 19 percent of inmates in federal prisons illegally entered the U.S.) First we must realize that given the length of our borders and the determination of our enemies, it would be virtually impossible to stop terrorists and criminals at the border. Keeping these people out of the country requires a focus that is months and miles before they show up at the border, rather than minutes and meters. As for those who come here looking for a piece of the great American pie, many good Americans—Republicans, Democrats, and independents—have very different ideas on how to deal with immigration and illegal immigration. One of the major problems with the debate about people is that the terms of reference are all too often used interchangeably when

they shouldn't be. Immigrants should not be confused with illegal immigrants, and illegal immigrants should not be confused
with terrorists and criminals entering America. Immigrants obey
the law, as my grandparents did when they came to Ellis Island
and became American citizens and taxpayers. Terrorists and international criminals come to America to cause us harm. Illegal
immigrants come because they want a chance at the dream. They
want to make a decent living and provide their children with a
better life. Illegal immigrants are not security threats. One can
certainly argue the economic, social, and political issues involved,
but these arguments should not be confused with those regarding terrorists.

The only time when the issue of terrorists and criminals inter-
sects with the issue of illegal immigration is when we are discussing *information*—the same weapon that terrorists and criminals
fear most is also a powerful means of controlling who lives and
works in America. Instead of attempting to control illegal immigration at our physical borders (primarily our southern border),
we need to move our thinking out of the eighteenth and nineteenth centuries and into the twenty-first. The best place to enforce our borders against illegal immigration is at the place of
employment.

Let's learn a lesson from the drug war. The long-standing debate is whether we should focus our efforts on supply or demand. After four years of working in the U.S. embassy just down
the road from the Golden Triangle in Southeast Asia, there is no
doubt in my mind as to which is the better choice. As long as
there is a demand in the U.S. for vast quantities of illegal drugs,
poor hill tribe farmers in Burma, Laos, and Thailand will continue to grow opium as their cash crop. They have no moral or
ethical problems with this enterprise, since they use opium in
their societies much the same as we use alcohol in ours. Our
State Department attempts to convince them to grow potatoes

and strawberries, but which would you rather carry down steep mountains, several hundred pounds of potatoes or a few ounces of opium?

Similarly, as long as organized crime continues to make enormous profits, drug trafficking will continue. This will not change until demand is significantly reduced, and the only way to accomplish that here in the U.S. is with a combination of strict enforcement, rehabilitation, and education. I am not suggesting that we stop spending money on drug interdiction overseas, only that it would be far more effective to focus on reducing demand rather than on reducing supply. Unfortunately, that is not our current strategy. (Homeland security is not the only area in which we have our priorities wrong.) The importation of illegal drugs is not a homeland security issue (as defined in this book), but it does highlight the supply versus demand debate. The issue of illegal immigration is another example. As long as there is a demand for illegal immigrant labor in the United States (read: "cheap labor"), there will be an ample supply. If we enforce our immigration policy at the place of employment, meaning that businesses and individuals could not hire illegal immigrants, the demand would be significantly reduced. But how could we accomplish this?

We certainly cannot do it with our current identity systems. While there are some employers who knowingly hire illegal immigrants, and some who abuse them at or near the level of slavery, the majority of employers have legitimate concerns and complaints regarding how they can accurately verify the citizenship status of prospective employees. I own a small business, but I don't know how to spot a fake driver's license or forged Social Security card. Do you? If the government is going to prosecute those who knowingly or unknowingly hire illegal immigrants, we must provide employers with a reliable identification system. Since we now live in a world where borders have a much broader meaning and scope than they did 200 years ago, or even fifty years ago, a reliable means of identification is becoming far more important. A national identity card would not only aid us in our fight against terrorism and with our challenges with illegal immigration, but it would provide great benefits for a number of other issues facing our nation today.

For example, national identity cards would be a powerful disincentive to identity theft. You can understand why bankers, credit card companies, retailers, employers, and individuals would benefit from a system that provided a positive means of identification. Additionally, a national identity system would make it far more difficult to collect more than one Social Security or welfare check. It would also require some cultural changes in certain states and cities. The longtime tradition of "vote early, vote often" would become a phenomenon of the past. While I say this with tongue firmly in cheek, I also acknowledge that the 1962 Supreme Court ruling in *Baker v. Carr* ("one man, one vote") is a fundamental principle in a democracy. Although this case was about reapportionment, the reasoning was based on the fact that each vote should carry equal weight. That is not the case when individuals vote more than once. Every eligible voter should be allowed to vote—but only once. Furthermore, those who are ineligible should not be allowed into the voting booth. Our current system of identification in this country does not properly protect this most important right and duty of U.S. citizens. I find it astonishing that you have to show a photo ID to board an airliner, enter federal buildings, or cash a check, yet the majority of states do not require a photo ID to vote (according to the 2005 report from the Commission on Federal Election Reform, co-chaired by Jimmy Carter and James Baker).

A national identity system is a protective measure that the terrorists would hate and fear, but many Americans seem to fear a national identity system almost as much as they do the terrorists. I always find the national ID issue to be one of the most interesting discussions I have with audiences. If the topic is not introduced during a Q&A period, I bring it up. The trend I see is that audiences that already have a form of national ID, such as business executives (passports) and the military, do not have a problem with the concept, and are generally supportive. People who don't travel outside the U.S. and spend little time on airliners inside the U.S. are not so supportive. One group of teachers I spoke to in Pennsylvania was disturbed to discover that I favored the idea, because these individuals considered a national ID system a serious threat to our right to privacy. The fact is, a properly designed national standard for identification is the best method to protect your privacy and finances.

One solution would be to implement voluntary programs, beginning with a traveler's identification system. One is already being tested in a few airports, and this program could be greatly expanded. Next we could implement a voluntary national identity system, which would allow us to work out the bugs and test various procedures and protocols, while simultaneously providing us with an immediate improvement in airline security. We could combine the national identity system with state driver's licenses. Yes, I understand this is a radical idea—asking the federal and state governments to work together—but technology now makes this possible, and the only barrier to such cooperation is the ideological entrenchment of these two government entities.

The REAL ID Act of 2006 was a step in the right direction, but many states are unhappy with the legislation, viewing it as just another unfunded mandate. While there might be legitimate financial concerns regarding implementation of this act, it is one of the more important homeland security initiatives. Federal funding to help states pay for this program will eliminate the majority of complaints from the governors and state legislators.

How we package a national ID system will be a critical element in getting the support of Americans. If the public understands that this system would increase our security by keeping terrorists off our airplanes and out of our country, protect our identity against theft, ensure the credibility of our democratic processes (no more "vote early, vote often"), and safeguard our social welfare systems against abuse, we might stand a chance of gaining the public confidence required to move forward with such a system.

I sometimes ask my audiences the question "How do you think members of the National Rifle Association would respond to a national identity system?" At a recent presentation, someone in the back of the room (perhaps a member of the NRA) said, "They'd shoot you." I'm not convinced. When I lived in Illinois, I discovered an excellent program to control gun sales. To purchase a gun, I had to provide a request and my fingerprints to state and local authorities, who then had two weeks to check me out. Was I a convicted felon? A mental patient? A habitual drug user? A wife beater? Once they determined I had a clean record, I was issued a photo ID. With this ID in hand, I could walk into any gun store and buy whatever gun I wanted, without the inconvenience of a waiting period (California, for example, has a ten-day waiting period for all types of guns). The only potential problem with this system would be the ID cards' vulnerability to alteration or counterfeiting. But with a national identity card that contained biometric information that made it virtually impossible to counterfeit or alter, I would be able to buy any gun, anywhere, at any time. Now why wouldn't the NRA endorse such a program?

This type of initiative would definitely require us to think anew. Today, Senator Alexander has changed his thinking, and now believes we should consider a national identity card. It may take us a decade to fully implement a national identity system that will successfully answer my four (or five) questions, but the time to start is now. We must not wait until the next major attack, even though it would certainly be an easier sell after such an event. In October 2001, more than two thirds of the American public said they were ready to consider a national identity system. However, if we wait until the day after the next large-scale attack, a hasty, knee-jerk reaction driven by fear will be unlikely to result in a program that will provide the four yeses necessary for success. (Can we ensure that ID credentials are properly issued? Does technology exist to prevent alteration or counterfeit? Can we build an affordable system? Can we protect privacy?)

NEW RULES

"The Wall"

Few, if any, terms used in homeland security have caused more confusion and misperceptions than the debate about "the wall." For those not familiar with the term, "the wall" has been used to describe the laws, policies, and cultural barriers that prevent or hinder the flow of information and other efforts in the fight against international terrorism.

Some problems are due to the complexity of the subject, some can be attributed to frequently changing laws, policies, and interpretations, some are caused by honest mistakes regarding the actual definition, and some are due to partisan finger pointing and intentional misrepresentation. The most blatant obfuscation came from Attorney General John Ashcroft during the 9/11 hearings, when he accused one of the 9/11 commissioners, Jamie Gorelick, of personally building this wall.

It is difficult to understand why a sitting attorney general would intentionally misrepresent such key information while testifying under oath. Some speculate he was trying to divert attention from him-self in the hearing. Others say he was responding in kind to a press leak from somewhere inside the commission the weekend before his testimony. The leak resulted in a *New York Times* story about the testimony of Thomas Pickard, who served as the acting director of the FBI from June 21 to September 4, 2001. Pickard told the 9/11 Commission that Ashcroft had not been focused on terrorism prior to 9/11. According to Pickard, Ashcroft told him to exclude terrorism from his FBI briefings, and refused to give the FBI the counterterrorism funding it had requested. Pickard asked if he could appeal the funding decision in writing, and Ashcroft agreed to reconsider. Pickard learned of Ashcroft's denial on September 12, 2001.

Regardless of his motivations, Ashcroft's accusation was a combination of partisan grandstanding, intentional misrepresentation, and, in my opinion, an attempt to deflect blame from himself for failing to prevent 9/11. (However, I need to make it perfectly clear that no single person, organization, or administration was solely to blame for 9/11—there is plenty of blame to go around.)

Here are the key facts, devoid of partisan politics. To borrow a quote from Lee Hamilton, co-chair of the 9/11 Commission, "There are neither Republican facts nor Democratic facts—just facts." Over the years, there have been many different "walls," some of which have been raised and lowered due to executive branch policy decisions, new legislation, new judicial interpretations, and individual action—some legal, some not.

The first wall was erected with the National Security Act of 1947, which created the Department of Defense, the U.S. Air Force, and the Central Intelligence Agency. It clearly stated that the CIA and other foreign intelligence organizations would not collect domestic intelligence. The term domestic intelligence is often misused and misunderstood. This prohibition on domestic intelligence has to do with who one is collecting against rather than where the collecting is being done. For instance, the National Security Agency cannot tap the phone of a U.S. citizen in Paris, France, any more than it can in Paris, Texas.

Without question, this wall has been lowered several times, particularly during the Vietnam War, when intelligence organizations designed to work overseas conducted operations inside U.S. borders against U.S. citizens. This is an example of an improper lowering of the wall, and these transgressions were uncovered during a series of hearings led by Senator Frank Church (D-ID) in 1975-76. The congressional committee's report on domestic intelligence activities (Book II, Section III) begins with this sentence:

The Committee finds that domestic intelligence activity has been overbroad in that (1) many Americans and domestic groups have been subjected to investigation that were not suspected of criminal activity and (2) the intelligence agencies have regularly collected information about personal and political activities irrelevant to any legitimate governmental interest.

There were many appropriate reactions to these findings, and as can always be expected, some overreactions. The Foreign Intelligence Surveillance Act (FISA) was one of the appropriate reactions to the Church hearings, and established a special court and special procedures for domestic intelligence operations against foreign powers. President Ronald Reagan signed Executive Order 12333—still in effect today—barring intelligence agencies from domestic spying. This was appropriate for the Cold War, but when bin Laden declared war on the United States in 1998, both legal and cultural walls existed that hampered the flow of information between the law enforcement and intelligence communities.

This was the setting for the 9/11 Commission hearings. While not actually naming Jamie Gorelick, a deputy attorney general during the Clinton administration, Attorney General John Ashcroft stated that one of the members on the 9/11 Commission was involved in building what he called "the wall." Ashcroft stated, "Someone built this wall . . . full disclosure compels me to inform you that the author . . . is a member of this commission." His accusation was based on the existence of two memos: one signed by Gorelick, and the other by former Attorney General Janet Reno.

The first memo, drafted in March 1995 and signed by Gorelick, provided guidance on two terrorism investigations, one of which was the 1993 bombing of the World Trade Center. This memo actually facilitated cooperation, directing agents on both the intelligence and law enforcement sides of the investigation to share information. It even specifically directed one agent to work on both teams to ensure that information was passed "over the wall." (This information is available in *The 9/11 Commission Report,* Chapter 8, page 539. If Gorelick were to be accused of anything, it could be of overstepping her authority in *lowering* the wall with this memo.) The other memo in question was signed in July 1995. A Department of Justice committee, including the FBI, prepared a memo that went through Gorelick to Attorney General Reno for signature. The purpose was to provide clear guidance to those working in the field who had to deal with these complex issues on a daily basis. There were numerous laws and interpretations by the courts regarding the sharing of intelligence information, and one cannot expect an FBI agent to read them all. That is the role of leaders: to provide guidance, once their staffs have thoroughly researched the issue, and that is precisely what the attorney general did. She did not make the rules; Congress and the White House accomplished that through legislation, which was then interpreted by the courts. Janet Reno merely provided operational guidance to those in the field.

This guidance can in no way be used by Attorney General Ashcroft as an excuse as to why proper investigations were not possible during his time in office prior to 9/11. As noted in *The 9/11 Commission Report* (Chapter 3, p. 79):

> *The 1995 AG [Attorney General] Guidelines (p. 1) required the FBI to notify both the Criminal Division and [Office of Intelligence Policy and Review] OIPR of information from FISA [Foreign Intelligence Surveillance Act] wiretaps reflecting a possible crime: "If, in the course of an . . . investigation, facts and circumstances are developed that reasonably indicate that a significant federal crime has been, is being,* or may be committed, *the FBI . . . shall . . . notify the Criminal Division. . . . The FBI shall inform OIPR when it initiates contact with the Criminal Division." (Emphasis added.)*

In fact, when the Ashcroft Justice Department considered the Reno guidelines, it endorsed them. On August 6, 2001, Larry Thompson, John Ashcroft's deputy attorney general, signed a memo in which he stated that the 1995 Attorney General Guidelines "remain in effect today." Once again, he didn't make the laws, he merely interpreted them.

These were the rules that were in place in 2001 when the FBI agents investigating Zacarias Moussaoui (later convicted of being part of the 9/11 plot) were seeking help from FBI Headquarters, and when agents in San Diego were searching for Khalid Almidhar and Nawaf Alhazmi (two of the 9/11 hijackers). The field agents' efforts were thwarted by officials in FBI Headquarters, but not because of memos from Janet Reno, Jamie Gorelick, Larry Thompson, the federal courts, or the U.S. Congress. The

problem was the FBI culture that was focused on investigation after a crime, as opposed to an intelligence-gathering operation before the crime was committed. Additionally, as often happens in
government agencies, subordinate organizations (in this case the
FBI), further interpret guidelines "from above" and make them
more restrictive. This is legal, but the guidelines cannot be made
less restrictive.

The unanimous conclusion of the bipartisan 9/11 commissioners agrees with my assessment of Attorney General Ashcroft's
comments. (FYI: As *The 9/11 Commission Report* notes, Gorelick
recused herself from all deliberations regarding the time period
in which she served as the deputy attorney general.) Neither the
March 1995 memo signed by Deputy Attorney General Gorelick,
nor the 1995 Attorney General Guidelines themselves were as characterized by Attorney General Ashcroft when he said that they were
responsible for the information-sharing problems in August 2001:

> *Attorney General [Ashcroft]'s testimony does not fairly
> or accurately reflect the significance of the 1995 docu-
> ments and their relevance to the 2001 discussions.* The
> 9/11 Commission Report, *Chapter 8, p. 539, n. 83.*

In Air Force terms, Attorney General Ashcroft's attack on Gorelick was the equivalent of "chaff and flares." (These are objects
ejected from an aircraft to distract radar and heat-seeking missiles.)
In Washington terms, his actions can best be characterized as partisan claptrap. There was a "wall" between intelligence and law
enforcement, but it was created over many years by laws, court
interpretations, and executive orders, not by Jamie Gorelick. Many
of the legal problems with this "wall" were corrected by the USA
Patriot Act.

I do not want to get into a lengthy legal discussion on the arguments for and against this act, but it is important to note that

while many people believe it faced major opposition, the facts provide a different picture. The U.S. Senate voted 98–1 in favor of this bill. At the time, Congress demonstrated great wisdom (yes, I do occasionally praise congressional actions) by including a sunset clause—meaning Congress would have to periodically reauthorize certain provisions. At a conference I ran in 2003, a senior representative of the American Civil Liberties Union began her presentation with these words: "The ACLU has no problems with 80 percent of the Patriot Act." This is not generally the impression that most Americans get from the news media. There are just a few sections of the Patriot Act that create controversy. The most hotly debated issues are the provisions that require periodic reauthorization.

I have no problems with roving wiretaps; however, the ACLU does. The previous rules were developed decades ago. Today, we all have and use many different phones. I have no problem with a judge signing a search warrant to tap any phone or computer device used by a suspected terrorist, as opposed to the old days when law enforcement personnel could only tap the numbers actually listed on the search warrant. Terrorists are smart. They buy cell phones at convenience stores, use them for a few days, and then throw them away. They use cyber cafés and public libraries with computers hooked to the Internet. For years roving wiretaps had been legal for the FBI when investigating organized crime. On October 25, 2001, during floor debate on the Patriot Act, and specifically roving wiretaps, Senator Joseph Biden (D-DE) stated, ". . . the FBI could get a wiretap to investigate the mafia, but they couldn't get one to investigate terrorists. To put it bluntly, this was crazy! What's good for the mob, should be good for terrorists."

I have no problems with "sneak and peek" warrants, but the ACLU does. Prior to the Patriot Act, if a search warrant was used to search a home, business, or warehouse, the FBI was required to notify the owner. The Patriot Act has a "sneak and peak" provision that eliminates this requirement. When the British searched a London warehouse in 2005, they discovered several tons of explosives. Their domestic intelligence organization, MI5, has sneak and peek authority, which allowed them to put 24/7 surveillance on the warehouse for a couple of months and eventually identify a dozen terror suspects. Had they been required to notify the owner shortly after the initial search, the majority of suspects would have been tipped off and avoided detection. Prior to the Patriot Act, the FBI in a similar situation would have had to notify the owners of the home or business being searched.

I do have some problems with the sections that, in my opinion, do not provide adequate oversight, and so does the ACLU. The most worrisome is something called "National Security Letters." They are issued by a special agent in charge, or deputy SAC, from one of the fifty-six FBI field offices. They provide, in effect, a warrantless search. This is the section that causes the controversy for librarians and Las Vegas hotels. In one highly publicized incident, the FBI demanded the information on hotel guests in Las Vegas for a one-week period. (And you thought what took place in Vegas, stayed in Vegas.) Furthermore, the individual receiving the National Security Letter has no means of appeal. The individual who wrote the guidelines at FBI for National Security Letters, Michael J. Woods (who no longer works in government), cautioned that they be used "judiciously." According to press reports, the FBI currently issues more than 30,000 National Security Letters each year. (The actual number is classified.)

I agree with the ACLU assessment that 80 percent of the Patriot Act was required to update obsolete rules and procedures. In fact, I have no problems with many of the remaining 20 percent of the Patriot Act provisions. However, I draw the line at warrantless searches. Checks and balances are one of the most important principles provided by our Founding Fathers. As we move into a world where borders have less meaning than before, and where the distinction between foreign and domestic intelligence becomes blurred, at times to the point of nonexistence, increased oversight is required.

A November 6, 2006, page-one article in the *Washington Post* offered similar criticism for the National Security Letters. The Justice Department quickly responded with a letter to the chairmen of the House and Senate judiciary committees. Assistant Attorney General William E. Moschella said that the *Post* report contained "distortions and factual errors." The letter contained a seventeen-point rebuttal. However, the *Washington Post* reporter, Barton Gellman, seemed to know more about the issue than the Justice Department.

Just three months later, the Justice Department's Inspector General released a report lambasting the FBI's management of the NSL program. Neither the Attorney General nor the FBI director disputed the findings. In a speech to the International Association of Privacy Professionals Privacy Summit (Washington, D.C.) on March 9, 2007, Alberto Gonzales, the U.S. Attorney General, stated:

In its examination of the FBI's use of National Security Letters, or NSLs, the IG found that the FBI did not have sufficient controls, did not provide adequate training, and failed to follow its own policies and Attorney General Guidelines.

There were two main problems: First, partly due to insufficient guidance and training, there was some confusion in the field about the rules, and that led to numerous instances of these letters being used in ways contrary to our policies and procedures. For example: in some cases the paperwork was filled out wrong; in some cases necessary approvals were not obtained or documented; and in some cases the third-party recipient provided the wrong information or information on the wrong individual. In addition, one FBI unit used a form letter to obtain information that should have been obtained by an NSL.

And second, the FBI did not have proper internal mechanisms to track the use of NSLs or to provide adequate oversight. Consequently, the FBI is unable to give an accurate number of NSLs issued . . . and thus our reporting to Congress has been inaccurate.

I was upset when I learned this, as was Director Mueller. To say that I am concerned about what has been revealed in this report would be an enormous understatement. Failure to adequately protect information privacy is a failure to do our jobs.

Law Enforcement or War?

Since the afternoon of 9/11, people have questioned how we should fight this new enemy. From an international perspective, there are two different approaches currently available for our struggle against al Qaeda and other similar terrorist organizations: law enforcement or war. During the Clinton administration, law enforcement was in the forefront of this effort, while the military was primarily in the business of launching cruise missiles, and the intelligence community collected, analyzed, and disseminated information. After 9/11, the Bush administration gave the military increased jurisdiction, augmented by significant operational support from the CIA, while the sixteen agencies that comprised the intelligence community refocused their efforts on the war on terrorism. Law enforcement was still on the team, but military and intelligence agencies had clearly taken the lead.

Many former officials from the Clinton administration argue that terrorism is a crime, and should be handled in the same manner as all other crimes—through law enforcement and our judicial system. They point to the cases of Ramsey Yousef and Omar Abdel-Rahman, the "blind sheik" from Brooklyn who conspired to bomb the Lincoln and Holland Tunnels and George Washington Bridge in New York City, as proof of the effectiveness of this approach. Both of these terrorists are currently serving life terms in federal prison. In contrast, the Bush administration and many of its supporters say that terrorism is a form of warfare, and believe that a war should be fought by the military, supported by intelligence operations. Obviously, all elements of national power must be fully engaged to defend our homeland. Some cases are better handled by law enforcement methods, and some by military and covert operations. However, the fundamental issue that must be resolved for the future has less to do with which team will assume the lead (military, intelligence, or law enforcement), than with the rules by which we will play.

The current international rules regarding the conduct of nation-states have evolved since the end of the Thirty Years War (1618–1648) and the Treaty of Westphalia (1648). This document is generally credited with establishing the principle—though it is not specifically stated—that nations are sovereign entities. The Geneva Conventions of 1949 are part of international humanitarian law. They established rules of warfare between nation-states, including the treatment of prisoners of war. One can debate the appropriateness and enforceability of these rules, but nevertheless they are recognized by more than 190 nation-states, which equates to almost every country in the world. Additionally, there are recognized standards for international law enforcement, and most nation-states have agreements for extradition and cooperative arrangements for pursuing international criminals and transnational criminal organizations.

From a legal perspective, war and law enforcement are completely separate entities, governed by completely different sets of rules, neither of which are best suited for our current struggle against al Qaeda. For instance, there is a raging debate in the U.S. and abroad regarding the legal status of al Qaeda terrorists we captured in Afghanistan. So what would we do if we captured bin Laden? Do we consider him a prisoner of war and follow the rules of the Geneva Conventions, or do we consider him a criminal, read him his rights, and ensure he has proper legal representation? The nature of terrorist organizations further complicates the matter. The Geneva Conventions clearly state that to be classified as a "soldier," one must wear a distinctive uniform, be a part of a traditional military organization, and follow the laws of warfare. Al Qaeda terrorists do not meet the legal standards of this classification, and therefore, there is a valid argument that they should not benefit from the protections afforded by the Geneva Conventions. There is precedent to this argument.

Terrorists and spies have often been treated differently than captured soldiers, even before the enactment of the Geneva Conventions. George Washington was faced with this situation during our Revolutionary War. Major John André, a British officer, was caught behind American lines, dressed in civilian clothes and carrying plans from General Benedict Arnold for the British attack on West Point. Despite pleas for mercy from many American leaders, including Alexander Hamilton, General Washington ordered him executed as a spy.

On the other hand, Judith Miller, former general counsel in the Department of Defense during the Clinton administration, argues that we must nevertheless follow the rules of the Geneva

Conventions in dealing with terrorist situations. First, she says that our compliance is necessary in order to protect our soldiers if they are captured. (To which some reply that the bad guys behead their prisoners.) Second, she believes that we need to follow the rules of the international community and the treaties we signed. Senator John McCain and former Secretary of State Colin Powell agree with her.

There are strong arguments for and against both approaches, but I think most observers will agree that the primary problem is that we are trying to fit square pegs into round holes. It is time that we begin to examine a new set of international laws and procedures to deal with today's unique security environment. The United States and our close allies should lead this effort. It will not be easy—the United Nations can't even agree on a definition of terrorism, much less the rules to deal with it.

Perhaps the best resolution would be to create a third model with rules that differ from those of either war or law enforcement. The best way to proceed would be to set a very high, or perhaps the correct term would be a very low, standard for the illegal behavior that warrants treatment under these new rules. Intentional attacks on civilian targets may be a good place to begin. Launching Katyusha rockets at Israel would not fit into this category, any more than would have Britain's night-bombing campaign of German cities in World War II, because the technology available at that time did not allow for precision strikes. The attacks on the Marine barracks in Lebanon, and the attack in Yemen on the USS *Cole* would also not qualify. Marine barracks and a U.S. destroyer are both military targets. (I have always objected to the attack on the Marine barracks being classified as terrorism. The U.S. had a battleship sitting off the coast, firing 1,600-pound shells at targets in Lebanon. A military conflict was ongoing, and a military target, a Marine base, was struck. It was a tragic loss of life for the U.S., and it was a horribly flawed operation in terms of force protection, but it was not terrorism—it was war.) On the other hand, when a suicide bomber walks into a pizza parlor filled with teenagers and families, surveys the scene, walks over to a woman pushing a baby carriage and detonates a nail bomb, then a line has been crossed. It is difficult to imagine that the U.S. could not get a majority of nations in the U.N. to identify such an act as falling outside the realm of protection by the Geneva Conventions. Furthermore, when a terrorist organization claims credit for such an action, and the bomber's family celebrates their son's or daughter's martyrdom (and in this particular case, when Saddam Hussein provided the family $25,000 compensation), we have a clear case for what can be referred to as a crime against humanity. This is not war, nor is it an ordinary crime.

By establishing the standards at this extreme level, to include hijacking airplanes and turning them into weapons of mass destruction for use on civilian targets, and placing bombs on trains and subways primarily targeting civilians, it would be far easier to gain international support. Since the nations of the world do recognize that certain types of killing in conflicts between nation states are legal, we should be able to muster broad support for a new enforcement regime against this type of mass murder.

I find that many individuals who have not served in the armed forces do not understand the internationally recognized laws of armed conflict. When I served as a helicopter gunship pilot in Vietnam, I was legally authorized under the Geneva Conventions to seek out and kill the enemy. I was not restricted by the rules of law enforcement, which dictate that a police officer can use deadly force only in cases of self-defense or in the defense of others. A police officer does not have the authority for the offensive use of deadly force. During armed conflict, a soldier does. My military ID card was, in effect, the "00" in special agent 007 James Bond's "license to kill." This is why many people do not want al Qaeda or any other terrorists to receive any protection under the Geneva Conventions, because if certain aspects of these rules apply, such as treatment of prisoners, then why not other provisions, such as recognizing a terrorist's right to use deadly force? Crimes against humanity must never fall under the category of warfare, nor should they receive the protections that govern wartime activities.

Debates about the 1949 Geneva Conventions (four treaties and three amendments) and terrorists generally include a discussion of Common Article 3. While the Conventions were primarily written for nation-states at war, Common Article 3 was included to cover civil wars within nations, but not international terrorism. It was designed to protect those who are not a member of a traditional military organization. It provides them protection from "violence to life, murder, mutilation, cruel treatment, torture and outrages upon personal dignity, in particular, humiliating and degrading treatment." It has been interpreted by some to apply to al Qaeda, but the guidance is both poorly defined and ill-suited to international terrorism.

Likewise, individuals and organizations engaged in crimes against humanity do not deserve the protection of international criminal law. I can see no way for the U.S. and most other nations to adapt criminal law in a manner that best suits the struggle ahead. It is time for new rules, and the British concept of "outlaw" may be a good place to begin. Many associate the term "outlaw" with the American Wild West, but it actually has its roots in British common law. Those individuals who committed "crimes against the realm" were banned from civil society and lost all protection afforded common criminals. Summary execution was common, and not only were citizens authorized to kill outlaws, they were often rewarded. (In the American Wild West, this was best exemplified with "wanted, dead or alive.") This provision lasted in English law up through the late nineteenth century and in Scottish law until 1940. Winston Churchill and others argued to resurrect the terminology in order to use it against Nazi war criminals, but American and Soviet leaders voted instead for war crimes tribunals.

Some suggest we look back to the international response to piracy in the seventeenth and eighteenth centuries. Piracy fell into that gray area between warfare and crime. For the most part, pirates were nonstate actors, although some of the most successful did receive state sponsorship (as privateers). While former rules for dealing with outlaws and pirates may provide some perspective, the fact remains that we need new rules for the twenty-first century. Using the rules for armed conflict between nations or criminal law to fight international terrorism is much like using the rules for the NFL and NBA in a game of rugby while the opposition uses knives and handguns. A new game requires new rules. The international community must develop rules for use against those who would engage in crimes against humanity. These rules would cover special procedures for offensive operations, capture, interrogation, detainment, trial, rules of evidence, and punishment.

The Press

I remember reading Jack Anderson in the 1970s and 1980s and never quite understanding how he was able to begin his newspaper columns with the words "A top secret CIA document crossed my desk this week" and not be guilty of violating some law. When I questioned such activity, I was told by legal scholars that it wasn't against the law for Anderson or any other reporter to see, possess, or write about classified information. Reporters were protected by the First Amendment. I would then ask, "What about the government employees who gave him the information? Were they committing a crime?" Invariably, the answer was, "Yes, of course."

In my youthful naïveté, I would continue, "Then why aren't they prosecuted?" No one ever provided me with what I considered to be a satisfactory answer to this question, but the responses generally went back to the First Amendment, and the fact that the government could not successfully prosecute government employees without forcing reporters to disclose their sources—or indeed revealing classified intelligence matters. Furthermore, expert "leakers" know how to provide classified or sensitive information to a reporter while remaining anonymous, or at least maintaining plausible deniability. This was the case during the Clarence Thomas confirmation hearing. Two Senate staffers who wanted to release sensitive information from FBI files to a reporter while still protecting themselves conveniently had a discussion on one side of a partition when they knew the reporter was standing on the other side. Not only is it illegal to release information from FBI files, much of it is unconfirmed and hence highly unreliable. All senators had access to this information, and if they wanted to bring it up at the hearings, they could have. The staffers' activities were at best shabby partisan politics, at worst, a serious crime.

What complicates matters, of course, is that administrations, both Republican and Democrat, classify information to avoid embarrassment. On the other hand, there have also been instances when classified information, the type that is vitally important to the security of the U.S., has ended up on the front pages of American newspapers. The most glaring example cited in *The 9/11 Commission Report* was the case of NSA eavesdropping on bin Laden's satellite phone. Shortly after the story appeared, bin Laden stopped using his phone. (This is a textbook example of what is meant by "protecting sources and methods." It wasn't the information we obtained from a particular phone intercept that was important to protect, it was how we obtained that information.) For this discussion, however, we will not consider those issues that shouldn't have been classified, or even those in the gray areas—only information that most observers would agree justifies protection. Why can't we do something about that? Actually, the 106th Congress tried.

Section 304 of the Intelligence Authorization Act for Fiscal Year 2001, passed by both houses of Congress in the fall of 2000, would have made it a crime to intentionally expose classified information via broadcast or print media. The government would have had to prove that the news organization was aware that the information was classified, and also that the information deserved classification, rather than it being an attempt to disguise government blunders. If both facts were proven in court, media exposure of this material would constitute a felony.

Most Americans do not seem to be aware that this is the standard throughout the Western World. The U.S. is the anomaly, and that can be directly traced back to the First Amendment. But is that what the Founding Fathers had in mind? I don't think so, and neither did the 106th Congress. According to the drafter of this legislation, Dan Gallington, a senior staffer from the Senate, Congress had been granted assurances from the Clinton White House that the president would sign the legislation into law. However, a last-minute lobbying effort by the media resulted in a veto. One can certainly hope the 110th Congress, which began in January 2007, will demonstrate the wisdom and courage to reintroduce this legislation. It is a difficult issue, but certainly one worthy of continued debate and consideration.

A cornerstone of the media defense is that they would never release information that would damage U.S. security. The facts, however, do not always seem to back this up. In her superb book *A Woman at War*, Molly Moore of the *Washington Post* makes this claim.

I call the book superb for two reasons. First, it is one of the best descriptions of the emotions of war that I have read. During the first Iraq war in 1991, Molly lived with the Marines in the field. She captured the fear, boredom, frustration, excitement, loneliness, and stress of ground combat better than any other reporter that I have read. Second, she also inadvertently illustrated the best argument for this type of legislation.

Throughout her book, she complains of the censorship enforced by Coalition Forces Commander General Norman Schwarzkopf, arguing that reporters should be trusted to know what should and should not be reported. Her greatest complaint is the fact that reporters accompanying troops in the field during the ground war were not allowed to carry their satellite phones. All reports to their bureaus had to go through military public affairs channels to ensure the sensitive battlefield information (intelligence from the enemy's perspective) did not end up on CNN and the front page of newspapers.

When the Iraqis began to flee Kuwait, the Marines were directed to change their battle plans. While standing outside a command center (a tent), Molly listened in on the new attack plans. Her account makes clear that were it not for censorship, she would have put the details of the new plans on the front page of the *Washington Post*. In her own words from page 259:

I eavesdropped on the war from my listening post on the other side of the canvas wall, frustrated that so much was unfolding before me and I had no way of reporting it because our convoy had become separated from [Major General William] Keys and his communications satellite. Right now it was 8 P.M. in Washington. The deadlines for the final editions of the Post *were hours away. I cursed myself for heeding Schwarzkopf's order barring reporters from taking satellite phones onto the*

battlefield. I should have just stowed it away under the
duffel bags in the back of the Blazer, I thought.

What she wanted on the front page of the *Washington Post*
was real-time information about battle plans as they unfolded.
Molly is typical of most American journalists. She is a good American who would never intentionally do anything that would risk
the lives of fellow Americans. But when under the stress of deadlines and getting the big story, there are times when members of
the press, especially those without decades of national security
experience, may not consider or fully understand the implications of their reporting.

A more recent example is the *New York Times* June 23, 2006,
report of the federal government's secret program to track terrorist money flow through the international banking system
(Society for Worldwide Interbank Financial Telecommunica-
tions, SWIFT). It made for big headlines—the type of story
that wins Pulitzer Prizes, but in the end, the federal government had done nothing illegal and the *Times* tipped off the
bad guys to one of our best methods for tracking their financial
activities.

On July 2, 2006, Byron Calame, the *New York Times* om-
budsman, defended the paper's decision to report on this secret
program.

My close look convinced me that Bill Keller, the execu-
tive editor, was correct in deciding that Times *readers*
deserved to read about the banking-data surveillance
program. And the growing indications that this and
other financial monitoring operations were hardly a se-
cret to the terrorist world minimizes the possibility that
the article made America less safe.

However, after it became clear to most serious observers that the program was not illegal, but was secret, highly sensitive, and productive, Calame retracted his defense on October 22, 2006. (Interestingly, this mea culpa was buried at the end of a column titled "Can Magazines of the *Times* Subsidize News Coverage?")

Since the job of public editor requires me to probe and question the published work and wisdom of Times *journalists, there's a special responsibility for me to acknowledge my own flawed assessments.*

My July 2 column strongly supported the Times's *decision to publish its June 23 article on a once-secret banking-data surveillance program. After pondering for several months, I have decided I was off base. There were reasons to publish the controversial article, but they were slightly outweighed by two factors to which I gave too little emphasis. While it's a close call now, as it was then, I don't think the article should have been published.*

Those two factors are really what bring me to this corrective commentary: the apparent legality of the program in the United States, and the absence of any evidence that anyone's private data had actually been misused. I had mentioned both as being part of "the most substantial argument against running the story," but that reference was relegated to the bottom of my column. . . . I haven't found any evidence in the intervening months that the surveillance program was illegal under United States laws. Although data-protection authorities in Europe have complained that the formerly secret program violated their rules on privacy, there have been no Times *reports of legal action being taken. In addition, I became embarrassed by the how-secret-is-it issue, although that isn't a cause of my*

*altered conclusion. My original support for the article
rested heavily on the fact that so many people already
knew about the program that serious terrorists also must
have been aware of it. But critical, and clever, readers
were quick to point to a contradiction: the* Times *article
and headline had both emphasized that a "secret" program was being exposed.*

I am a strong supporter of the First Amendment protection for
the freedom of the press. I am a member. I have my own weekly
public radio show. I believe that a free press is one of the important checks and balances in our constitutional system. But there
has always been a difficult balance between the need to protect
critical government secrets and the right for citizens to know.

The information age makes this an even more difficult challenge. Does every blogger have the same protection as the *New
York Times*? Can a blogger refuse to testify in a court of law to
protect their sources? If so, can anyone freely disclose classified
information? Do we just fire up a blog and give all of our most
sensitive information to our enemies? Can we all be Jack Ander-
sons in the twenty-first century?

I have no answers for these questions; in fact, on this most
difficult issue, I am still working on asking the right questions.
This debate will continue. The press will howl with indignation
and disbelief if the 110th Congress even considers passing the
provision that caused President Clinton to veto the initial FY
2001 Intelligence Authorization Act. They will claim that the
press is the "guardian of liberty." Only the press can protect the
citizens from illegal government actions. There is truth in their
claim, but there is also truth in the words of the Roman poet
Juvenal, *"Sed quis custodiet ipsos custodes?,"* "But who watches
the watchers?" (A question also asked by Plato and Socrates.)

If the law is changed, there will remain other courses of action. If the press discovers illegal activity, it could provide this information to an appropriate organization within the federal government. For instance, if the press believes that the executive branch is doing something wrong, such as SWIFT, it could provide this information to appropriate members of Congress, or perhaps, the oversight organization recommended in the next section. But the question remains, if the investigation does not result in a front-page story, then why do it?

NEW ORGANIZATIONS

Domestic Intelligence Organization

America has very limited domestic intelligence capabilities. The responsibility falls under the purview of the FBI, which is not organized, trained, equipped, or even particularly interested in such a mission. According to Keith Slotter, the FBI Academy's deputy assistant director for training, "We didn't have any intelligence training before 9/11" (*Washington Post,* August 17, 2006). This is not surprising since it was not a high-priority mission prior to 9/11. However, most Americans would likely be shocked to discover that five years after 9/11 the 700-hour curriculum at the FBI Academy for new recruits contains only one hour examining "Islam, Arabic culture and understanding the terrorist mind-set." New recruits do receive extensive training on traditional skills: 114 hours learning to shoot, 78 hours on arrest techniques, and 36 hours on forensics.

Director Mueller says the FBI is taking its new mission very seriously. I greatly respect the integrity and sincerity of Bob Mueller, but the task of reinventing the FBI is a major challenge. Progress has been limited. To borrow a phrase from Mark Twain, I would say this effort is currently comprised of more "nouns than verbs."

- In the first five years after 9/11, there has been a virtual revolving door in the FBI's counterterrorism office. It has had seven different leaders (Dale Watson, Pasquale J. D'Amuro, Larry Mefford, John Pistole, Gary Bald, Willie Hulon, and Joseph Billy, Jr.).
- According to the FBI's own assessment (published in the October 11, 2006, *Washington Post*), not a single one of the 12,000-plus FBI special agents was rated as a "native speaker" of Arabic. Only ten agents were rated at the "General Professional" or "Advanced Professional" levels.
- As described in a *New York Times* op-ed article (October 17, 2006) by Jeff Stein, during a deposition in a whistleblower case, observers were shocked at the basic lack of knowledge displayed by senior FBI counterterrorism officials (including Gary Bald) regarding even the most basic issues of Islam. Bald commented that it was far more important to be a good manager than to have expertise about the enemy (clearly a law enforcement, rather than an intelligence or counterterrorism, perspective).
- The new FBI intelligence training center is not scheduled to open until 2014.

The FBI is not properly organized for an intelligence mission. Since its creation in 1908, it has been, and remains today, a decentralized organization. Agents in the fifty-six field offices focus their efforts on working closely with the assistant attorneys general in their regions to investigate crimes and prosecute the perpetrators. The FBI's primary, almost exclusive, focus has been building cases to take to court. The FBI is the appropriate organization for this type of mission, which is why the legislative and executive branches chose it for the task. By comparison, an intelligence organization collects information and sends it to a central organization for compilation, analysis, and distribution to key leaders in the administration and Congress, and other operators in the field. This type of mission was, and remains today, totally outside the FBI's culture of investigation. The "I" in FBI will always stand for *Investigation*, not *Intelligence*.

On September 4, 2001, Robert Mueller became the sixth director of the Federal Bureau of Investigation. On the morning after 9/11 he walked into the Oval Office to meet with President Bush, and he said, "Mr. President, we are going to find out who did this." President Bush replied, "Bob, we know who did it. They're dead. Your job is to make sure it does not happen again." I am sure that Director Mueller understood that the nineteen hijackers were dead, and was actually referring to those who had ordered and funded the attack. Nevertheless, he was doing the traditional FBI mission: investigating crimes and prosecuting the perpetrators. The president changed ninety-plus years of tradition with his one sentence that morning when he gave the FBI the new mission of prevention.

America has given the FBI more than five years to adapt to this new mission, and one could argue that it has succeeded. As of this writing, with the exception of the anthrax incidents of October 2001, there have been no new attacks on our homeland. But no one can say why this is true. Undoubtedly, taking away al Qaeda's sanctuary in Afghanistan, killing and capturing many of al Qaeda's top leaders, and making it more difficult to transfer money and information, as well as move personnel in and out of countries (including our own) have all played a part in keeping us safe since 2001. However, al Qaeda may have had no intention of attacking during this period. Remember, it was eight years between the first and second attacks on the World Trade Center.

I'm not convinced that either the FBI or the CIA is the right organization for the job of domestic intelligence. During the question and answer period of my testimony to the 9/11 Commission I stated, "If the FBI knocks on my door at two in the morning with a search warrant, I want all of the legal protections that our laws, court interpretations, and cultural values provide. On the other hand, I want the CIA to be an organization that has extensive freedom to find terrorists overseas, and when possible, kill them or take other actions to neutralize the threat." The combination of the culture within the FBI and our societal values for what American citizens expect and demand of the FBI and the CIA makes both incompatible as domestic intelligence organizations. We must think anew in order to create a type of organization and culture that can collect and analyze intelligence inside the U.S.

What type of role would a true, independent domestic intelligence organization play? Its sole mission would be prevention. The key to success would be that a domestic intelligence organization would have a significantly different culture from the FBI. It would have no arrest authority. The agents could not testify in a federal or state criminal court. (The reason being that their probable cause standards would not be as restrictive as those of the FBI.)

This would be a relatively small organization, exclusively focused on working with the director of national intelligence to provide a seamless effort in tracking terrorists as they move from other countries into the U.S. This organization could conduct surveillance operations against any person inside the United States, including American citizens, something the intelligence community cannot do today. Its sole mission would be prevention. This is the type of organization that could have prevented 9/11, and one that could prevent the next major attack. And with proper oversight, it could be an organization that would not violate our cultural norms.

Aggressive oversight of a domestic intelligence organization would be critical to maintaining public support. This oversight could be provided by the FISA Court, created under the authority of the Foreign Intelligence Surveillance Act of 1978. It provides a means for the FBI to conduct a wide range of surveillance activities on foreign persons inside the U.S. On the other hand, oversight could be provided by a new organization. In fact, this new organization could provide oversight for both foreign and domestic intelligence operations.

I cannot overstress the importance of aggressive, nonpartisan, and effective oversight of all intelligence operations. This is a pursuit that began for me on September 12, 2001. On the morning after 9/11, I was asked to provide a two-hour tutorial to Senator Edward Kennedy (D-MA) on homeland security. While we were talking about how to prevent the next attack, Senator Kennedy asked, "Should we allow the CIA and NSA to operate inside U.S. borders?" It was a question many people in Washington were asking, or at least thinking about. My answer to that question today and tomorrow is and will be the same as it was on September 12, 2001: "Whatever we do in terms of domestic intelligence operations, it must be accompanied with appropriate oversight . . . above partisan politics." This oversight is even more important when considering the fact that these operations might include surveillance of U.S. citizens and legal residents.

An intelligence operation within U.S. borders is an entirely new ball game. It will require new rules, a new organization, and a far better system for oversight. If we decide to continue down the path of focusing our efforts and spending on the two minutes prior to an attack, then we really don't need to worry about creating a new domestic intelligence operation. If, however, we decide to focus efforts on preventing attacks, as the British did when they foiled the plot to blow up ten U.S. airliners over the Atlantic in August 2006, then we need a new domestic intelligence organization, and we need a far better system for oversight—one that will not only allow for the types of intelligence operations that are required, but also for the simultaneous and aggressive defense of our civil liberties and privacy.

Frankly, I do not think the American people will support the creation of an independent domestic intelligence organization, at least not until after the next attack. Maybe then the public and our elected officials might decide that a better system for domestic intelligence is needed, and if that day comes, we must ensure appropriate oversight.

Oversight Commission

Over time, our elected officials have come to realize that some critical processes of our federal government work most effectively when management and oversight are placed outside the realm of politics as usual. Three examples of this type of organization are the Securities and Exchange Commission, the Federal Reserve System, and the newest model, the Base Realignment and Closure Commission.

Congress created the SEC in 1934 as a means to enforce two newly passed security laws: the Securities Act of 1933 and the Securities Exchange Act of 1934. Prior to the Great Crash of 1929, there was little support for government oversight and regulation of the stock market, but after investors and banks suffered from this catastrophe and the Great Depression that followed, public confidence hit an all-time low. In an effort to restore faith in our capital markets, Congress passed these two acts, which were based on two main premises: first, that the public has a right to know information about the businesses selling securities, including the risks involved in investment; second, that those selling and trading securities be required to treat the investors fairly by putting the investors' interests first. Today, the SEC has approximately 3,100 employees, led by five presidentially appointed and Senate-approved commissioners. One of the five is designated by the president as chairman, and in order to remain a bipartisan organization, no more than three commissioners can belong to the same party. The SEC's commissioners' responsibilities include interpreting federal security laws, enforcing and amending existing laws, and proposing new rules as needed.

The Federal Reserve System, more popularly known as the Fed, was founded by Congress in 1913 in an effort to provide the United States with a safer and more stable monetary system. Since its creation, its role has been significantly expanded. Today, its responsibilities include regulating banking institutions, providing financial services to the U.S. government, and establishing the prime interest rate to regulate the economy. The Fed is comprised of a central government agency based in Washington (the Board of Governors), and twelve regional Federal Reserve Banks. Because the Fed's decisions don't have to be ratified by the president or anyone else in the executive branch, it is considered to be an independent, central bank. However, it is still subject to congressional oversight. The Board of Governors is comprised of seven presidentially appointed, Senate-confirmed members.

Imagine what it would be like if Congress controlled interest rates. Do you suppose the majority party might benefit from interest rates going down prior to an election? It is in the best interest of our nation for certain aspects of governance to be removed from partisan politics. This was the reasoning behind the creation of the SEC and the Fed, and the same principle applied to the Base Realignment and Closure Commission (BRAC).

As the Cold War ended, both Congress and the administration realized that the Defense Department required a massive restructuring, including base closures. A successful program would not only provide America with a more efficient military, but it would also guarantee the so-called peace dividend to the American taxpayer. There was just one problem—the U.S. Congress. Powerful members, in particular committee and subcommittee chairmen, could prevent base closures in their home districts and states.

In 1989, the first BRAC began work. This commission was designed to conduct extensive research, listen to all sides of the debate, and offer recommendations to the administration and Congress. The commissioners were selected from the public and private sectors, and were representative of a wide range of professional expertise and a broad spectrum of political backgrounds and affiliations. The BRACs (1989, 1991, 1993, 1995, 2005) were successful due to the fact that these commissioners placed the interests of an effective and efficient Defense Department and the American taxpayers above their own political, professional, and geographic loyalties.

Once the Commission submitted its recommendations to the administration and Congress, neither could make any changes. They could only approve or disapprove in whole—amendments were not allowed. (Some will say the process was a bit corrupted in 1995 when President Clinton made some minor changes to the recommendations for a base in Texas and one in California.)

The success of the BRAC model was demonstrated during the first three BRACs when five bases from the Ninth Congressional District of California were selected for closure and/or realignment. The district was represented by Ron Dellums, the chairman of the powerful House Armed Services Committee, and this would never have occurred if Congress had been in charge of the process.

This BRAC process may be a model for other difficult decisions we will face in the next few decades. Since Social Security is well known in Washington as the third rail of politics (an analogy about subways where the third rail is electrified—touch it and you are dead), the only way we will be able to make major changes, the type necessary to prevent us baby boomers from destroying the economic future of our grandchildren, will be with a BRAC-like process. Consider it adult supervision, something required at times during the political process.

Direct democracy works for a local PTA, but it is not appropriate for a large electorate. Our Founding Fathers understood this, which is why they created a republic: a system of government where the electorate sends its representatives to the seat of government. The creation of organizations such as the SEC, the Fed, and the Base Realignment and Closure Commission is a further refinement of the democratic process. For the most part, they removed partisan politics and pork from key functions of government that are essential to our society. It is now time to further expand this process, and the next area for consideration is that of intelligence oversight.

Until the mid-1990s, the House and Senate intelligence committees practiced what they preached: "Partisan politics stop at the water's edge." They maintained a reputation far above that of most other committees because of their strong bipartisan spirit and commitment to professional expertise. Additionally, members remained on these two committees for considerably longer periods of time than other committee assignments, gaining significant expertise.

I have been critical of many members of Congress in this book, but in their defense, let me be clear about the difficulties they face. In the period of one week's time, members might be asked to make key decisions on issues ranging from Social Security and defense spending to taxation, banking procedures, highway funds, and education reform. We have a large and complex government, and we expect our representatives to understand the issues on which they must vote. This is without question a difficult challenge, and why it is so important that the House and Senate intelligence committees establish professional credibility and work diligently to maintain a collegial, bipartisan approach. Unfortunately, the system no longer works the way it should. The professional competence may have survived, but the bipartisan collegiality has not, and therefore it is time to place the critically important function of intelligence oversight in the hands of a new organization.

Highly sensitive intelligence operations are currently briefed to the intelligence committee chairs and senior-ranking minority members, and the remainder of the "Gang of 8," which includes the speaker and minority leader of the House, the majority and minority leaders of the Senate, and the chairmen and ranking members of the congressional intelligence committees. During the past few years, we have watched how partisan politics has dominated this once respected process.

The cure for this disease is the creation of a permanent commission, much like the SEC or Fed. The blurring of the line between domestic and foreign intelligence, the need for more aggressive intelligence operations, and just as importantly, the absolute requirement of protecting our privacy, civil liberties, and cultural values, require that a truly independent commission of distinguished, well-qualified citizens provide this new function.

The purpose of the commission would be to provide oversight of the executive branch, and appointment of members would be solely in the hands of Congress. There would be a balance between Republican and Democratic representation, just as there was on the 9/11 Commission, and if the right people are selected, we will see a comparable result: Republicans and Democrats coming together to create a unanimous set of bipartisan recommendations. The U.S. Commission on National Security/Twenty-first Century (also known as Hart-Rudman) is another successful example of this type of endeavor. Even though the commission's membership spectrum ran from as far left as Andrew Young to as far right as

Warren Rudman, its fifty recommendations were unanimous. The key to creating a successful oversight committee is to select members who not only share the same professional credentials and high ethical standards as those on the Fed, SEC and BRAC, but who also are devoid of partisan agendas. The only way to ensure that is to appoint members who are not seeking elected office. If they're not immersed in running a campaign and winning an election, they are much less likely to be embroiled in the daily partisan squabbling that has become so pervasive in Congress.

Leaders such as Tom Kean and Lee Hamilton (co-chairs of the 9/11 Commission), and Chuck Robb and Laurence Silberman (co-chairs of the Commission on the Intelligence Capabilities of the United States Regarding Weapons of Mass Destruction) are just a few examples of America's wealth of intelligent, dedicated individuals capable of serving in this capacity. Additionally, this commission should include business executives, college presidents, and other distinguished citizens from outside the Beltway. Once this commission is in place, there would be no excuse for the White House to avoid sharing information on critical intelligence operations. While I disagree with how certain operations were handled by this administration, I understand its reluctance to throw red meat to the opposition. Americans want to be secure. We want the intelligence organizations in this country to be aggressive in defending our homeland. But we also want to ensure that any aggressive action does not become a greater threat to our privacy, civil liberties, and cultural values than the terrorists. By design and circumstance, the U.S. Congress is no longer the best-qualified organization to provide oversight for highly sensitive intelligence operations. Congress would maintain the important functions of intelligence appropriations and issues regarding organization, but would delegate oversight authority of operational matters, such as the NSA wiretapping and data mining issues of 2006, to this commission.

This standing commission would be operating in many gray areas. If at any time an intelligence operation, either domestic or foreign, did not receive the support of two thirds of the membership, the matter could be referred to the House and Senate intelligence committees for resolution. This is an opportunity for Congress to demonstrate, in a bipartisan fashion, its wisdom and foresight in creating the new organizations necessary to the defense of our nation.

Director of Biodefense

According to a 2005 study by the Center for Biosecurity-UPMC, there are twenty-six presidentially appointed, Senate-confirmed individuals working in a dozen different agencies that are actively engaged in biodefense, but none of these people has biodefense as a full-time job. Perhaps it's my three decades of military service, or perhaps it's just common sense that makes me feel uneasy about the fact that no one is in charge of defending America from what most agree is one of its greatest threats.

I recommend the creation of a director of biodefense. This individual will have authority over policy, budget, and in times of public health crises, operational control of all federal organizations engaged in biodefense. This would not be just another reshuffling of the boxes on the organizational wiring diagram, but a major overhaul of America's biodefense capabilities on the scale of the Goldwater-Nichols reforms of 1986 for the Department of Defense and the Intelligence Reform Act of 2005 that created the director of national intelligence (DNI). There are great lessons to be learned from both of these major initiatives.

The National Security Act of 1947 was a major step forward in preparing America for the security challenges of the post-World War II era. The Department of War, which included the Army and Army Air Corps, and the Department of the Navy, which included the Navy and Marine Corps, were combined to create the Department of Defense. The Army Air Corps became a separate service, the U.S. Air Force. The act also created the Central Intelligence Agency. The Department of Defense went through several other evolutionary changes during the next two decades, but there were still major organizational problems, particularly in the operational chain of command. Three major events highlighted these deficiencies: the failure of the rescue mission in Iran (frequently, but incorrectly, referred to as Desert One), the invasion of Grenada, and the attack on the Marine barracks in Lebanon.

A congressional hearing held aboard a Navy cruiser sitting off the Lebanese coast within sight of the former Marine base highlighted the most significant obstacle to force protection, as well as the problems that plagued the other two incidents in question: the chain of command. There were forty-four levels of command and staff between the commander-in-chief in the White House and the Marine colonel who commanded the Marine Expeditionary Unit (MEU) in Lebanon. Until the 1987 Goldwater-Nichols Act provided a revolutionary change, guidance from the president would have to wind its way through this byzantine process. Following implementation of Goldwater-Nichols, the chain of command from the commander-in-chief to a deployed MEU commander was reduced tenfold. The chain now consists of the president of the United States, the secretary of defense, the regional combatant commander, and the deployed MEU commander. This radical reorganization was implemented throughout the Defense Department, and the effects of this extraordinary change were witnessed during the next two highly successful military operations: Just Cause (Panama, 1989) and Desert Shield/Desert Storm (liberation of Kuwait, 1990–91). Today, all flag officers (generals and admirals) sing the praises of the Goldwater-Nichols reforms during their congressional testimony, but what is often forgotten is the extent to which the flag officers fought these reforms back in 1986. The chief of naval operations (the senior naval officer) was so opposed to these reforms that in an emotional appeal during a congressional hearing he stated, "This . . . this is un-American." In a separate meeting during the hearing process, two other service chiefs refused to shake Senator Goldwater's hand.

Bottom line, the Defense Department would have never made these reforms on its own initiative. It fought with great passion to prevent these changes that today are universally praised. As much as I tend to beat up Congress for its partisan pranks, pork barrel waste, and general lack of strategic perspective, let me say loud and clear: "Thank God Congress showed the courage and wisdom to get this one right." We need Congress to demonstrate that same courage and wisdom today to face the slings and arrows of an entrenched bureaucracy that will howl in protest against the creation of a director of biodefense. All of those who will oppose such reform should get their talking points from the four service chiefs who opposed Goldwater-Nichols. Their arguments will be similar—and just as wrong.

In response to 9/11, and what many refer to as a major intelligence failure, Congress and the president agreed to a major structural reorganization of America's intelligence community with the creation of the director of national intelligence. Some (including former Senators Gary Hart and Warren Rudman) claimed this was not necessary, since the National Security Act of 1947 had already created such a position. There is some credibility to this argument. When Porter Goss assumed duties as the director of the Central Intelligence Agency on August 10, 2004, he actually assumed two positions, the same as his eighteen predecessors. He became the director of the Central Intelligence Agency and the director of central intelligence (DCI). In this second job, he allegedly controlled all sixteen agencies that comprise the intelligence community. This may have been true in theory, but over fifty years of neglect in attempting to exercise such authority had turned this position into nothing but a figurehead. Goss had no authority to control budgets, personnel, or reorganizations.

This was somewhat the case for Admiral William Crowe, the chairman of the Joint Chiefs of Staff, when Goldwater-Nichols was passed by Congress and signed by the president. Prior to Goldwater-Nichols, the chairman of the Joint Chiefs had surprisingly little authority without the unanimous consent of the four service chiefs. However, Admiral Crowe seemed content with the status quo, and made no serious attempts to implement and enforce the new procedures during the remainder of his tenure. The same was not true for his successor, General Colin Powell. Powell's greatest contribution in his nearly four decades of service to the Department of Defense was the force of his personality and leadership style in implementing and enforcing Goldwater-Nichols. Powell and his successors became the chief executive officers of the uniformed services. Had the first few directors of central intelligence taken the same action in the late 1940s, there might not have been a need for the Intelligence Reform Act of 2005.

Learning from these two examples, we must now move forward to create a director of biodefense (DBD). To be as successful as Goldwater-Nichols, there are several key issues that must be addressed:

- The person selected by the president and confirmed by the Senate to be the director must be chosen based on professional competence, not political pedigree. He or she must not be a lawyer from the horse show industry, but someone with the professional credentials necessary to immediately gain the confidence of the medical, public health, and scientific communities. The director must

also be someone with considerable experience inside the
Beltway.

- The director must have authority similar to that of the director of national intelligence, with the power to control
policy, personnel, and spending programs. The director
will be responsible for developing a national strategy, supporting policies, and budget submissions for biodefense.

- There must be a provision for the president to declare a
national bio-emergency. Once declared, the DBD will, in
military terms, become the "supported combatant commander." In Desert Shield/Desert Storm this position was
held by General Norman Schwarzkopf. All other combatant commanders (four-star generals and admirals who
command America's primary war fighting units) became
"supporting commanders." In other words, the designated
civilian biodefense assets of the secretaries of Health and
Human Services, Homeland Security, the Department of
Agriculture, the Department of Justice, and other senior
leaders such as the administrator of the Environmental
Protection Agency would all fall under the operational
control of the DBD during a presidentially declared biological emergency.

This would most certainly not solve all of the operational
issues, since unlike military operations, state and local governments would play a major role in any response to a biological crisis. However, state and local government leaders would have a
single leader within the federal government to look to—a leader
who is professionally competent, and in control of all federal
resources. Perhaps the creation of a director of biodefense at
the federal level might encourage similar reorganizations at the
state level.

Unfortunately, this position is not likely to be created until America experiences a biodisaster, because that is the way things tend to work in a democracy. You didn't have to be a flag officer or a senior member of an armed services committee in Congress to realize that a major reorganization was required to improve the effectiveness of the Defense Department. The failures at the Marine barracks in Lebanon, at Desert One in the Iranian desert during Operation Eagle Claw, and the serious coordination failures during the invasion of Grenada created the tipping point that forced Congress to take action. Likewise, 9/11 brought about the Intelligence Reform Act that created the director of national intelligence. It is unfortunate that it will most likely take a biodisaster before action is taken to properly prepare America for this most troubling threat.

Some insiders will scoff at this recommendation. They will say the issue is too complex, and that there are too many organizations involved in biodefense to put one person in charge. However, no one who has ever commanded on a field of battle will say this—it would be the equivalent of suggesting that the invasion of Normandy on D-Day was too complex to have one person in charge. Nonsense! I am sure General Eisenhower would have disagreed. There were dozens of vigorous debates on key issues among the various senior-ranking generals involved, but ultimately, one leader had to make the final decisions. But we don't even have to use the military analogy. Imagine trying to tell Jack Welch that General Electric was too large and complex to be led by a single individual. It is specifically because of this very complexity and its relevance to the survival of our nation, our families, and our economy that we must have someone in charge.

We can create a director of biodefense either before or after a biological emergency. If one believes that it is only a matter of time until such an event occurs, then why wait until after the fact? Doing it before will not significantly increase the cost of biodefense, but it will most certainly improve our safety. If the administration and Congress adopt only one recommendation in this book, it should be this one. We are already spending vast amounts of money on biodefense, but it will all be for naught if no one is in charge.

NOTE: During the past decades, few individuals have accomplished more to improve the biodefense capabilities of this nation than Dr. Robert P. Kadlec. As an Air Force physician, Bob spent much of his career in special operations. The three-star general (and former Delta Force commander) who spoke at Colonel Kadlec's retirement ceremony said, "Unfortunately, I can't talk about most of Bob's accomplishments in an unclassified setting." Bob is only one of three U.S. servicemen to have personally received a Bronze Star for service in Iraq in the Oval Office from the president. During the past decade, he served in biodefense positions in the Joint Special Operations Command, Office of the Secretary of Defense, United Nations Inspection Teams, White House, and in Congress as the staff director of the Senate Subcommittee on Bioterrorism and Public Health. In 2006, Bob fought one of the toughest battles of his life to move comprehensive biodefense legislation through Congress. In December 2006, President Bush signed the Pandemic and All-Hazard Preparedness Act. With strong bipartisan support from Senators Richard Burr (R-SC), Ted Kennedy (D-MA), Bill Frist (R-TN), and Harry Reid (D-NV), plus Representatives John Dingall (D-MI) and Mike Rogers (R-MI), this legislation provided a major effort to improve America's biodefense capabilities and push the decimal point to the left. Nevertheless, the requirement for a director of biodefense remains.

Chapter 7

Corporate America

Their Responsibilities

THERE ARE SOME PEOPLE IN THE BUSINESS COMMUNITY WHO SEEM TO THINK that homeland security is the government's responsibility. When I hear this sentiment, I share with them a story I heard from a vice president of General Electric. We were on a panel at a conference just two months after 9/11. In his opening remarks he said:

> *For those of you who don't think corporate America is involved in homeland security, let me tell you about GE and 9/11. The two airplanes that hit the World Trade Center—all four engines were built by General Electric. Both airplanes were owned by General Electric, and leased to United and American Airlines. General Electric was a secondary insurer for World Trade Center Towers 1, 2, and 7. And General Electric owns NBC, which had no advertising revenues for several days after 9/11.*

That was Jeffrey Immelt's first week on the job as CEO of General Electric.

Businesses have become the prime target for international

terrorists. According to the U.S. State Department, between 1996 and 2003, there were 2,479 terrorist attacks worldwide. Businesses were the target for 2,074 of these attacks (230 targeted diplomatic facilities, 123 targeted government, and 52 targeted the military). To paraphrase Leon Trotsky's maxim, "Business may not be interested in terrorism, but terrorism is interested in business."

Corporate America played a vital role in securing the U.S. during the twentieth century. Most notably, it provided the technology and hardware for the "arsenal of democracy." America's two greatest security victories in the last century, World War II and the Cold War, were directly linked to the might of corporate America. Continuing this tradition, corporate America will supply the technology and hardware required to secure the American homeland, but that will be only one of four important missions:

1. Protecting employees and business processes (business continuity planning).
2. Building partnerships in local communities to improve resilience within the private and public sector.
3. Providing technology, hardware, and services (the traditional mission).
4. Providing both financial and intellectual capital through not-for-profit partnerships in order to accomplish those missions no longer best suited for the government.

BUSINESS CONTINUITY PLANNING

During my last six years of military service, one of my specialties was what the Air Force calls ATSO, the military acronym for ability to survive and operate. This is an essential function in all military organizations, and a tremendous amount of resources are expended providing this capability. Military organizations have plans for an amazing array of emergencies, from hurricanes, tornadoes, earthquakes, all the way through the full spectrum of wartime contingencies.

During my years on active duty, a typical command post on an Air Force base would have a wall filled with three-ring binders containing the various plans for that base. These plans are written, reviewed, and in most cases tested, on at least an annual basis. Today, many of these plans are computer-based, but the procedures to develop, review, test, and update remain the same. There are two types of planning in the military: deliberate planning (before something happens) and crisis planning (when something is about to happen or has happened). Military organizations of all sizes and types expend significant resources building, reviewing, and testing these plans. This type of planning, known as business continuity planning (BCP), already exists in many large corporations and will also become the standard for small and mid-sized corporations—at least for those who want to survive.

According to the Small Business Administration, the majority of companies that do not reopen within two weeks following a disaster declare bankruptcy within one year. According to a study at Tulane University by Dr. Laura Steinberg, an associate professor of civil engineering, nine months after Katrina, 80 percent of businesses in New Orleans had not reopened, including fourteen of twenty-two hospitals and 61 percent of restaurants. One could say that these incredibly high numbers for New Orleans were the result of conditions and events beyond the control of the businesses in that community. Without question, Hurricane Katrina was an extraordinarily devastating event for the corporations and businesses in New Orleans, but one could say the same for corporations based in the World Trade Center Towers on 9/11. Let's look at two of them: Morgan Stanley, which offers a superb example of protecting employees, and Cantor Fitzgerald, which has become a classic in the field of protecting business processes.

In 1990, Morgan Stanley hired Rick Rescorla as its security officer. Rick was a highly experienced combat veteran who had worked in South Africa before coming to the U.S. and joining the Army. His military tour of duty took him to Vietnam, where he fought in the Ia Drang Valley battle of 1965. Many of you have seen the movie *We Were Soldiers* with Mel Gibson, which was based on the book *We Were Soldiers Once . . . and Young*, by Lieutenant General Harold G. Moore (Ret.) and Joseph L. Galloway. The picture of the soldier on the cover of that book was Rick Rescorla. After many years in the military, Rick left to become a corporate security officer, and in 1990 he came to work for Morgan Stanley in the World Trade Center.

Rick's first project was to conduct an initial security evaluation, and it only took him a couple of days to identify a serious security threat. He sat down with Morgan Stanley's CEO, and informed him that terrorists could easily drive a truck bomb into the basement parking garage, inflicting serious damage to the Twin Towers and threatening the lives of thousands. (Remember, this was in 1990.) Rick suggested that the company move across the river to New Jersey, and base its operations in four- to five-story buildings. He pointed out that most of the employees lived in New Jersey anyway, and would be happier with a shorter commute. More importantly, security would be significantly improved, perhaps to such a degree that the company wouldn't require the services of a highly paid security consultant. The CEO understood Rick's concern, but identified two reasons that prevented Morgan Stanley from relocating to New Jersey: a long-term lease, and the prestige of the World Trade Center. Nevertheless, he appreciated Rick's concerns and told him, "I will do anything else except move. Tell me what we need to do."

Rick designed a plan (deliberate planning) for evacuating the 2,700 Morgan Stanley employees from floors 44 to 74 of the South Tower, including plans for evacuating them without electricity and with smoke in the stairwells. And then they practiced. Of course, some of the employees thought this was a little too much like grammar school—fire drills, floor monitors, head counts. Rick had the steps in the stairwells marked with iridescent paint, and formed people into teams that would stick together and assist one another down the countless flights of stairs. Three years later, Ramsey Yousef drove a rental truck into the second level of the basement parking garage under the North Tower of the World Trade Center. The explosion ripped a hole the size of a basketball court through four levels of the garage. The electricity and telephone systems went out in both towers, and acrid smoke rose to the ninety-third floor. Nevertheless, as Rick Rescorla sang Irish folk songs into his bullhorn, just as he had during the exercises, all 3,700 employees of Morgan Stanley were safely evacuated—because they had a plan, and because they had practiced.

Eight years later, shortly after Mohamed Atta flew American Airlines Flight 11 into the North Tower, a Port Authority employee in the South Tower made an announcement over the public-address system that all employees should remain in their offices: "Go back to your desks, do not evacuate." But because Rick had spent the time in deliberate planning thinking about various scenarios, he decided the greater risk would be to remain in the tower, and ordered an immediate evacuation. Rick gave that order from his office on the forty-fourth floor, and then climbed to the seventy-second floor to assist.

Just twelve minutes later, Marwan Al-Shehhi flew United Airlines Flight 175 into the South Tower, destroying floors seventy-eight to eighty-four. With bullhorn in hand, Rick sang "God Bless America" and Cornish folk songs as the darkened stairwells filled with smoke. When he reached street level Rick called his wife to let her know he was okay. She was in a state of panic. Like many Americans, she had watched the second plane hit the South Tower. Moments later, Rescorla discovered that three employees were unaccounted for.

A true professional, with the extraordinary courage that had impressed his superior officers, peers, and subordinates in Vietnam, Rick led his security team back into the building. He and three members of his staff (Wesley Mercer, Jorge Velazquez, and Godin Forde) were killed when the South Tower collapsed. Out of the 3,700 Morgan Stanley employees who worked in the World Trade Center, only six died.

The most important lesson learned from Morgan Stanley on 9/11 is recognizing that few companies will ever find themselves in a more challenging situation, yet the decision made by the CEO in 1990 to build appropriate plans and test them, combined with the courage and wisdom of Rick Rescorla and his team, allowed for the phenomenally successful evacuation of Morgan Stanley personnel. This was a perfect example of the first mission of business continuity planning: protecting people.

Now let's take a look at the second mission, protecting business processes. This corporate story comes from Cantor Fitzgerald, which was one of the country's larger bond trading companies, trading over a trillion dollars a week. The company had 1,050 employees, and was housed on the 101st, 102nd, 103rd, and 105th floors of the North Tower of the World Trade Center. American Airlines Flight 11 struck the building, causing catastrophic damage to floors 93 to 98. That morning, only 658 of the Cantor Fitzgerald employees were at work when the plane slammed into the North Tower at 8:46 A.M. Howard Lutnick, the CEO, was not there; he was delayed, dropping his son off at

Richter Scale) rocked central Taiwan. It killed more than 2,400 people, injured 10,000, and destroyed or severely damaged 17,000 buildings. Parts of the island were without power for ten days. One area particularly hard hit was a region that produces 12 percent of the world's semiconductors, 66 percent of computer motherboards, 40 percent of laptops, and 60 percent of monitors. This was certainly a major human and economic tragedy for Taiwan, but it also shut down assembly lines for Dell and Hewlett-Packard in Texas and California. What would have been a local tragedy forty years ago was in fact an economic quake felt around the world.

Let's peel the onion a little more on business continuity planning and examine its link with ATSO—ability to survive and operate. After six years of study in homeland security, I retired from the military in the summer of 2000, and expanded my studies to include homeland security issues in the private sector. In my new life as corporate vice president and officer, I discovered a whole new world. The rules, culture, and priorities were quite different from those in the military, and I often found these differences to be beneficial. For example, I had spent an entire year in the military trying to fire an incompetent civil servant, but in the end, the best I could achieve was getting that person transferred. During my second month in the private sector (in Virginia, which has at-will employment), I discovered that it only took one minute and one signature to dismiss an incompetent employee. Even more importantly, I discovered that I could rapidly promote and financially reward my superstars, which is impossible to do in the military because of what is known as "time-in-grade" requirements. Regardless of how talented, dedicated, and valuable the individual may be, there are minimum time-in-grade requirements necessary for promotion.

There were many other differences between the military and corporate worlds, positive and negative, some of which I exkindergarten. Upon hearing about the disaster on the rad proceeded to the World Trade Center, only to be nearly when the South Tower collapsed.

It is difficult to imagine what must have been going th his mind that morning. He had to assume that the majo his employees had been killed. At some point, he also I consider the survivability of his company. For those (Fitzgerald employees who had not yet arrived at the World Center, and for those working at other locations, the only that could make matters worse would be standing in an ployment line the following week while still grieving for who had been lost. I remember traveling to New York couple of weeks after 9/11, and seeing the long lines of at Madison Square Garden attending a job fair—all were employees of companies in the World Trade Center co However, there were no Cantor Fitzgerald employees st in that line, because the firm had conducted deliberate ning, and then quickly transitioned into crisis planning on the afternoon of the disaster. When the financial n reopened on September 16, 2001, Cantor Fitzgerald ope business. That first day's trading was nowhere near the I activity of September 10, but by mid-November, Cantor I ald was back to their pre-9/11 bond trading level of more trillion dollars a week.

America's best military units could learn much abou ience through deliberate planning from Morgan Stanley sis planning from Cantor Fitzgerald. These are both rem and inspiring stories, but we must also remember that b continuity planning is not just for terrorism. In fact, it is f; likely that your company will benefit from such plannin sponse to a natural disaster or crisis than one from a t organization.

On September 21, 1999, a massive earthquake (7.6

pected, and others that I had not. One of the most interesting surprises was the similarity between military ATSO and corporate business continuity planning. Despite the huge cultural differences between the for-profit world and the public sector, I discovered that the questions military leaders asked about ATSO were virtually the same as those that corporate leaders asked about BCP. The major difference between the two communities was that virtually all military organizations engage in ATSO, while the majority of businesses do not employ BCP.

According to a 2005 survey of small businesses by the Ad Council, 88 percent of respondents stated it was important to have a business continuity plan; however, only 39 percent said their company had such a plan. According to the Small Business Administration, 99 percent of all employers in the U.S. are small businesses who employ half of the private workforce. However, being a small business is not a good excuse for failing to plan for disaster. It makes no difference if you are a Fortune 500 company or a fifty-employee machine shop; prior planning can make the difference between life and death, and business continuity and bankruptcy.

Most of the large corporations have superb business continuity plans that are developed by in-house experts who do this as a full-time job. Some of the most notable, such as Wal-Mart, have crisis command centers that rival many military organizations. These centers constantly monitor the weather and other industry-specific conditions that could cause problems for supply chains or account for differences in customer spending patterns.

One of the lessons Wal-Mart has learned over the years (and

it has a tremendous "Lessons Learned" program) is that when hurricanes are between forty-eight to seventy-two hours from landfall, people in the regions that are threatened rush to their local Wal-Mart to buy bottled water and strawberry Pop-Tarts. Therefore, Wal-Mart knows that when a hurricane is ninety-six hours from landfall, it needs to push strawberry Pop-Tarts, bottled water, and other items, such as batteries, to the threatened area. In other words, it is more than just protecting employees and supply chains; it is getting the customers what they need.

Four days before Katrina slammed into the Gulf Coast, Home Depot's hurricane center in Atlanta was preparing to respond. According to then CEO Bob Nardelli, extensive planning and preparations enabled Home Depot to reopen twenty-three of thirty-three stores in the impact zone within just one day. Within a week, all but four had been reopened. FedEx was another major corporation that demonstrated its commitment to disaster planning. FedEx employees prepositioned 30,000 bags of ice, 30,000 gallons of water, four two-ton building repair kits, and eighty-five generators in Baton Rouge prior to Katrina's landfall.

The advice in this book on business continuity is not designed for large, successful corporations. They already have plans. That's not to say they can't be improved upon, but at least these people are asking the questions, developing plans, and routinely testing them. The companies that are best at the practice of BCP go far beyond the basics of preparing for yesterday's threats, and attempt to anticipate tomorrow's crisis. Mellon Bank and TIAA-CREF tested their employees' capabilities for telecommuting in preparation for an influenza pandemic. This method of conducting business will not only prove to be of great value in case there's a global pandemic, but may also be of value during the annual flu season, or during a major oil crisis that sends gas prices to astronomical levels. (Mellon Bank's initial assessment was that 37 percent of employees could successfully telecommute during a crisis.) Unfortunately, the same is not true for small and mid-sized businesses, because they don't have the plans or the capability. This fact is not only a threat to their survivability, but to the U.S. economy as well. As we have seen, on numerous occasions bin Laden has clearly stated his goal of disrupting and destroying America's economy. This means that business continuity planning for large and small businesses is not only important to the CEOs, proprietors, stockholders, and employees; it is also important to America.

For those corporations below the Fortune 500 threshold, military-quality planning may be beyond reach. Military organizations generally have an enormous array of plans, but this is not practical for small corporations. Could a company consisting of 100 employees actually develop and maintain separate plans for a hurricane, tornado, chemical spill, chemical attack, transportation disruption, and a pandemic flu? No. But that does not mean small and mid-sized businesses should entirely forgo disaster planning. An all-hazards disaster plan, or what could be called the "85 percent solution," would provide the best answer for the vast majority of businesses. If you own or lead a company (or any organization in the private or public sector) that does not currently have disaster plans, the first step is to develop an all-hazards plan. Your most substantial benefit will be provided through *the process of building that general plan*. The process itself will be of far more value than the actual plan in the three-ring binder on your bookshelf.

Plans are particularly useless when companies or certain government organizations (e.g., the city of New Orleans) pay a consultant or a contractor to come in and build a plan for them. CEOs say, "Oh, we need a real expert to do this." And so the experts come in, study the business or government organization, determine threats and vulnerabilities, and then develop a plan. This plan is briefed to the leadership, who pays the consultants and then puts the three-ring binder on the bookshelf, confident that the business continuity planning is now complete. This is a surefire method of ensuring a very limited result, and one of the contributing factors in the devastation of New Orleans following Katrina. New Orleans had a hurricane disaster plan. I am not convinced, however, that the city's leaders were cognizant of the details—even though they had supposedly tested it during an exercise fourteen months prior to Katrina. The plan stated that officials would need to order an evacuation forty-eight hours prior to a hurricane making landfall. In the case of Katrina, the order was given less than twenty-four hours prior. The mayor claimed that he had been reluctant to give the order because of the possibility that the hurricane could change course, in which case the city might be vulnerable to lawsuits for lost revenue from businesses in the tourist industry. This is exactly the type of issue that should be identified, discussed, and resolved during an exercise, from a brown bag, two-hour lunch with executives sitting around a table to a full-scale field exercise with executives in their command posts, first responders moving throughout the city, simulated victims taken to hospitals, and selected military units deploying to the city. Once critical issues, shortfalls, and other deficiencies have been identified, they can be carefully and calmly researched prior to a crisis, not during one as we witnessed with Katrina.

A major lesson learned from Katrina: Plans and exercises are of little value unless conducted properly. In the military we call it the "5 Ps": *Prior planning prevents piss-poor performance.* General Eisenhower was a bit more eloquent:

> *I have always found that plans are useless. The planning is indispensable.*
>
> General Dwight D. Eisenhower

Ike was right. The plan itself is useless, because the war, crisis, or disaster never happens quite the way you anticipated. But what is valuable is the planning process (assuming it is accomplished at a higher standard than that in New Orleans), and therefore, the leadership throughout the corporation must be involved. It is during the planning process that you learn which questions to ask and why. The answers may change, but most of the questions will not. During the "Mother of all Briefings" following Operation Desert Storm, General Schwarzkopf talked about war plans. He compared warfare to a grand ballet, where every minute, every second, is carefully choreographed and orchestrated, but when the conductor raises the baton for the first note, two homicidal maniacs jump out of the orchestra pit onto the stage with bayonets and begin chasing the ballerinas—that is warfare. Much the same is true for disaster planning. Nevertheless, because you went through the planning process, you understand the key challenges, the key questions, and the critical issues regarding your specific business—and that is what will give you the flexibility to adapt in a crisis.

And as I said earlier, this is what I found most interesting when comparing my military experience with ATSO with the corporate world's BCP process—that the questions are similar. One of the most important questions for a corporation or military organization is, "What are my core functions?" There is a lot of planning going on right now for how corporations would deal with a flu pandemic. One of the best descriptions I have heard of what a flu pandemic would be like for a corporation comes from Dr. Michael Osterholm, the former state epidemiologist for Minnesota, who said, "Imagine a blizzard in your community that lasted for three, four, or five months." We all understand the challenges of a blizzard, where life in a community is at a standstill or in slow motion for three, four, or five days. Now imagine that condition lasting for months. What would happen if 40 percent of your employees didn't come to work tomorrow, or next week, or even next month? Clearly you would have to scale down your business operations, but what are the necessary functions that must continue?

We're in a very lean business environment. Corporate leaders frequently deal with the challenges of manpower caps, but what happens to an already lean organization if it is suddenly hit with a 40 percent no-show rate? If you wait until the crisis begins, some of the top leaders will be included in that no-show group. The same people who are needed to ask the right questions and provide the answers that will make the difference between survival and bankruptcy will not be available if this planning is not conducted prior to the event.

In 2006, the Vice President of Government Affairs for Con-Way, Inc., Randy Mullet, was assigned the task of building a pandemic flu business continuity plan. Con-Way is a $4.2 billion transportation corporation with 21,800 employees working out of 440 locations across the U.S. Working with senior leaders (from human relations, internal and external communications, operations, strategic planning, finance, information systems, and training), Mullet helped Con-Way create a comprehensive plan that includes everything from stockpiling 500,000 N95 masks (individually packaged, meaning there is no expiration date) to operations plans for periods of quarantine (including alternate operating locations) and HR policies, such as the pooling and distribution of sick leave.

As Field Marshall von Moltke wrote more than a hundred years ago, "No plan survives contact with the enemy." While still true today, whether talking about war plans or flu plans, those who have gone through the process of developing a plan will be miles ahead of those who have not.

Perhaps the best aspect of Con-Way's flu planning is that the company's CEO, Douglas W. Stotlar, believes that the shareholders have already received a good return on investment from these efforts. Stotlar is convinced the company's education program on basic public health procedures, such as frequent hand washing and proper cough etiquette (upper sleeve, not hand) will reduce the number of sick days at Con-Way during routine flu seasons.

The better the deliberate planning prior to an event, the easier the crisis planning will be during the event.

The deliberate planning process will lead to significant improvements in corporate resilience, and may provide insights for daily operations. Examining processes under great stress can lead to breakthroughs in improvements for routine operations. Likewise, some highly efficient routine operational techniques and procedures can be extremely valuable during a crisis.

Standardization of procedures is one method that UPS has used to improve efficiency in its daily operations, but that has also proven quite efficient during a crisis. UPS has standardization practices that surpass even many military standards, and it goes far beyond the trademark brown uniforms. Why is standardization so important? Let me give you an example from my experience in the military.

The Air Force has very strict standardization procedures for crews on large airplanes. One such example is the challenge and response checklist, where one pilot gives a command, and the other pilot responds. (Pilot: "Flaps 40 percent." Co-pilot: "Flaps 40 percent, slats extended.") This is done not only to improve safety, but also to significantly improve flexibility. During my two tours flying the Air Force's largest plane, the C-5 Galaxy, I frequently flew with mixed crews—where the pilot, co-pilot, flight engineer, scanner, and loadmasters were from different units, and in some cases, even split between active duty and Reserve personnel. The standardization of procedures—all the way down to what words were used on the flight deck—provides enormous flexibility in scheduling, particularly during a crisis. The same is true for UPS pilots.

The 2,700 UPS pilots follow these same standardization procedures, but standardization at UPS goes far beyond the pilots, who make up only one half of one percent of the workforce. UPS tells its drivers which fingers they should use to hold the keys when opening the door to their step vans. The company's standardization procedures almost reach the point of being obsessive-compulsive, but they exist for a very specific and important reason. The machinery used in the major sorting facilities, as well as that used throughout the UPS system, is all standardized. This allows for great flexibility, particularly during a crisis. The best example was back in 1990, when a devastating ice storm hit Louisville, Kentucky.

Because winters are relatively mild in Louisville (the primary UPS hub), all snowplows had rubber bottoms on them to help protect the streets. However, rubber blades are virtually useless when there is three to four inches of ice on the highways. The mayor ordered the city to be shut down. Even ambulances could not get out on the streets. But while the city was paralyzed, the sophisticated equipment at the airport had the runways opened by the next morning—a Monday—yet none of the UPS employees could get to work. Louisville was paralyzed due to an "Act of God," clearly beyond the control of local authorities and UPS. Nevertheless, the people throughout the rest of the nation (and the world) still expected on-time delivery. The fact that there was a big ice storm in Louisville didn't make any difference to the person in Pittsburgh who needed important machinery parts, or the person in Bangkok, Thailand, who needed grandma's birthday gift delivered to New York City. But UPS wasn't able to get its Louisville employees to the primary sort facility at the airport because the mayor said, "Don't go to work."

At moments like this in the Air Force, we used to say, "Flexibility is the key to airpower," and standardization is the key to flexibility—that, and prior planning. UPS demonstrated both. On Monday, UPS employees were flown in from other locations around the country to run the sorting process in Louisville. On Monday night, UPS planes carried packages to Louisville, where they were sorted, reloaded, and flown to their destinations. This was possible because of standardized procedures. The blizzard of 1990 was a once-in-a-hundred-years storm, but UPS was still able to continue its core processes. It was unable to conduct all normal functions, but on-time delivery of time-critical packages became the sole focus. Have you identified the absolute essential functions in your company that must be maintained?

For many businesses experiencing a routine ice storm that makes travel dangerous, the correct decision might be to simply tell everyone to stay home. (Hopefully, you have a system to do this, such as telephone calling trees or an Intranet site like many schools now use.) It may make the most sense to protect your employees from the hazards of travel during winter storms, when little work would be accomplished at the office due to local disruptions. However, for some companies that bill time to public and private sector organizations, it is important to have a formal procedure. A few years ago, a new CEO at a company in northern Virginia elected to declare a "weather day" following an unexpected snowstorm. In terms of safety for the employees, it was a good call. However, this company was a government contractor and had no formal plan for telecommuting. None of the employees could therefore bill for their work that day, and the company lost $425,000. (Remember those 5 Ps?) The company now has a plan, but a few hours of deliberate planning *prior* to the snowstorm would have provided a very handsome return on a rather small investment of time. When building an all-hazards plan, there are three critical areas to analyze: function, personnel, and supply chains. Let's take a look at each individually.

First, you need to differentiate between your core functions and those that are nonessential and can be shut down for the short term. Keep in mind that your determination of the latter might change depending upon the length of the crisis. Will the functions you deem nonessential during a one- or two-day crisis still be identified as such if the crisis lasts weeks, or even months? How can you improve upon the resilience of your core functions? Spend time asking and answering these questions. For instance, while assisting a small company (twenty-five employees with $6 million per year in gross revenues) walk through this deliberate planning process, we discovered that the financial management office could be closed for at least two weeks without a serious disruption to the operations. In fact, automated payments of utilities, direct deposit of employee paychecks, and telecommuting from home would allow near-100 percent capabilities if the company was forced to move to an alternate, smaller facility for an extended period.

For small and mid-sized companies, one soon discovers this is not "rocket science." Most problems can be resolved with a little deliberate planning. During this particular process the corporate leaders discovered that no one knew how to turn off the heating/ventilating/air-conditioning system for the building (critically important during a chemical or radiological attack or a nearby building collapse, for instance), nor had anyone considered a plan for sheltering-in-place or procedures for employees to systematically back up key computer files. Asking the right questions identified these deficiencies, and they were quickly corrected.

The next important area is personnel. Who are the key people in the company? Perhaps an even more critical question, one that the military affords great consideration, is in which areas of the company is the operation only one, or perhaps two people deep? In other words, you might have a smooth-running business today, but if one person has a heart attack, if one person is called to military duty, or if one person decides to take a job in another company, will the wheels come off the wagon? Obviously, larger corporations have a bit more flexibility in this area because they may be two, three, or four people deep. Where this issue becomes critical is in smaller companies, which represent 99.4 percent of all employers in the U.S. A small company might not be able to afford to have two strong information technology people on salary, despite the fact that IT is one of the company's core functions.

The third factor to consider is supply chains. Who are your critical suppliers? There is a classic supply chain story about the 1995 Kobe earthquake in Japan. This was the largest earthquake to ever hit a densely populated urban area. It destroyed more than 80,000 buildings, killed more than 5,000 people, and injured more than 25,000. The effects, however, reached far beyond the physical devastation of the 7.2 magnitude earthquake. All of the brake shoes used in Toyotas for the Japanese domestic market were manufactured in a factory destroyed by the earthquake. Within a couple of days, Toyota was forced to shut down its domestic production line, and quickly realized a loss exceeding $200 million. Because of this incident, many large corporations spend more time today thinking about supply chain interruptions, whether caused by Mother Nature or by man-made incidents, such as a terrorist attack. Following a keynote address to a large transportation security conference, I was asked the following question: "Don't you think there is a high probability that the government will overreact after the next terrorist attack—an overreaction that will seriously disrupt our supply chains?" I said, "No. I disagree. There is not a high probability; it is a sure thing. So there is no excuse for being surprised or unprepared."

Businesses' concerns are not unfounded, and my statement was not mere speculation. During a 2003 meeting at the Center for Strategic and International Studies (a D.C. think tank), the secretary of transportation, Norman Mineta, said that he would shut down all seaports in response to a major attack on a single port until he could assure the president that all containers entering the U.S. were safe. This action would cause far more damage to the U.S. economy than most terrorist organizations could ever hope to inflict. If your business is dependent on just-in-time deliveries across international borders, you might want to consider a backup plan, but make sure you ask the right questions.

Here are two brief examples of the supply chain issue from the auto industry. One company hired a major consulting firm to conduct a homeland security exercise for the executive leadership team. During the exercise, terrorists destroyed the Ambassador Bridge between Windsor, Ontario, and Detroit, Michigan. This 7,500-foot bridge carries 25 percent of all merchandise trade between the United States and Canada. (To put this 25 percent in perspective, consider this: Canada is our largest trading partner.) More than 12,000 trucks cross the bridge each day, many of which move auto parts both ways across this international border. When provided this challenge, the vice president for operations stated, "Well . . . I guess the Army Corps of Engineers will have to build a pontoon bridge. I assume they could do this in a few days."

While it is a good sign that this corporation conducted the exercise to examine the threats to its business processes, it was also obvious that this type of scenario had never been seriously considered. The 7,800-foot pontoon bridge on the Hood Canal in Washington state took three years to build. Combat-style pontoon bridges can be built considerably faster, but require tugboats to hold them in place against the current, and would have great difficulty carrying even one tenth of the traffic that uses the Ambassador Bridge each day.

Another U.S. auto manufacturer has an assembly plant that now requires all parts suppliers to be located within 500 miles, with the additional stipulation that none can be located in Canada. Following the reactions to 9/11, this company did not want its production to be dependent on the ability to quickly move materials across international borders. This supply chain requirement guarantees better protection of the company's business processes from transportation disruptions, but it may also produce higher costs. One might question their answer (the decision to use only domestic parts), but I will not criticize their foresight to ask the right questions.

One thing is certain: There will be no quick, easy, or inexpensive answers to these questions. America's corporations were designed and built to operate in an environment that had few worries about terrorism, but that has changed. Safety has been a high priority for many decades, but now, corporate leaders must also think about security. Many of the changes required will be long-term initiatives. Incorporating security into new designs of facilities and processes is far less expensive than redesigning those already in existence. Security needs to become as intrinsic to corporate America as safety and quality.

Because of concerns regarding government overreactions and other forms of disruptions to supply chains, some companies elect to maintain multiple suppliers, but often that is not possible or economically feasible. Intel Corporation demonstrated an alternative solution, consisting of what my grandmother called "putting your eggs in a single basket, but protecting that basket."

In his superb book, *The Resilient Enterprise*, Yossi Sheffi tells the story of an Intel manufacturing plant in Oregon. A shutdown of this plant would cause company-wide disruptions. And while the plant is not in America's most active earthquake zone, earthquakes are still a possibility. When the plant was constructed, it was designed to withstand 90 percent of the expected earthquakes in that region. On the other hand, Murphy's Law (if anything can go wrong, it will) is always lurking just around the corner. In fact, people in my line of work think Murphy was an optimist. During the planning process, Intel's execs asked an important question. It wasn't the most intuitive one, but it was the right one. Given the information I just provided, what do you think they asked? Do you think they said, "We don't have to worry about 90 percent of the earthquakes, but what do we do if we get hit with a really big one?" No, they did not. Instead, they asked the most important question a strategist, either military or civilian, ever asks: "And then what?"

Before Intel focused on the most unlikely scenario, it asked what would happen after a small or mid-sized earthquake, which was a realistic possibility. The answer was that the building would most likely survive with little or no damage, but might have to remain closed until state inspectors could certify it safe. In the event of a significant earthquake, state inspectors would have to examine hundreds, if not thousands, of buildings. It might take days before they got to Intel. But because Intel's executives asked the right question, they found the right answer: They sent three of their personnel to a training program to be certified as state inspectors. If an earthquake hits tomorrow, Intel's inspectors would begin the required inspections almost immediately, and the factory could be back in operation within hours. As an example of good corporate citizenship, Intel has volunteered its inspectors to help throughout the rest of the state, once the inspection of their facility is complete. They effectively become part of the posse.

It makes no difference if you are responsible for building a business continuity plan for a corporation, an ability to survive and operate plan for a military unit, or a continuity of government plan—it all begins with asking the right questions. But you can't start to ask these questions after the crisis begins. During my two years in command of the 89th Operations Group (America's fleet of VIP aircraft) at Andrews Air Force Base in Maryland, I was not aware of a single incident where one of the 125 pilots experienced an in-flight emergency that he or she had not already seen numerous times in a flight simulator. Not only had the pilots dealt with these simulated emergencies in high-fidelity training devices, they had also spent hours "hangar flying" these situations—talking through them with other pilots. This practice was not unique to the 89th; it is standard procedure for top-quality flying organizations in the military and civilian world. Unfortunately we don't have sophisticated simulators for CEOs and business owners. However, the planning process allows for a company to "hangar fly" the crisis, ask the right questions, build checklists, and practice. Pilots prepare for emergencies because it means the difference between life and death. For corporate America, it could very well mean the difference between business continuity and bankruptcy.

For more information on what small and mid-sized business can do to improve resiliency, see www.prep4disaster.com. For assistance in evaluating business continuity plans for large corporations, see www.cpxllc.com. A small investment in time and money can provide an enormous return.

BUILDING PARTNERSHIPS IN LOCAL COMMUNITIES

On the morning of 9/11, when Americans realized that our homeland had become a battleground, many people began ask-

ing, "What can we do to help?" Several of my employees walked
into my office that morning and asked me that question. At first,
I didn't know what to say, but I realized that people wanted—
needed—to do something. Since I had no idea as to the extent
of the casualties or the possibility of further attacks, I suggested
they give blood. As it turns out, many Americans had the same
idea. The Red Cross received far more blood donations than it
was prepared to handle and had to destroy a large amount of it
after its forty-two-day shelf life. The system was overwhelmed.
Chapter 8 discusses the role of citizen volunteers in local communities, but there is also a volunteer role for businesses. Deliberate planning in local business communities can significantly
augment the response capabilities of local governments, and
prevent well-meaning, but ultimately wasteful gestures such as
the blood situation with the Red Cross.

When Hani Hanjour flew American Flight 77 into the west
side of the Pentagon, the 36,200 pounds of jet fuel ignited a fire
that burned for several days. As soon as local restaurant owners
in northern Virginia learned that first responders would remain
on-scene for several days at the Pentagon, they began sending
free food. Again, it was a wonderful, but wasted, gesture—most
of the food was discarded. There were plenty of good people
wanting to help, but unfortunately, there was no system in place
to maximize the potential of this goodwill.

Shortly after Katrina, the Department of Homeland Security
established the National Emergency Resource Registry (NERR).
An e-mail blast was sent to thousands of companies asking them
to sign up online if they would donate or sell equipment that
could be of use during the response. In just one month, 77,000
individual items were registered. As described by one insider, "It
was a huge funnel at the top, and a little neck at the bottom. In
the end, only a few thousand items were ever deployed to the

disaster area." One participant described it as a "Herculean effort that showed little or no results."

The most important lesson learned from these three incidents is that systems need to be established and tested prior to an event. Prior planning can make the difference between failure or success of individual and corporate goodwill during a disaster. Some companies have long-standing plans for disaster assistance. One of my favorites is Miller Brewing Company. You have probably seen their TV commercial. The narrator talks about how Miller helps local communities respond to natural disasters: Bottlers in a local community just outside the disaster area immediately stop bottling beer, and instead put water into the bottles. Miller drivers then deliver the bottled water to the disaster relief personnel. At the end of the commercial, a relief worker (who looks like he has been awake for about a week) thanks Miller for its public service. He then says, "But guys, every once in a while, you could put beer in some of the bottles you send us." Not only does Miller get credit for its public service, but it also gets high marks for marketing. Whenever I walk down the beer aisle at my local grocery, I think of that commercial. Individual efforts by corporations are certainly of value to local communities, but coordinated response efforts in the private sector will provide local communities with greatly expanded response capabilities at a very low cost. This type of cooperation is a fundamental element in a successful homeland security strategy.

According to the National Response Plan, developed by the Department of Homeland Security, when disaster strikes, a Joint Operations Center is formed. The JOC is a consortium of federal, state, and local government officials, all working in one command center to coordinate efforts. This is a major improvement from where we were just a decade ago, but to further improve this system, we need to develop a private sector BEOC (Business

Emergency Operations Center) to work in coordination with the government JOC. The BEOC, which would have a direct link to the government JOC, would be activated by the local government in the event of a disaster. Once the JOC assesses the situation and identifies critical requirements, such as the need for more trucks, it would make one phone call to the BEOC to issue the request. The BEOC would be standing by with representatives from Ryder, U-Haul, Penske, Budget, and other truck rental companies, and need only ask the JOC, "How many, what size, where, and when?" These assets could be provided on a contractual basis to the local government, or in some cases, they could be provided pro bono.

If the JOC realized that a 24/7 operation was going to be required, it would contact the BEOC and request food for the first responders. In this case, the BEOC would have representatives from McDonald's, Burger King, Pizza Hut, and other volunteers from local restaurants, and the delivery of food could be provided in a coordinated manner to minimize waste. But business participation extends far beyond making sure that first responders are well fed. In some scenarios, the corporations themselves become the first responders for local communities. This concept is being developed and tested in several communities, such as Atlanta, where the not-for-profit Business Executives for National Security has one of the more successful models.

During an exercise conducted in 2006 to test Atlanta's ability to quickly dispense a Push Pack (remember, that is the 97,000 pounds of medical supplies—primarily antibiotics—that would be used in response to a bio-attack such as anthrax), the federal, state, and local officials quickly learned the harsh truth. As described earlier, the feds will do their part. They create the Push Packs, store them, rotate inventory, and quickly deliver them to a county when needed. But that is where the problems begin. Few communities have the capability to properly dispense the antibiotics in a timely manner. In this particular exercise, state and local public health officers used 40 percent of their staffs to dispense a mere 10 percent of the antibiotics expected to be required in response to a major bio-attack. Remember, the best we can hope for after a bio-attack is to move the decimal point to the left. Failure to efficiently and effectively distribute a Push Pack is a prescription for moving the decimal point to the right.

As Ern Blackwelder of BENS, Business Executives for National Security, said, "You do the math. The state and local public health officials have only a fraction of the staff they need to treat the whole population within forty-eight hours—something that could make an enormous difference in a biocrisis. It could mean the difference between thousands of deaths and a few hundred deaths." So what's the solution? In D.C.-think, the answer would be to spend more money to significantly beef up public health staffs. ("Ready! Shoot! Aim!") Or, as some have suggested, we should consider using the National Guard. But both of these answers are wrong. Why? Because we're asking the wrong question. The correct question is: "How can we posse up to solve this problem?" Thanks to BENS and Lockheed Martin, Atlanta now has a Push Pack posse. (In this case, 3 Ps are definitely better than 5 Ps.) With BENS coordinating the effort, Lockheed Martin became the core of the posse. In a response to a bio-attack, Lockheed Martin employees and their families will be the first to receive the antibiotics, after which they will report to dispensing sites around the city to help distribute medication to the general public. This test in Atlanta should serve as a model for America. Prior planning and a Push Pack posse can save thousands of lives, perhaps hundreds of thousands, and at a cost that we can afford.

Some might ask, "Why would a company be interested in participating in such a program?" Actually, there are several very good reasons, both intrinsic and extrinsic. From the employees' perspective, they and their families will be among the first to receive treatment, and by volunteering at the dispensing sites, they also get to play a key role in defending their own community. From the corporate perspective, being a good corporate citizen certainly has its own rewards in terms of favorable publicity. Additionally, the quicker a community recovers from a disaster, the quicker the business environment will improve. Once people get back to work, they will start to purchase goods and services again. Another benefit is mutual support. States accomplish this through agreements called EMAC (Emergency Management Assistance Compact). EMAC allows governors in unaffected states to share state resources, such as National Guard troops, with other states experiencing a disaster. These are arrangements that must be coordinated in advance to be most effective.

Applying this EMAC concept to the business community would not only provide great benefits during major disasters, but also during a crisis within an individual company. The system would be most effective for small companies (once again, 99.4 percent of companies in America), especially in terms of personnel. For example, if one of the participating companies suddenly loses its single IT expert, it could use an EMAC arrangement to obtain short-term assistance. This is all accomplished on a voluntary basis with appropriate financial reimbursement. EMAC for the business community would serve all participants during natural and terrorist crises, as well as individual companies faced with the day-to-day challenges unique to small business owners.

EMAC is also the model we need for local governments. We cannot afford to buy every piece of equipment that every fire, police, and EMS department would like to have. We must learn how to leverage mutual support on a regional basis.

PROVIDING TECHNOLOGIES, HARDWARE, AND SERVICES (THE TRADITIONAL MISSION)

Since the early days of the Industrial Revolution, the private sector has played a fundamental role in national security. The new technologies and vast quantities of world-class hardware it provided to the U.S. military played a major role in America's three major military victories in the twentieth century: World War II, the Cold War, and Desert Storm. The private sector will continue to provide essential technology and hardware for America's military and homeland security forces in the twenty-first century, and it will also play a significantly expanded role in providing services to government organizations engaged in security operations. This expanded role in operational services will hopefully build upon the success of programs such as the Civil Reserve Air Fleet (CRAF), which was one of the best investments the American taxpayer has ever made in this type of endeavor. In the early days of the Cold War, war planners in the Pentagon determined that the amount of airlift capacity required to respond to a Soviet invasion of Western Europe would be far too costly to maintain within the U.S. military. A relatively small fleet of cargo aircraft was needed for peacetime airlift and for training; however, even with the surge capacity maintained in the Reserve and National Guard forces, there remained no economically feasible formula for maintaining sufficient capacity within the Department of Defense. In 1957, CRAF was created. It was, and remains today, a program where the military maintains sufficient surge airlift capacity within the private sector at a fraction of the cost of an exclusively military fleet of airplanes.

There are three elements in CRAF (passenger lift, cargo lift, and aeromedical evacuation), and three phases of activation (Stages I, II, III). Stage I activation would cause little disruption to normal airline operations. Stage II would provide the military with more airplanes, and would cause significant disruptions to certain normal airline operations. Stage III would only be used for a large-scale global war, and would, of course, cause major disruptions to all normal airline operations. (At this level of conflict, airline operations would already be significantly disrupted.)

The program was never used during a crisis until Operation Desert Shield. On August 15, 1990, CRAF Stage I was activated. During the next five months, 64 percent of the 500,000 military personnel and 27 percent of air cargo transported to the Persian Gulf was carried on commercial airliners. A partial activation of CRAF Stage II was ordered on January 15, 1991, in order to provide aeromedical airlift capability. However, these planes were not required, due to the low casualty rate in Desert Storm. No modifications of passenger airplanes were required.

A commercial airliner can be pulled from routine passenger service in the morning, and carry soldiers halfway around the world that same afternoon. Military cargo, however, tends to be heavier per square foot than most commercial air cargo, so the military paid to have stronger floors installed on the CRAF fleet of planes. This added some weight, which resulted in increased fuel consumption for the commercial cargo carriers during peacetime. The military paid the participating companies a subsidy to offset these extra fuel costs. Additionally, the military covered the cost of the modifications required to quickly convert airplanes into an aeromedical airlift mode (pulling out the seats and installing beds and medical support equipment), and the government signed contracts with CRAF that required federal employees to travel on these airlines for routine trips during peacetime. These benefits, plus other small subsidies, made CRAF an attractive program for the airlines, and a good investment for the American taxpayer. Surge capacity was maintained within the private sector, and everyone benefited from the arrangement.

CRAF is the model that we must adopt for disaster response in America. The government's response to Hurricane Katrina was in stark contrast to this efficient and proven model, relying instead on emergency, open-ended, no-bid contracts, many with companies the government had never done business with before. When CRAF was activated on August 15, 1990, no contract negotiations were required, and no open-end, no-bid contracts were let. Every detail had been negotiated in advance (remember those 5 Ps: prior planning prevents piss-poor performance). A CRAF-type system would have been invaluable to the preparation, evacuation, and response to Katrina. However, we must be careful that we do not learn the wrong lessons from that catastrophe. A few weeks after the disastrous federal response to Katrina, I was doing an interview on MSNBC with Monica Crowley. She said, "No one does logistics better than the military. Shouldn't we put them in charge of logistics for disaster response in America?"

Wrong Question

The correct question would have been, "Who should be in charge of logistics during a major disaster?" It is not the military. The fact is, no one is better at logistics than Wal-Mart, FedEx, Dell, UPS, and Target. The government should look to the private sector to provide food, water, shelter, and transportation during a natural or man-made crisis. CRAF is the model that will work, and the model America can afford.

PROVIDING FINANCIAL AND INTELLECTUAL RESOURCES THROUGH NOT-FOR-PROFIT PARTNERSHIPS

Dr. D. A. Henderson led the ten-year World Health Organization effort to eradicate smallpox—a disease that killed more than 300 million during the first seventy-five years of the twentieth century. Since 1980, not a single human has suffered from this disease that had been a scourge dating back to the pharaohs. This was one of the greatest humanitarian and scientific achievements of all time, and it was accomplished with a new type of organization. While WHO continues to lead the governmental efforts in global public health, private organizations are also beginning to play key roles, such as the Bill and Melinda Gates Foundation's effort to eradicate malaria. The freedom from cumbersome government bureaucracies and the enormous wealth of visionary philanthropists make this private sector initiative a potential model for new homeland security initiatives. There is also precedent from the 1930s.

Just before the Crash of 1929, Alfred Loomis, a wealthy Wall Street investor, liquidated his stocks and became one of America's wealthiest individuals during the Depression. In the mid-1930s, he became convinced that America would eventually fight a war with Nazi Germany, and he initiated a privately funded program to identify and develop technologies that could prove useful in this conflict. With his own money, he hired 4,000 scientists and engineers to begin the research and development on these new technologies. He held lavish weekend parties at his estate in Tuxedo Park, New York. His weekend guests included Nobel Prize winners, professors from America's leading universities (such as Albert Einstein), and visionaries from industry. These guests were asked to brainstorm new ideas and assess current research.

Many ideas, concepts, technologies, and products had their beginnings in Tuxedo Park, the two most notable being nuclear power and radar. This privately funded effort provided enormous benefits. Actually, it is not possible to even measure the return to the American taxpayer, since no government funds were used. But for Loomis, whose only interest was in increased security for the U.S., the return was beyond measure.

This is a model that could prove useful. The federal bureaucracy is slow, lumbering, and generally inefficient. There are some notable exceptions: the development of nuclear weapons (twenty-nine months to design and build the first bomb), and the race to the moon (a little more than eight years from the first U.S. manned space flight to the success of Apollo 11), but these programs had a simple, single focus and extraordinary budgets. This is not the case for the current requirements in homeland security, but there is opportunity for a new-style Tuxedo Park program.

In July 2006, I received an e-mail from Mark Lampert, a Silicon Valley entrepreneur who had enjoyed reading an op-ed piece I had written for *The Wall Street Journal*. Like many who study homeland security, Mark was frustrated with the lack of progress by federal, state, and local governments. We discussed the Tuxedo Park model from the 1930s, and how it might be adapted to our current needs. Mark then posed a fascinating question. He said, "I have read much of what you have written in publications and congressional testimony during the past five years. You make more sense than anyone else I have read or heard. If you had access to $100 million, could you make a difference in homeland security?" Of course this little voice in the back of my head said, "YES!" However, I controlled my impulse, and replied, "I don't know, let me think about it for a couple of weeks." The fact is, I had never thought of such a concept, and wasn't sure $100 million could really make a difference. My only guidelines from Mark were:

1. The investors would demand a significant return on investment—not in terms of dollars, but in terms of increased security for America.
2. The investors were not interested in competing with the government. This effort had to focus on what the government couldn't or wouldn't do.
3. The investors were not interested in paying for a traditional think tank. They wanted action.

After a couple of weeks of thought, and many discussions with some of America's best homeland security experts, I wrote a proposal for Mark. Here is a summary version.

PROPOSAL

Problem: No organization exists today, either inside or outside the government, to conduct prototype testing of homeland security operational concepts. One small organization exists within the Department of Homeland Security, but it lacks the freedom to move quickly, and it is, by design, a reactive organization. Its charter is to develop new technologies and operational concepts in response to a crisis. What America needs is an organization that can stay two or three steps in front of emerging problems, not one step behind. Furthermore, this is just one small office in a large bureaucracy. While it can have some influence vertically in the Department of Homeland Security, America's problems must be resolved horizontally across the entire federal government, plus state and local governments and the private sector. No organization within the government is capable of meeting this challenge. The primary problem is that no one is in charge. (See *Washington Post* op-ed, "Years After 9/11 . . . No One Is in Charge of Fighting Our Two Biggest Threats," May 20, 2005.)

Solution: Create an action-oriented 501(c)3 not-for-profit corporation to fund and supervise operational prototype development and testing. In fact, this may be one of the true silver bullets for homeland security.

Unlike traditional D.C. think tanks, this 501(c)3 would be hands-on, operationally oriented, and solely focused on:

- Identifying key requirements that are not being satisfied by federal, state, or local governments (much of this work has already been accomplished).
- Soliciting and selecting proposals for concepts of operation that could be deployed in a small-scale, prototype environment (significant cash awards, up to $1 million, would be given to individuals or organizations whose proposals were selected for prototype testing).
- Directing the testing of deployed prototypes.
- Hiring independent auditors to evaluate the prototypes.
- Submitting the independent evaluations to key congressional committees, appropriate government agencies (such as the Department of Homeland Security, Centers for Disease Control, and Health and Human Services), and the media.

Following an initial proof-of-concept project, I envision that this 501(c)3 could run three to four different prototype programs simultaneously around the country. In my estimation, we could "fail" in up to half of our prototype endeavors (i.e., half might not go beyond initial testing), but even those prototype systems would be of extreme value to the nation as "lessons learned" for application to follow-on prototype testing.

The Tuxedo Park of the twenty-first century will not likely resemble that of the 1930s. There are no *technological* silver bullets for homeland security, or at least none that this type of organization could hope to fund. Even something as simple as developing a new antibiotic costs between $600 million and $1 billion.

What this project could afford would be operational prototypes, such as testing a community's capabilities to organize, train, and equip volunteers. Could a convention center be turned into a 1,000-bed hospital? What supplies would be required? If these were stockpiled, could they be rotated through the routine supply chain to ensure that they did not exceed acceptable shelf-life periods? What legislative actions would be required to provide indemnification for those volunteers? (Maryland does this by putting volunteer medical personnel into the Maryland Defense Force. Other states such as New Jersey have similar programs, including some for corporations that donate facilities.) What training would be required? During the smallpox eradication program, D. A. Henderson taught illiterate villagers how to give smallpox vaccines in little more than fifteen minutes. (I am convinced retired Air Force pilots could learn in as little as thirty.)

Bottom line: A 501(c)3 is the only type of organization that could successfully run this kind of program. Government organizations are not likely to go down this road; certainly not with the freedom one would have in the private sector—freedom from bureaucratic gridlock and partisan/pork barrel politics. No *for-profit* organization would find this type of program attractive. However, to a group of investors who were primarily interested in a return on investment measured in terms of significant improvements to the security of the American homeland, this is a program that will exceed their expectations.

―――――――――

This is just one example of how the private sector could fulfill a new role in America's security mission. No matter which models are eventually selected, the financial and intellectual talent of the private sector must play an expanded role in providing the creativity and flexibility that will never be possible in government programs. The Bill and Melinda Gates Foundation and the Nuclear Threat Initiative funded by Ted Turner are the Tuxedo Parks of this century. More are needed. These types of organizations have the visionary leadership and the resources to produce results that are not possible with a lumbering bureaucracy, hamstrung with outdated rules, regulations, and processes. Funding these types of organizations is not only a responsibility for corporate America; it is also in its best interests. Stanley Weiss, the founder of BENS, Business Executives for National Security, explained to many Fortune 500 CEOs why they should be interested in national security during the Cold War: "Being dead is bad for business." Today, we can tell America's CEOs: "Meeting your responsibilities for the security challenges of the twenty-first century is good for business."

Chapter 8

Local Communities

911 Is a Local Call

THE FACT THAT THE UNITED STATES IS COMPRISED OF 87,000 JURISDICTIONS at the federal, state, and local levels makes the challenge of homeland security even more difficult. Countries with a national system of government, such as Thailand and France, have fewer challenges adapting to this new security environment. Thailand has one police department; the United States has 18,000, all of which are independent.

In previous chapters, I recommended the creation of several new organizations within the federal government, but I most certainly do not recommend changing the Constitution. The Founding Fathers did not trust an all-powerful national government, and neither do I. But we must develop a better understanding of how the federal government can work as a team with state and local governments during all phases of a crisis, and we must determine who will plan, who will pay, and who will be in charge. One concept all Americans must understand is that 911 will always be a local call—governors and mayors will tell you that they are always in charge. The Constitution was specific with regard to this issue, and governors can quote the Tenth Amendment better than anyone:

The powers not delegated to the United States by the Constitution, nor prohibited by it to the States, are reserved to the States respectively, or to the people.

On the other hand, sending federal dollars to state and local governments to do with as they please is not a panacea for homeland security. If the federal government had provided New York City with $5 billion of homeland security funding prior to 9/11, New York would not have been able to prevent the attacks on the World Trade Center, would not have been able to prevent the collapse of the Towers, or have been able to significantly reduce the casualty figures. Likewise, most of the equipment that the federal government bought for New Orleans was underwater and useless just hours after Katrina made landfall. The primary federal role is far more complex than just writing checks. The federal role in homeland security is not about protecting any one city or state, but protecting the nation as a whole, and providing the appropriate type of support to state and local governments. Since 9/11, there have been some significant improvements in this area.

SUPPORT FROM THE FEDERAL GOVERNMENT

When most people think of the federal government's role in disaster response, they think of money, and without question, "more money" is the number one request made by state and local officials. Federal funds provide grants for training and equipment prior to a disaster, plus grants and low-cost loans during recovery and rebuilding. This has been a federal government mission for decades, but two new programs initiated by the Department of Homeland Security since 9/11 have resulted in significant improvements in federal support for state and local governments. These programs addressed two important issues: creating standards and a common knowledge base, and developing a common template for disaster response procedures and processes. Let's take a look at both.

It is the federal government's responsibility to provide America's first responders with standards for equipment and procedures that guarantee the best use of federal funds while also enhancing interoperability. Interoperability is what allows first responders to work with others both inside and outside their normal jurisdictions, and the federal government is the only organization capable of providing this service. Prior to 9/11, interoperability was a glaring deficiency. The lack of equipment standards for first responders is a problem I first encountered in the summer of 2000 while visiting the Center for Domestic Preparedness in Anniston, Alabama. This is a world-class training facility for firefighters, police officers, and EMS personnel that provides instruction on a wide range of skills. It is also the only civilian training program in the U.S. that allows trainees to suit up and work in an environment contaminated with lethal chemical agents, such as nerve gas. (I politely turned down an offer to participate.)

L. Z. Johnson was the director of CDP at the time of my visit. One of the deficiencies that he identified and wanted to resolve was the fact that there was no single place to determine what worked and did not work. This lack of a "standard-bearer" caused three significant problems: It threatened the safety of the first responders, it reduced their capability to properly respond—which was a threat to the citizens they were sworn to protect—and it wasted taxpayer dollars. This would seem like sufficient motivation for action. However, CDP was at that time part of the Department of Justice. This provided a close link to law enforcement personnel, but creating standardization for firefighters and EMS personnel was not part of the agency culture or mission.

In response to the 1993 bombing of the World Trade Center and the 1995 bombing of the Murrah Building, the federal government provided grants to local fire departments. But because there were no national standards and no equivalent of the Underwriters Laboratory for first responders, fire departments around the country spent millions of dollars on equipment with marginal capabilities, or that was inappropriate for the task. Many of the small and mid-sized departments did not have the expertise to ask the right questions. For example, it was not uncommon for some departments to buy equipment for use in a response to a chemical incident that would protect them against liquids but not vapors. This oversight was an honest mistake made by first responders, but for the less-than-reputable vendors who were selling substandard equipment to these departments it was misrepresentation at best, and in some cases it constituted outright fraud.

However, you will be glad to know this deficiency has been corrected. In 1999, the congressionally funded Memorial Institute for the Prevention of Terrorism (MIPT) was created (www. mipt.org). Located in Oklahoma City, the institute was born from the desire of the survivors and families of the Murrah Federal Building bombing to assist other communities in preventing terrorist acts, improve response capabilities, and to share lessons learned with communities across the nation. This small, not-for-profit, but influential organization provides a range of valuable services to agencies in federal, state, and local governments, but few more important than the Responder Knowledge Base.

MIPT is a unique organization. The original design concept for the Responder Knowledge Base differed greatly from the finished product, because once the employees went into the field and talked to first responders, they did something unusual—

they actually listened to their customers' input. Consequently, MIPT scrapped its original plan, and redesigned and fielded a system based on the true needs of their customers. Due to these changes, first responders are better prepared, your families are more secure, and tax dollars are better managed. Because of this database, if a fire department in Pueblo, Colorado, needs to purchase new protective breathing devices, it can determine which equipment authorized for purchase with federal funds also meets its specific needs. Additionally, contact names and phone numbers of other fire departments throughout the country that have already purchased this equipment are provided so that potential buyers can request direct feedback about the product.

The Responder Knowledge Base is just one of the many programs operated by MIPT. While we always seem to hear about the wasteful programs, this database will help to prevent the incredible waste that we have read about. Mimi Hall of *USA Today*, one of America's best homeland security reporters, has documented numerous cases of sparsely populated rural counties receiving exotic high-tech equipment that sometimes isn't even found in major cities. This equipment was purchased with federal funds for communities that had no critical infrastructure (major airports, nuclear power plants, chemical plants, military installations, and so on). Thanks to the Responder Knowledge Base, we won't be reading as many of these stories as we have in the past.

Another federal contribution to state and local governments is the improvement in procedural and process standards, provided by the Department of Homeland Security through the development of the National Incident Management System. Thanks to the leadership of Bob Stephan, the assistant secretary for infrastructure protection, NIMS became the national standard in 2003. NIMS provides a consistent nationwide template to enable all government, private sector, and nongovernmental organizations to work together during domestic incidents. Stephan didn't create this system from a blank piece of paper, but from a variety of lessons learned in various organizations at the federal, state, and local levels over many years of disaster response. With the creation of NIMS, these lessons learned became the national standard for the first time.

This standardization of procedures and processes facilitates regional response to disasters by allowing first responders from outside local and state jurisdictions to deploy to a disaster scene and know exactly where and how they fit into the complex, dynamic process.

This is a wise policy from both an operational and financial perspective. We cannot afford to buy every piece of equipment that each first responder organization has on its wish list, and more importantly, we don't need to if we coordinate and standardize efforts.

In 2003 I discussed this issue with Mayor Edward Garza of San Antonio, Texas, who is a leading advocate for a regional approach to disaster response. He said, "San Antonio can't afford and doesn't need to buy every piece of first responder equipment that we may use only once in a decade." What the mayor needed was the confidence that this equipment was located within a reasonable distance and available for use during exercises and actual events. This "good neighbor" approach to disaster response is a system we can afford.

However, the good neighbor approach requires that this type of system be regularly tested during exercises. As the former commissioner of health for the City of New York, Dr. Peggy Hamburg, said more than a decade ago, "We should not be exchanging business cards on the first day of a crisis." Cross-jurisdictional cooperation will only work during a crisis if we practice.

One of the primary roles of the Texas State Homeland Security chief is to coordinate this type of support. Steve McGraw has served as the chief since August 2004 and has developed a benchmark system for this service. He began by ensuring that every piece of equipment purchased in Texas with federal money is placed into a database. If a mayor calls and says she needs a dozen 80 KVA generators, the database will not only provide the location information, but also the contact information for the individual responsible for that equipment. This system proved highly effective during Hurricane Rita in 2005, providing communities with a significant improvement in response capabilities. But these benefits were not limited to the citizens of Texas. Considerable personnel and equipment from Texas were deployed to Louisiana during the response to Katrina, including Texas Task Force One, the largest state-level disaster response force in America (of course it's the largest—it's from Texas).

Steve McGraw is a strong champion for cross-jurisdictional support. For instance, when federal funds are used to purchase equipment for the fire department in Lubbock, McGraw considers this a statewide asset, not just a local one. The equipment can even be shared with other states.

These first two initiatives, standardization of equipment and procedures, are not of the variety that make for good headlines in newspapers, but nevertheless they are wise investments of your tax dollars, and provide major benefits to first responders and the communities they serve.

One particular area of federal support to state and local governments has not been improved upon since 9/11. Although related to the standardization of equipment and procedures, it is far more controversial than the Responder Knowledge Base or the National Incident Management System. Approximately 90 percent of funding for the National Guard comes from the federal government. This should not change, but the primary mission of the National Guard should. Today, the National Guard is well organized, trained, and equipped—for the Cold War. We need to reshape and realign this force for the challenges of the new century, and we should begin this effort by shifting the Guard's focus to activities conducted inside the United States. This was the Guard's original mission, and it's time for it to return to its historic roots. Let's begin this discussion with some recent history.

The Reserve Component of the U.S. military is comprised of the Army, Navy, Air Force, and Marine Reserves (federal forces always under the command of the president) plus the Army and Air National Guard (which serve under the command of governors, unless federalized). After Desert Storm in 1991, several changes were made to the Reserve Component of the Defense Department, particularly within the Army Reserve. The majority of combat support (defensive units) and service support (the logisticians) was placed in the Reserve, while combat arms units (offensive units) were transferred to the National Guard. This is exactly the opposite of what we need today.

Ask yourself this question: If you were the governor of your state, which would you rather have under your direct control, units with M1 tanks and F-16 fighter jets, or military police, civil engineer, transportation, and medical units? I know what my choice would be. National Guard units are also the best suited for use beyond their own state boundaries. A National Guard military police unit from Montana can quickly coordinate efforts with a National Guard military police unit from New York while they are both operating in Louisiana. Additionally, using the organizational structure and equipment of the National Guard provides the standardization that allows for the most effective utilization of resources, and the fact that many people in the National Guard have similar duties in their civilian jobs allows them to leverage their civilian experience. You cannot tap into that experience base when you utilize active duty military units.

Furthermore, all states are now members of the Emergency Management Assistance Compact. This agreement allows governors to share state resources, including the National Guard, with other governors. States also have specialized National Guard units trained to respond to attacks with weapons of mass destruction. These units, called WMD Civil Support Teams, are manned with full-time Guardsmen capable of deploying anywhere in their respective state within a matter of hours. These units can also be shared between states.

Emergency response to man-made or natural disasters within the U.S. should not be a mission for the active duty and Reserve military forces, which should be exclusively organized, trained, and equipped to fight wars outside the U.S. It is time we begin restructuring the National Guard for the homeland mission by increasing its percentage of civil engineer, military police, transportation, and medical units, and designating these units for use only inside the U.S.

Some senior National Guard leaders have told me that this would cause a problem for recruiting. While this may have been true during the Cold War, times have changed. A National Guard limited to domestic missions would have great appeal to some people who would never consider joining a traditional military force. Furthermore, we need to reexamine the militia concept.

Today, twenty-six states have "organized militias." These units are separate from the National Guard, but under the control of the state adjutant general (head of the state National Guard). Some of the members are too old or physically unfit for military service, but can still be of great value during a disaster response, as can many retirees and other groups such as the 40,000 nurses in Texas who are not currently working in health care. The key is to make sure these groups are properly organized, trained, and equipped.

There is considerable difference in militia size, training, and expertise in the twenty-six states, so it is difficult to say what services a "typical" state militia provides, but as an example, the Maryland Defense Force is comprised of volunteers who provide a variety of services including training and crisis response for medical, legal, and disaster counseling, and disaster-related damage assessment. In 2005, 200 members of the Maryland Defense Force were deployed in relief efforts following Hurricane Katrina. These medical professionals and support staff worked in six remote medical pods in Jefferson Parish, Louisiana, and provided medical treatment to more than 7,000 victims.

Another area where many state and local governments look to the federal government for support is on the issue of communications. They point to *The 9/11 Commission Report* and other studies that address communications problems among first responders.

One of the classic stories was the response to the 9/11 attack on the Pentagon. Ed Plaugher, the chief of the Arlington, Virginia, fire department, was in charge of the emergency response. Because of the multi-jurisdictional nature of the first responders, and the inability to communicate across a wide range of radio frequencies, Chief Plaugher had to resort to a communications system exactly like that which had been used on the battlefields of Gettysburg and Antietam during the Civil War: He wrote notes, and gave them to runners to communicate to other leaders.

There are certain areas within communications where the federal government can provide assistance, such as providing increased frequency spectrum for first responders. Legislation to accomplish this, which will provide more and better frequencies for first responders, has made it through Congress and has been signed by the president. It will not take effect until 2009, which is later than it should, but it's a step in the right direction. The second area is in developing and coordinating standards, and sharing lessons learned. Finally, the federal government can provide funds for systems that will assist in developing communications during multi-jurisdictional, large-scale disasters. During Katrina, when virtually all the local communication systems were destroyed or severely disrupted, the federal government should have had the capability to airlift into the area a self-contained, satellite-based communications system. This communications suite would have provided digital voice and data communications to state and local officials—from top elected officials all the way down to first responders. Many of the situational awareness and coordination problems could have been resolved if such a communications package had been available during Katrina.

However, the most important issue to understand about first responder communications is that the federal government cannot resolve the most difficult challenges. Spending billions of dollars on new radios will not improve crisis communications between organizations that cannot communicate when seated across from each other at a conference table. During an interview on *Homeland Security: Inside and Out,* Howard Safir, the only man to serve as both the New York City fire commissioner and police commissioner, talked about the cultural barriers to communications and cooperation between the NYPD and FDNY. A $500 million state-of-the-art communications system will not significantly improve communications between organizations that don't want to talk. Cultural and parochial differences can only be resolved at the state and local level, not by throwing federal money at them. (To listen to all of Commissioner Safir's comments, go to www.hlsinsideandout.org.)

Many in Congress view the communications issue as a means

to an end: pork and votes. Communications is a highly complex and important issue. We must understand that "Ready! Shoot! Aim!" will not solve the problem, and technology will not resolve cultural and parochial barriers. Communications problems are primarily a state and local issue.

SUCCESS STORIES FROM THE FRONT LINES OF HOMELAND SECURITY

I introduced Sheriff Donald Sowell ("Posse up") in Chapter 1. During Hurricane Rita, Sowell demonstrated how leadership and prior planning can make the difference between a successful response and a dismal failure during a disaster. The residents of Grimes County, Texas, and the several hundred thousand evacuees who passed through all owe him a tip of their Stetsons.

When Sowell first received notification that forecasters were predicting 105-mile-per-hour winds in his county, he activated his plan to batten down and posse up. Understanding that the first crisis Grimes County would face would not be the winds of Hurricane Rita but the exodus of hundreds of thousands of coastal residents, he focused on facilitating a swift transit through his county to the prepared evacuation sites further north. His first action was ordering a large stockpile of gasoline brought to the county and placed under his control, after which he turned to the task of forming his posse. Step one in building that posse was activating his reserve deputies, who were trained, armed, and licensed, and routinely worked with the full-time staff. He then looked to his primary sources of personnel from outside his county: Texas game wardens, who are licensed peace officers, and deputy sheriffs from other counties. Through prior arrangement, each request would only require one phone call to Austin. Actually, after the first call to the state game warden,

Sheriff Sowell did not have to make another one; the director of Fish and Wildlife in Austin agreed to send eighty-three game wardens and sixty-six boats. With an emergency supply of gasoline and a posse for traffic control and law enforcement, Sheriff Sowell was confident that he could handle the crisis.

Nevertheless, the evacuation wasn't pretty. Evacuations rarely are. The number one obstacle to an efficient evacuation was that many people took to the roads with gas tanks that were less than half full. A large percentage of the people who arrived in Grimes County were frightened, hot, frustrated, and out of gas—factors that could have quickly led to ugly scenes on the highway. However, there was not a single arrest or report of a serious crime during the entire evacuation through the county because Sowell's posse supplied the evacuees with enough gas to get them further north to where gas stations were still operating. And the highly visible presence of peace officers was crucial to maintaining law and order. Fortunately, Rita turned northeast and spared Grimes County. Once the evacuation had slowed to a trickle, the game wardens and their boats were sent to assist those in northeast Texas that did bear the brunt of Rita's destructive forces.

On 9/11 in New York City, Diane Lapson demonstrated that you don't need a badge to form a posse. In 2001, she was the vice president of the Independence Plaza North Tenant Association. This organization represents 3,500 residents of three high-rises and a group of townhouses located three blocks from the World Trade Center that had a high concentration of senior citizens.

September 11 was election day in New York City, and Diane's friend Kathryn Freed was running for city council. Diane and Kathryn were walking to the local polling station when American Flight 11 slammed into the North Tower of the World Trade Center. Diane describes that first hour as a bit of a "horrific blur." She and Kathryn assisted in the evacuation of the local schools, and then headed toward the nearest police station. The one officer left in the station told them, "We can't help you. Do what you have to do."

Diane and Kathryn went back out on the street to help move the crowds uptown. Staying busy and helping others kept their minds off the horrors of that September day. After returning to their complex, they discovered that Building 9, a thirty-nine-story condominium close to Ground Zero, had lost electricity and phone service. In response, the association's leaders established command posts in the lobbies of their three largest buildings. The team was relieved to have an organization to fall back on, but all wished they had received some training in disaster response. The ideal combination is an organization with plans, training, and practice under its belt. This management team had completed step one, but everything else was developed on the fly.

The sick, disabled, and elderly were identified as the team's top priority, what they called the A list. The second priority was for floor captains to contact all residents to see who was missing and who else might need assistance. On the morning of the 12th, when city authorities ordered the evacuation of Building 9, Red Cross volunteers and floor captains focused their efforts on assisting those on the A list. At this point there was no electricity, phones, or water, and all local stores, including pharmacies, had been closed. Providing food, water, and prescription medication to the A list became the mission of the day. On September 14, Kathryn smuggled the owner of the local drugstore into the controlled area around Ground Zero, and with tenant volunteers running the cash registers, the owner filled prescriptions delivered by floor captains. Social workers began arriving to provide counseling to the traumatized residents; within a few days, Diane learned one of the lessons of the Oklahoma City bombing:

Those providing assistance are in as much need of trauma counseling as the victims.

Looking back on her experience, Diane talks about lessons learned. She is grateful that they were organized, but while none of the tenants questioned the authority of the elected leaders, she did. Were they qualified? Why hadn't they taken Red Cross training? Why didn't they have emergency supplies? On the evening of September 14, Diane took a break from her near nonstop duties and walked out into the street to look at where the World Trade Center had stood. She says she remembered someone once asking her, "How do you live in the middle of a city? There is no landscape, no hills, no forests—just concrete and glass." That night she reflected on her response: "That's true, but in New York City, the people are the landscape."

Sheriff Sowell had a posse and a plan. Diane Lapson had only a posse, and while heroic work was still accomplished due to courage, grit, and quick wit, she'd tell you without a moment's hesitation that she wished she'd had a plan. She's not alone. Barry Johnson, a former Army officer, lives atop one of the largest fault lines in the U.S. Barry learned at an early age the value of organization and plans, but when an unexpected event occurred in his community, Barry and the rest of the residents found themselves without a plan.

In late November 2005, Barry's community, an upscale suburban development of eighty-six single-family homes in Oakland, California, called Fountains-on-Estates, experienced three burglaries in a single night. This was extraordinary for a community that hadn't seen a single burglary in anyone's memory. A meeting was called by a few local residents, and Brenda Ivy of the Oakland police department talked about creating a community watch program. She also suggested the need for disaster preparedness.

One resident stepped forward and volunteered to create a

neighborhood watch group, and Barry offered to use his computer skills to develop a database and assist with leadership and organization. Information on all eighty-six houses, including digital photos, was loaded into the database, and he divided the community into six blocks and recruited block captains and assistants. The community purchased walkie-talkies for the leadership team, and created a mobile command post that could operate in Barry's driveway without electricity. A master plan was developed for the community, and specialty teams (communications, damage assessment, search and rescue, and first-aid) drew up their own individualized plans, including requirements for training.

Fountains-on-Estates had a posse and a plan; now they had to practice. Training was provided by Citizens of Oakland Respond to Emergencies (CORE), and was conducted in three phases: CORE I—personal and home readiness; CORE II—neighborhood readiness; and CORE III—search and rescue, triage, cribbing (shoring up a house after an earthquake), fire suppression, and darkened room searches. Similar programs are available throughout the U.S. through the Community Emergency Response Team program. CERT was originally developed by the Los Angeles fire department in 1985, and FEMA made this training widely available in 1993. CERT training, now available in fifty states and six territories, is a twenty-hour course that includes classroom instruction and hands-on exercises. CERT teams are frequently formed with businesses, residential communities, and even schools. Maryville Middle School in Maryville, Washington, created a Student Emergency Response Team that has been trained in first-aid, CPR, and earthquake preparedness. The team will be available to assist Red Cross personnel in the event of a local disaster. For more information on CERT, see www.citizencorps. gov/cert/.

Within just four months from that initial meeting, the

Fountains-on-Estates Disaster Preparedness Group, consisting of eighty-six homes and 200 people, was organized, trained, and equipped. In April 2006, the Fountains community participated in a citywide earthquake disaster drill, which tested the group's ability to communicate within their local community and with first responders, as well as its response to twenty simulated incidents scattered throughout the community. If an earthquake, wildfire, or other disaster occurs, they will be far better prepared than before their wake-up call from the burglars in November 2005. The investment of money was minimal, and although there was some time investment required for the organization and training meetings, residents say it was time well spent. As Barry says, "Even if we never have a disaster, it was certainly worth the time. I had lived in this community for ten years and knew less than a dozen of my neighbors. I am now on a first-name basis with forty, and have met virtually all of the adults in the Fountains community of eighty-six homes."

You could spend the time doing all the research that Barry did to build his Ready Watch program, or for less than $200, you can buy the software and planning manuals at www.readywatch. com. There are other Web sites (you can find with a Google search) where you can obtain less-sophisticated software and manuals for free. What's important is that you take action to build a posse and a plan prior to a disaster in your local community, not during or after the event.

SAINTS OR SINNERS?

How will people in your local community react during a major crisis or disaster? Will they be saints or sinners? There is empirical evidence supporting both possibilities. The heroic actions of first responders and ordinary citizens in lower Manhattan on 9/11, Oklahoma City following the attack on the Murrah Building, southern California after the North Ridge earthquake, and in the London Underground in 2005 support the saint argument. If you have not seen the movie *World Trade Center*, I suggest you do so. The heroism of the rescuers at Ground Zero surpasses any I witnessed during three decades of military service.

Dr. Monica Schoch-Spana from the Center for Biosecurity–UPMC has done considerable research in this area, and is convinced that, in most cases, "private citizens are inclined to show compassion for, and offer assistance to others in their communities. A stereotypical portrayal of a 'panicked public' undermines the potential for policymakers and local planners to include citizens in crafting thoughtful response measures that can ultimately shape the way a disaster unfolds in a community." Dr. Schoch-Spana states that academic research overwhelmingly supports the argument that people generally act during disasters as they do during normal activities. Parents take care of children, and employers (at least the good ones) take care of their employees. Society does not break down when the lights go out.

On the other hand, the riots in American cities during the 1960s, the Rodney King riots in Los Angeles in 1992, the crime spree that broke out in New Orleans following Katrina, and even the hooliganism we see from fans at European soccer matches and in America following victories and losses in major sporting events, demonstrate the potential for the darker side of human nature to emerge. One of the most dramatic and well-documented cases of mass panic occurred in 1995 in Surat, India. Several patients in three different hospitals in Surat were diagnosed with plague. A couple of local radio stations picked up the story and it was quickly, and incorrectly, attributed to a terrorist attack. In what proved to be one of the most extraordinary public responses to radio reports since Orson Welles's *War of the Worlds* radio broadcast the day before Halloween in 1938, an estimated 500,000 people fled the city, including most of the health care workers.

Some analysts and observers predict that the better angels of the human spirit will emerge during a major disaster, while others fear the darker. My experience during three decades of military service, which included combat, natural disasters such as floods in Thailand and Bangladesh, hurricanes, widespread power failures, earthquakes, ice storms, civil disorder, and airplane crashes, has led me to agree with the academic literature cited by Dr. Schoch-Spana. However, I am also convinced that there are situations such as the one in Grimes County, Texas, during the Hurricane Rita evacuation when leadership and planning prevented the loss of civil order. The New York City police department learned this lesson the hard way from the blackout of 1977, which produced widespread looting and arson. A congressional study reported total damage of $300 million and nearly 4,000 arrests. When the power went out in the Northeast again on August 15, 2003, Mayor Michael Bloomberg put the entire NYPD on the streets in uniform. The crime figures for that night were lower than a normal weeknight in the city. The difference in crime statistics between these two events is evidence of the impact leadership and planning can have on a crisis situation.

I began this chapter by saying that 911 is a local call. When talking about pandemic flu at a conference in Denver (March 25, 2006), Mike Leavitt, the secretary of health and human services, said, "Any community that fails to prepare with an expectation that the federal government will come to their rescue will be sadly disappointed." A senior Department of Homeland Security official who asked not to be identified told me, "If anybody thinks that calling area code 202 [Washington, D.C.] in a crisis will solve their problems, they'd better think again." (This statement was made before Katrina.) While everybody seems to understand that 911 is a local call, we must also realize that in a major crisis, most 911 callers will get a busy signal. The more you do now to prepare your local community, the better off you will be when you get that busy signal. Furthermore, you need to prepare your family.

Chapter 9

Your Family

Be Prepared

EVERY FAMILY IN AMERICA SHOULD PREPARE FOR DISASTER. THIS IS NOT JUST my recommendation, but that of the American Red Cross, the Department of Homeland Security, and every Boy Scout and Girl Scout in America—whose motto is "Be Prepared!" Preparation includes education (most of which has been accomplished by reading this book), training (available through your local Red Cross chapter), and the development of three things every family and individual should have: a transportation plan, a communication plan, and a readiness kit. (See the tear-out sheet at the end of the book for a checklist.)

I am not suggesting that you build a bomb shelter, buy a year's supply of food, or join a survivalist group. I will not recommend any actions I have not taken or recommended to my family. I am a strong believer in the 85 percent solution. For most families, my recommendations require an initial commitment of six hours of Red Cross training, an hour or two of planning, and a small investment in supplies and equipment for a readiness kit. This kit might prove to be the best investment you will ever make, and it will not require a large-scale terrorist attack to reap the benefits. My kit came in quite handy when

Hurricane Isabel hit Washington in 2003. When the electricity went out and the city water supply became contaminated, I was not one of those people standing in line complaining. I had everything I needed.

Each floor of my house has a plug-in flashlight that automatically turns on when the power goes off. I used my small black and white TV that runs on D batteries, and my crank radio for AM/FM and shortwave. I had my nonperishable food, my water supply, and I was sitting in my leather easy chair, drinking a glass of scotch. Life wasn't too bad, considering we had a hurricane over the city. I was fortunate; I was only without power for about eighteen hours. Neighbors just up the hill from me did not have any power for four days. While not a big survival issue, they were certainly dismayed when they lost all the steaks in their freezer—a situation that could have been avoided if they had properly prepared by buying ice before the storm hit. But this chapter isn't about saving steaks; it is about saving your family, so let's begin with training.

I recommend that every member of your family, twelve years of age or older, go through Red Cross training programs. At a minimum, they should receive training in CPR and first-aid. During the summer break, or when the kids have a day off from school, you should go as a family. I recently took my twenty-three-year-old daughter for CPR and first-aid training. The class was her first exposure to this, and for me it was a great refresher for what I learned in the military. Who knows; someday she may save my life, I may save hers, or maybe we will never have to use that training. But when we walked out of that class, we were confident that if we were the first to arrive at an auto accident or saw someone having a heart attack, we would know what to do: *Check. Call. Care.* (If you aren't familiar with the actions required in each of these three life-saving steps, you should sign up for the course.) And even if we never use our training, it was a good day together as father and daughter.

Many people do not understand the difference CPR can make. Cardiovascular disease, which causes heart attacks, strokes, and heart failure, is the leading cause of death in America for men and women. There are certain types of heart attacks that will prove fatal even if you are in a hospital surrounded by cardiopulmonary specialists. However, properly administered CPR saves lives every year. In many cases, even improperly administered CPR can make a difference. A friend of mine who is a physician told me about an individual who had a heart attack at a party. The host called 911 while everyone else just stood around waiting for the paramedics to arrive. By the time they did, the individual was dead. An autopsy determined that the heart attack had been mild enough that had one of the guests just put his or her foot on the victim's chest and pushed down fifteen to twenty times per minute, he might have survived until professional help arrived.

Of course, properly administered CPR from a trained individual is the ideal situation, and that is exactly what happened to Charles (Bo) Floyd on November 16, 1992. Bo had just returned to his office in Baltimore and was talking to his assistant when he began experiencing chest pains. Moments later he was on the floor, unconscious and close to death. His assistant called 911 while two young co-workers who had recently completed Red Cross training began giving Bo CPR until professionals arrived. This was such a textbook example of how simple training can save a life that Bo's story was documented in a Red Cross training video. The video made him a bit of a celebrity, at least with his family and friends.

However, a real celebrity and one of America's favorite comedians, Jeff Foxworthy, saved his brother's life a few years ago with CPR, proving that even "rednecks" can be trained in proper CPR techniques. The Red Cross CPR and first-aid courses last about six hours. If you attend as a family, you might complete the day with a family meeting and a discussion of transportation and communication plans.

TRANSPORTATION PLAN

Transportation plans fall into three categories: sheltering-in-place, returning to home from work or school, and evacuating from the local area. Remember General Eisenhower: "Plans are useless. The planning is indispensable." Having a family discussion about transportation plans will allow you to ask the right questions. As you discuss the various scenarios, everyone can participate and thereby learn what questions they should ask during an actual event.

Sheltering-in-Place

The first option to consider in an emergency is to stay where you are, referred to as sheltering-in-place. I receive numerous inquiries from the press about mass evacuations, but there are few scenarios that require such a response. With just a little preparation, sheltering-in-place may be the safest action to take following a chemical attack or industrial accident that releases toxic chemicals, a radiological release (dirty bomb), or even a nuclear detonation.

Let's start with one of the worst scenarios, a nuclear weapon. If you survive the blast, heat, and immediate radiation—a likely possibility if you are a mile or so away from ground zero of a Hiroshima-style bomb—understanding the Rule of 7 may mean the difference between life and death for your family. There are two types of radiation: immediate and intense, and the long-term fallout. The immediate radiation dissipates within seconds. The fallout (particles of radioactive dust that fall back to earth) dissipates at a much slower rate, but can be just as deadly if proper protective actions are not taken. The radiation in fallout from a nuclear detonation dissipates at a rate that is easy to calculate and remember:

- 90 percent will dissipate within 7 hours
- 99 percent will dissipate within 48 hours
  (Remember 7 x 7 = 48—well, close enough for government work)
- 99.9 percent will dissipate within 2 weeks
  (Remember 2 days x 7 = 14 days)

$$7 \times 7 \times 7$$
$$7 \text{ hours} \times 7 = 2 \text{ days} \times 7 = 14 \text{ days}$$

The blast from a nuclear detonation from a Hiroshima-sized bomb would kill only a small percentage of the residents in a major city, but a much larger percentage of the population would be threatened by fallout. Protecting your family from this fallout for the first seven hours is the most critical step. Protecting them for the first two days virtually negates the threat, as long as you then leave the area. You may never return to your home, job, or school, but if you are alive and free from radiation sickness, you and your family can rebuild and replace everything else.

I am in no way suggesting you go out and build a fallout shelter. The likelihood of a nuclear weapon detonation in your community is extremely remote. (It will be even less likely if we take the appropriate actions.) However, understanding the basics of protecting your family from radiation can make a significant difference in the event that the unthinkable happens.

Emergency planners at the federal, state, and local levels know that appropriate actions by citizens can provide significant protection from radiation exposure. Many officials have expressed their frustration about how to communicate this information to the public after a nuclear detonation, due to the fact that local radio and TV stations could be disabled by the electromagnetic pulse. Call me crazy, but wouldn't a better solution be to share this vital knowledge with the public *before* such a crisis? The good news is that you now have most of the information you need. The only information you do not have is wind direction and velocity, which can cause significant variations in the fallout pattern. Nevertheless, sheltering-in-place is the 85 percent solution.

Anything you do to keep those particles of radioactive dust away from your body will significantly improve your chances for survival. For sheltering-in-place in response to a nuclear detonation, there are two critical elements to remember: distance and time. The further you are away from the radiation, the better, and the less time of exposure, the better. Plastic sheeting and duct tape will provide very little protection; however, several feet of concrete or dirt will provide a significant amount. If you are in a concrete building, you should go to a basement-level room. Remain there for two days—which is why it is important to have a readiness kit in your office. Several feet of concrete and/or dirt puts a lot of "virtual distance" between you and the radiation. After two days, 99 percent of the radiation will have dissipated. At that time, put as much actual distance between you and the radiation as possible.

My scientific friends will say that this issue is more complex. They are absolutely right, from a scientific perspective. They will say more information is required. This is a partial list of the questions they will ask:

- What type of material was used in the bomb?
- How many kilotons/megatons did the blast produce?
- Where was ground zero? Underground? Street-level? At the top of a high-rise building?
- Was it an airburst? If so, how high?
- What were the atmospheric conditions at the time of the explosion?
- How far away from ground zero are you?
- What is the type of construction of the building you are in?

If one had immediate access to all this information, a more sophisticated response scenario could be developed that would increase the probability of survival. However, what is the likelihood that you will be able to know the answers to these questions in the first minute after a nuclear explosion and will have access to a team of scientists who could then advise you? Zero.

This is always a challenge when dealing with scientists. In 2003, I was asked to design a one-day tabletop war game for a team of fifteen world-renowned Environmental Protection Agency scientists. Dr. Paul Gilman had just created the National Homeland Security Research Center. One of its key missions is to provide rapid scientific analysis during a crisis; however, this exercise was for EPA scientists in other research centers. Due to the complexity of environmental research, rapid analysis is a somewhat foreign concept. This is not a criticism, it is a fact of life in most areas of complex scientific research. Paul told me, "If you ask these people to determine the public health consequences of a large chemical release on a community, they will say, 'We'll get you an answer in eight to twelve years.'"

However, in a major disaster, EPA will likely be asked to provide rapid analysis. As the exercise began they all were shocked when I told them that I could only provide limited information about two events that had just occurred, and that they had to produce an assessment to give to the president in six hours. I then explained, "Look, there is more than 400 years of scientific experience seated at this table. You can provide the president with your best assessment and recommendations, or you can let a political appointee with no scientific background whatsoever provide recommendations to the president. Regardless, in six hours the president will have to make a decision that will affect the welfare of one million citizens." Those of us who ran the exercise, as well as the EPA senior leadership, were pleasantly surprised at how quickly and effectively the EPA scientists responded to what was for them both a difficult technical problem and a novel operational challenge.

The advice I give in this chapter is the type and level of advice given to troops on the field of battle. If a nuclear weapon is exploded in your community, you will be on a battlefield with very limited access to the facts. The actions I recommend here are the ones I would want my family to take.

For sheltering-in-place in response to any disaster other than a nuclear detonation, my advice is that you maintain a small readiness kit at your office, with enough supplies to last at least two days. Detailed information on sheltering-in-place is available at www.redcross.org, but here are the essentials:

- Make sure that your readiness kit is inside the house/office.
- Turn off all fans, heating, and air-conditioning systems.
- Close and lock all windows, exterior doors, and fireplace damper.
- Use duct tape and plastic sheeting to seal all cracks around exterior doors.

Returning to Your Home

If sheltering-in-place at your office is not required, the next challenge will be getting home. It was certainly a difficult experience for many here in Washington on 9/11. The Metro subway and bus systems were shut down. The government then closed the bridges between D.C. and Virginia, and shortly thereafter another government agency told all the federal workers to go home. A friend of mine walked from downtown Washington to our office building in Virginia—a distance of nearly six miles. She walked those six miles in high-heeled shoes, and had blisters to contend with for a week. If she had to do it again, I'd bet she would stop and buy some walking shoes. In fact, it's a good idea to keep a pair of walking shoes in your office. Many people who work in Manhattan walked home on 9/11, and on the day when the power went out in 2003.

Those who drive to work in large metropolitan areas generally know alternative routes home in order to avoid gridlock, but the younger drivers in your family may not. My youngest daughter was a college freshman on 9/11. During the next couple of days, we discussed different routes, and the importance of sheltering-in-place.

If you have young children, you have more serious transportation issues to consider than just blisters and inconvenience. What is your plan if you can't get home that night? Who will pick up the kids from day care or school? Don't assume that you can work this out by phone once the crisis begins, because there may not be any phone service available. You also need to understand the transportation and communication plans of your children's schools. Many facilities will go into lockdown during a crisis. If this is the case, you do not want to attempt to pick up your children. If your school system does not have emergency plans, or you think they should be improved upon, you might want to look at the system developed in Fairfax County,

Virginia, at www.fcps.edu/emergencyplan/. You can also check out www.ed.gov/emergencyplan.

Perhaps you don't have small children, but what about pets? If you can't get home for a couple of days, who will feed them? Have you made arrangements? These are the types of questions you need to consider during your transportation planning.

Evacuation

You should also discuss two types of evacuation: local and distant. A disaster at a chemical facility or an overturned rail tank car could necessitate an evacuation of the immediate area, but not require that you leave the state. Pre-coordinated plans with relatives or friends on the other side of town, with reciprocal agreements, could be of great benefit. Once again, don't think you can just work this out once the disaster begins. A five-minute discussion before an event is all it takes to coordinate a local evacuation for mom, dad, and two teenagers who are all starting from different locations. "If for some reason we can't go home and can't talk on our cell phones, go to Aunt Loretta's. Everyone try to call her on a landline." (Do you have calling cards in the glove box of each car?) Transportation plans are generally not complicated unless you have family members with special needs. A half hour of discussion once or twice a year will provide you with that 85 percent solution.

An evacuation from a hurricane may require more planning and preparation. The three to four days' advance notice of an approaching hurricane allows sufficient time to protect your house and prepare your family for evacuation. In addition to planning the evacuation, it is just as important that you make the decision to evacuate while there is still time. When Hurricane Floyd was approaching Charleston, South Carolina, in 1999, many residents delayed their evacuation, perhaps hoping that it would turn to a more northerly track. As stated before, hope is not a strategy. When thousands fled at the eleventh hour, many ended up riding out the hurricane sitting in their cars on gridlocked highways. For most residents, remaining in shelters would have been a far safer alternative.

COMMUNICATION PLAN

What is your plan for communication? It makes no difference if you are from the city or country, rich or poor, a senior executive or a minimum wage employee; when a major disaster occurs, we all want to communicate with our loved ones. Just moments after the second airplane struck the World Trade Center Towers, Secret Service agents bolted into the national security adviser's office. They literally picked up the diminutive Condoleezza Rice and carried her to an underground bunker. Condi says she thinks her feet may have touched the ground a few times during this short journey, but she's not entirely sure. When they arrived, aides were setting up the makeshift command center. Condi walked over to an unclassified phone and called her aunt and uncle in Mississippi. It was a very short call, "I'm okay, don't worry about me," but it is what we all want to do at a moment like that. The problem that most of us learned on 9/11 was that many calls, particularly those placed by cell phones, will not get through.

> One thing your teenage children all know that you may not: When cell phone systems jam, the text messaging function often continues to work.

Today, many people will be able to use the Internet to communicate via e-mail. Cell phone systems will quickly overload;

we see that in D.C. whenever we get two inches of snow—the traffic is gridlocked and the cell phones jam. However, landlines generally continue to work. One of the best communication plans is to use landlines. Amazingly, it is sometimes easier to place a long-distance call than a local one. Identify one or two relatives or friends outside your local area that everyone can call. "Uncle Bob is retired and lives in Florida. Everyone call him and leave a message regarding your whereabouts and your plans." Parents can leave messages for their children with instructions for what they should do.

I recommend that every home have a noncell phone hardwired to the wall (not a cordless model, which requires electricity). Mine has none of the fancy services and costs me less than $30 per month. However, when the electricity is out and the cell phone circuits jam, I can still make a call.

If you use the Internet for your phone service, as many now do, make sure that you have taken the proper steps to reach your local 911 call center. If not, you may reach a 911 facility in another city. When Internet phone service was first installed at Dallas–Fort Worth Airport, a gate agent called 911 and requested law enforcement assistance. It was several minutes before she realized she was talking to the 911 call center in Baltimore.

READINESS KIT

One of the top priorities for a readiness kit is prescription medication. Some people take up to a dozen different medications per day. What would happen if a disaster occurred just a day or two before you were to pick up your new prescription? What would happen if the pharmacies were closed for a week?

This could be the result of a major terrorist attack or a natural disaster.

Ideally, you should keep a fourteen-day emergency supply in your kit. There may be a few scenarios in which this would not be a sufficient quantity, but not many. Also, make sure your supply is in the bottles you received from the pharmacy, which will make it far easier for medical personnel to refill the prescription if you end up in an evacuation shelter. There were major problems during Katrina when people with chronic diseases showed up at the evacuation centers without proper documentation of their multiple prescriptions. Thanks to the great efforts of the Markle Foundation, which worked with corporations such as Wal-Mart, Walgreens, CVS, and other retailers, some pharmaceutical records were reconstructed. Nevertheless, you don't want to find yourself in this situation. Remember the five Ps? Take your prescriptions with you.

Some people I have spoken to say that their insurance plans will not allow them to have such an emergency supply on hand. I offer two possible solutions. First, I imagine that with the cooperation of your physician, it would not be difficult to figure out a means for you to obtain an extra two weeks' supply of medication that would still be covered by your insurance plan. Second, if this is not possible, ask your physician to write a separate prescription for you to take to the pharmacy, and pay for it out of your own pocket. Sure, there will be some expenses associated with preparing for a disaster, but if this medication is really important to your health, or the health of someone in your family, then I would call this an important investment in your security.

Regardless of how you obtain your extra medication, remember to rotate your emergency supply. If you have to use your kit two years from now, you don't want to be taking two-year-old medicine.

While on the subject of medicine, I might as well address one of the more controversial subjects. A question that I have routinely heard ever since the anthrax crisis of October 2001 is: "Should I have a supply of antibiotics for my family?"

I received this question one night while being interviewed on *Larry King Live* during the anthrax crisis, and I gave the caller the politically correct answer: "No." At that time, every politician and medical doctor on TV and radio gave the same answer, but it bothered me that I had said no, because I knew that many senior government leaders and doctors had supplies in their homes. It seemed dishonest to respond as I had.

So here is the answer I now give my audiences when I am asked about maintaining an emergency supply of antibiotics in one's home for use during a biological attack: "This is a decision for you and your personal physician. If your physician thinks that it's in the best interest of your family, then he or she will provide you the prescription."

Cipro is the antibiotic of choice, because the U.S. government believes it will work against some of the agents created by the former Soviet Union that had resistance to many of our antibiotics. There is some concern that terrorists could gain access to these former Soviet bioweapons. (The anthrax mailed around the U.S. in October 2001 was not resistant. Most antibiotics, including penicillin, ampicillin, doxycycline, and even tetracycline were effective.) You may not want to give Cipro to small children or pregnant women. Your physician will know which antibiotics are acceptable for different age groups.

I also receive questions about potassium iodide, particularly from people who live near nuclear power plants. First, people over the age of fifty and women who are pregnant should not take potassium iodide. Second, it only works if you take it prior to exposure to the radiation. Third, even if you do take it in time, its only value is that it may prevent thyroid cancer from developing twenty years after exposure. (This delayed effect is the reason most physicians do not recommend potassium iodide for people over age fifty, because people in that age group will most likely die of some other cause before they develop thyroid cancer.)

> If you do maintain an emergency supply of medication in your home, it is very important that you do not use it until you are advised to do so by competent medical authorities. Improper use can cause serious harm to your family.

If you have a serious medical condition, you might consider maintaining copies of your medical records, either in hard copy or on a CD or flash drive. For an example of a flash drive device see www.capmed.com/consumer/buynow.asp.

Many people talk about maintaining a large supply of food, but I tend to disagree with this suggestion. In Air Force survival training we were given the Rule of 2s as a guide to what humans require to survive. You can survive:

- 2 minutes without oxygen
- 2 hours without shelter (in extreme conditions)
- 2 days without water
- 2 weeks without food

These are guidelines, not exact numbers, but you can see that food is clearly the least important factor for survival. You will get hungry after just a day (for me, four hours), but an adequate supply of water is far more important. In virtually all scenarios, you will be able to obtain food within a week of even the most catastrophic of attacks.

I recommend that you maintain at least a three- to four-day supply of nonperishable food per person in your household (3,000 calories per day). This is easy and inexpensive. My survival kit contains peanut butter, canned tuna, canned fruit, nuts, energy bars, and crackers (salt-free are best). The menu will get boring after a few days, but we're talking about survival, not fine dining. You should pick nonperishable foods that you can rotate through your normal food supply. If you have infants, specialty items such as baby food, formula, and disposable diapers should be in your readiness kit. Additionally, the Red Cross recommends comfort foods. If you have children, make sure you have cookies in your kit. All Air Force survival kits have coffee. I was surprised when I first discovered this, since coffee is a diuretic. The instructors at the survival school said that coffee was included because morale is important in a survival situation. I agree with this philosophy, and have included a bottle of Johnnie Walker Gold in my survival kit. But use caution, because scotch and coffee are both diuretics. Maintaining proper hydration is important, particularly when under great stress.

The Red Cross recommends one gallon of water per day, per adult, as a sufficient supply for drinking and personal hygiene. Under ideal conditions, you should drink two quarts of water a day. I recommend several cases of bottled water per person for your drinking supply. (Obviously, you will want to rotate this.) Your hot water heater can provide water for personal hygiene, and so can your hot tub. (Use this line on your spouse as additional justification for purchasing a hot tub. "Honey, it's part of our survival kit.") Keep in mind that small hot tubs hold 100 gallons of water, and large ones can hold up to 500 gallons. Sounds to me like the best excuse, I mean reason, yet.

In a catastrophic event, your supply of bottled water may run out. For those of you who did not make it through Eagle Scouts, here are a couple of methods to turn nonpotable water, such as river water, into safe drinking water. Depending on the river, it may not taste great, and it may not be as safe as normal tap water, but it will kill most microbes and remove most heavy metals and chemicals. When possible, employ more than one type of treatment.

First, let suspended particles settle to the bottom of the container, and then strain the water through a clean cloth. Afterward:

- Boil the water for five minutes and/or,
- Disinfect with household bleach—sixteen drops per gallon—and let stand for thirty minutes. Do not use bleach that is scented, color-safe, or contains added cleaners.

An N95 mask could be one of the most valuable items in your readiness kit. This is a simple mask, similar in appearance to a surgeon's mask, but far better at filtering out small particles. They can be purchased at medical supply stores and in many hardware stores. According to a 2004 study by RAND (*Individual Preparedness and Response to Chemical, Radiological, Nuclear, and Biological Terrorist Attacks,* available at www.rand.org), a properly fitted N95 mask would be of use in protecting your family from:

- Dust from the collapse of a large building.
- Radiological particles from a dirty bomb, particularly one built with plutonium.
- Airborne particles during a biological event, man-made or natural.

Dr. Julie Gerberding, the director of the Centers for Disease Control, said that if SARS (severe acute respiratory syndrome) comes to America, anyone entering a hospital with a cough will be given a mask to wear. She was referring to a surgical mask, cheaper and easier to wear properly than an N95 mask. In the case of contagious diseases, most health experts agree that it is more important for those who are sick to wear masks than those who are healthy, because it would prevent the sick from spraying droplets into the air that contain either the bacteria or virus. Obviously, if someone is having difficulty breathing, any type of mask could worsen the problem, so use caution.

Surgical and N95 masks can only be worn for a few hours before they become saturated, uncomfortable, and smelly. It is impractical to think that you and your family could wear them for extended periods of time, but they could prove highly valuable while leaving a contaminated area. I carry one in my briefcase, several in my car, and have a box of twenty in my readiness kit. A box of twenty N95 masks at Home Depot costs $19.95.

If you have pets, obviously pet food and additional water is required. A few years ago, evacuation operations were not pet-friendly. This seems to have changed somewhat, but with 87,000 jurisdictions in America, I can't predict what rules you might encounter. Steve McGraw, director of homeland security in Texas, told me that Texas is a very pet-friendly state. There are even contingency plans in place for large animals, such as horses.

As a part of my readiness kit, I have cash, coins, and extra credit cards. Important documents such as birth certificates, wills, life insurance policies, and passports, plus bank account, credit card, and investment account numbers are maintained in a single, watertight, secure container.

Copies of all my documents and information are also stored

with an out-of-state relative. Electronic copies of key documents and information can also be of great value. While writing this book I maintained copies of my work on a flash drive and routinely e-mailed copies to myself.

Note: Keeping extra credit cards and cash in your document container can prove to be of great value during large and small disasters. About two hours before an important business trip, I discovered I had lost my wallet. The proper thing to do was immediately cancel all credit cards in my wallet. But how would I possibly fly coast to coast, hire a taxi, and check into a hotel with no cash, credit cards, or driver's license? Simple. I went to my safe, pulled out a credit card that had not been canceled, took out several hundred dollars in cash, and left for the airport. My passport is always in my briefcase, so I had all the identification I would need. It doesn't take a terrorist attack or natural disaster to enjoy the benefits of being prepared.

Candles might be romantic, but they are also dangerous. Instead, I recommend battery-powered and crank-powered lights. I spent just $39 on an AM/FM shortwave radio that also has a bright spotlight and can run on D batteries or the crank. I also paid $17 for a black and white TV that runs on D batteries. Both are available at most department stores.

I store my readiness kit in the garage for several reasons: I don't have to carry it up the stairs, it's easy to rotate the stock with new items I buy, and it will be convenient to put in the car for an evacuation.

Every home needs a good first-aid kit. Here are the Red Cross recommended items:

- (20) adhesive bandages, various sizes
- (1) 5″ x 9″ sterile dressing
- (1) conforming roller gauze bandage
- (2) triangular bandages
- (2) 3″ x 3″ sterile gauze pads
- (2) 4″ x 4″ sterile gauze pads
- (1) roll 3″ cohesive bandage
- (2) germicidal hand wipes or waterless alcohol-based hand sanitizer
- (6) antiseptic wipes
- (2) pair large medical grade nonlatex gloves
- Adhesive tape, 2″ width
- Antibacterial ointment
- Cold pack
- Scissors (small, personal)
- Tweezers
- CPR breathing barrier, such as a face shield

If you do not want to build your own kit, you can purchase one from the Red Cross or from numerous other vendors.

Since I frequently ride subways, I also keep a small head-lamp in my briefcase. Several years before 9/11, I was riding the subway in D.C. when the train suddenly stopped. The lights went out after just a few seconds, and it was so dark I could not see the person standing just inches in front of me. When I got off of the Metro, I went straight to the mall and bought a headlamp for about $20. Its bulb is a light emitting diode (LED), which means there are no batteries to lose power. The next time I am in a subway or building when the lights go out, I will not be the person cursing the darkness.

I owned guns long before I heard the term homeland security, but I now consider them an essential element in my readiness kit. I do not think I need guns to fight the terrorists, but I

Other Items You May Wish to Include in Your Readiness Kit

- First-aid manual
- Aspirin or nonaspirin pain reliever
- Antidiarrheal medication
- Antacid
- Syrup of Ipecac (used to induce vomiting if advised by the Poison Control Center)
- Laxatives
- Activated charcoal (used to block the absorption of poison in the stomach if advised by the Poison Control Center)
- Contact lenses and supplies
- Extra eyeglasses
- Tool kit
- Toilet paper, towelettes
- Soap, liquid detergent
- Complete change of clothing (including a long-sleeved shirt, long pants, and sturdy shoes—consider additional clothing if you live in a cold-weather climate)
- Matches in a waterproof container
- Feminine supplies and personal hygiene items
- Denture needs
- Mess kits, paper cups, plates, and plastic utensils
- Paper towels
- Paper and pencil
- Books, games, puzzles, or other activities for children
- Fire extinguisher

may need them to defend my home from looters. I would rather have one and not need it than the other way around. I have owned guns since I was a teenager, and have received instruction in their use, including extensive safety training. If you have not had professional training in the use of firearms (all professional programs include extensive safety training), I do not recommend that you buy a gun, because you would be a greater threat to your family than looters or other criminals.

Comments and a recommendation on the infamous color codes: Late-night talk show hosts and stand-up comedians probably benefited more from this system than anyone else. The public and media demanded some sort of system after 9/11, but unfortunately, there were two major errors in the implementation. First, the color code system (from highest to lowest: Red, Orange, Yellow, Blue, Green) attempted to measure two factors with one scale: likelihood of an attack, and type/scale of attack. What color would be used if there was a high probability of a single car bomb attack somewhere in the U.S.? What color would be used if there was an increased probability (but still a relatively low overall probability) of a nuclear attack? Would both cases warrant a code Orange? According to this flawed system, yes.

During the first four years of the color code program, there were six nationwide Orange alerts. The Department of Homeland Security eventually refined its use of the system in an attempt to avoid nationwide alerts. When possible, Homeland Security attempts to make the alerts industry-specific (e.g., airlines) or region-specific (e.g., Northeast).

The second problem is that the system is primarily useful to those in both the public and private sectors who are responsible for preventing attacks, not to individual citizens. However, when the news media goes into hyperdrive, individual citizens ask, "What should we do?" My recommendation for individuals and families is that an Orange alert level should be used as a reminder to review your transportation and communication plans and check your readiness kits. Then, "get back on the bus."

Bottom line on preparing your family: A small investment of time and money in education, training, planning, and supplies will significantly increase your ability to survive a manmade or natural disaster. Some of these actions may make your life more comfortable during a disaster, while others may save the life of someone you love.

Chapter 10

Conclusions

*For the Oval Office, the Front Office,
and Your Family*

Only the dead have seen the end of war.

—Plato

THE CHALLENGE OF DEFENDING OUR HOMELAND IN THE TWENTY-FIRST CEN-
tury is not about al Qaeda, Hezbollah, Jemaah Islamiyah, Islamic
Jihad, mass murderers such as Timothy McVeigh or Ted Kaczynski, Aum Shinrikyo or other apocalyptic cults, abortion clinic
bombers, or even transnational organized crime syndicates. All
are a threat to our lives and economic future, but the greatest
dangers we face are only possible due to the technology that
now allows small, nonstate actors to threaten a superpower. As
long as the human race has walked this planet, there have been
wars and acts of terror. Unfortunately, Plato was right. We have
not seen the end of war and armed conflict. Violence against
humans and terrorist acts that disrupt the economic, social, and
political order will continue, driven by territorial disputes, economic inequalities, oil, water, politics, and religion.

For more than a decade I have studied this new international security environment best described by President Bush as the "intersection of ancient hatreds and modern technology." Every day I think about the questions that most Americans asked themselves on the evening of September 11, 2001: How vulnerable are we? What are the real threats? What can we do to protect our families, communities, economic future, and our nation?

My goal is to provide insights on perspectives, priorities, key issues, and actions you can take to improve the security of your family and local community. I realize that some of my recommendations will spark controversy, which was precisely my intention. I've always found that the best ideas emerge from vigorous debate and inquiry. Hopefully, you are now better prepared to participate by asking your own questions and finding the right answers. There are a few important issues that I would like to reemphasize.

We must always ensure we are asking the right questions. A classic example of a wrong question was pointed out to me by my colleague and good friend, John Train:

On the evening of December 6, 1941, our government knew three essential elements of information:
1. *Japan always started a war with a powerful surprise attack.*
2. *They simultaneously delivered a formal declaration of war.*
3. *Our code breakers had determined that the Japanese would deliver a formal declaration of war at noon on December 7.*

Many asked the question: Where was the strategic location that the Japanese would deliver a crushing blow? The Philippines? Guam?

Alas, the right question was not asked: Where is it

dawn in the Pacific when it is noon in D.C.? (Torpedo and low-level bombers prefer to attack at dawn, coming in to their targets out of the sun.) The answer, of course, was Hawaii.

The title of the definitive history of that morning is *At Dawn We Slept*. America needs to wake up and start asking the right questions, before we experience a twenty-first-century Pearl Harbor.

We must focus on appropriate reactions, yet avoid overreactions. We do not know when, but without question, terrorists will again attack our homeland. The appropriate reaction for all Americans should be shock, but not surprise. Americans will always be shocked when ruthless, immoral cowards intentionally kill innocents, but we can no longer justify being surprised.

Several years before 9/11, I listened to a gentleman describe his final conversation with his father. The father was a survivor of Nazi death camps; however, he had never discussed his experiences with his family. Sitting next to his father's bed, just moments before he would finally succumb to congestive heart failure, the son said, "Dad, you have never talked of your experiences. I understand why you have not, but is there something from your experience you want me to pass on to your grandchildren and great-grandchildren?" Lying on his deathbed, eyes partially closed, in a voice near a whisper, his father replied: "When a man tells you he is going to kill you, pay attention."

We need to pay attention, not only to bin Laden's threats, but most importantly to the new security realities. However, do not confuse attention with preoccupation. Tonight there will be Little League and soccer games. This weekend there will be weddings, birthday parties, NASCAR races, ballet, opera, fishing, and most importantly, time with our families and friends. We should enjoy them all. We should not live in a world of doom and gloom, but we must understand the realities we face, and we must prepare. We will never again have the excuse of being surprised.

Also, do not confuse frantic but unguided action with attention. We must not overreact, but remember instead to "wind our watches." A couple of suicide bombers in a shopping mall, a chemical attack in a subway, or a bomb on an airplane would be a tragedy for those killed and injured, and for their families and friends, but it would only be a national crisis if our overreactions make it so. We must not be accomplices to terrorism. We must all be ready to get back on the buses the next morning.

We must also demand a substantial return on our investments in security. In his October 29, 2004, warning to the American people, bin Laden said the 9/11 attacks cost al Qaeda half a million dollars, while the economic impact on the U.S. had exceeded $500 billion. 9/11 was an incredibly efficient attack on the U.S. economy. We cannot afford to further al Qaeda's war with unsound, knee-jerk spending programs. Wasting money with good intentions makes us no more secure.

One great challenge I have dealt with during the past decade has been finding the balance between Ockham's razor and H. L. Mencken's assessment of simple solutions for complex problems. Ockham's razor is the principle proposed by William of Ockham in the fourteenth century: *"Pluralitas non est ponenda sine necessitate,"* or "entities should not be multiplied unnecessarily." Some interpret this as, "keep it simple, stupid" (KISS); however, it is a bit more complex than this. Ockham's razor tells us that when two or more theories are equally successful at predicting results, choose the simplest. This is not meant to be a guarantee, but useful for establishing priorities. On the other hand, H. L. Mencken told us that "for every complex problem, there is a solution that is simple, neat, and wrong."

Some have accused me of recommending simple solutions for

complex problems. When I push back a bit in the debate, I generally discover that the issue has more to do with questions than answers. I am often told that the best way to keep nukes out of the U.S. is to build a "multilayered defense." This gets a lot of support because everybody gets a piece of the action (read: "money"). In reality, if we ask the right question, "How do we keep al Qaeda from becoming a nuclear power?," the answer is far more simple—don't let al Qaeda get its hands on nuclear material. This leads to, "And how do we do that?" The answer to this question is far more complex. In other words, I try to simplify and clarify the questions. Some answers are simple, others are not. While I understand the necessity of purchasing some radiological detectors for use here in the United States and in overseas ports, our top priority with regard to both spending and policy must still be to prevent terrorists from obtaining nuclear material.

For the broad range of dangers we will face, a realistic and all-encompassing strategy will allow all organizations and citizens to understand where and how they fit into the homeland security playbook, from the Oval Office to the front office to your kitchen table. We have made progress in several areas, but partisan politics, cultural and legal barriers, organizational deficiencies, lack of education and common sense, the ongoing technological revolution, and a thinking enemy make significant progress difficult.

I have discussed the biological threat in this book more than any other, for good reason. It is the most significant danger we face, and the one for which we are least prepared. I often think about that study the U.S. Navy completed just six months before the Japanese attack on Pearl Harbor. It concluded that the water depth in Pearl Harbor was too shallow for the effective use of air-dropped torpedoes. On the morning of December 7, 1941, Japanese bombers dropped torpedoes specially modified for shallow water, scoring numerous hits on our battleships: *California* (2), *Vermont* (2), *West Virginia* (7), *Nevada* (1), and *Oklahoma* (4).

Two light cruisers, *Raleigh* and *Helena*, were also hit by the air-dropped torpedoes.

It wasn't just the Navy that got it wrong in 1941. The Army Air Corps, convinced that sabotage was the greatest threat, parked the airplanes at Hickam Field wing tip to wing tip so they would be easier to guard. This strategy made them easier targets for the Japanese planes on their strafing runs. Nearly half of the airplanes at Hickam were destroyed or severely damaged. To make sure future generations of Air Force officers do not forget the lessons of December 7, the .50-caliber bullet holes in the headquarters building at Hickam AFB have never been and never will be repaired.

When I say we must never again be surprised, I am talking about strategic surprise, not tactical. This means we can no longer say, "It is difficult to believe that there are people in this world who want to come to America and kill our families." It also means we can never say, "I didn't think they could or would use biological weapons." On the other hand, there will always be tactical surprises. Both opponents can see every piece on a chessboard, and know every possible move. Still, there is considerable surprise and deception in the game of chess. No matter how much we improve the effectiveness of our intelligence community, we must understand that there will still be tactical surprises.

Between the summers of 1998 and 2001, George Tenet, the director of the Central Intelligence Agency, frequently told the U.S. Congress and both the Clinton and Bush administrations that al Qaeda had declared war on America and was going to attack our homeland. The first Hart-Rudman Commission report, released in 1999, warned of terrorist attacks on our homeland: "Americans will likely die on American soil, possibly in large numbers." America's leaders in federal, state, and local governments, Republican and Democrat, failed to pay attention. On the morning of 9/11, they experienced both strategic and tactical surprise.

During the hours and days after the 9/11 attacks, there were additional surprises that were not provided by al Qaeda. Jim Moseley, a former deputy secretary of agriculture, told me about the surprise he received on 9/11. Shortly after the second plane struck the World Trade Center, when we all realized America was at war, the secretary of agriculture was taken to a secure area outside Washington as part of the continuity of government plan. (The secretary of agriculture is number nine in the line of succession for the presidency.) Deputy Secretary Moseley assembled all the key Department of Agriculture leaders in the main conference room. He asked a simple question: "What is our plan for protecting America's food supply during wartime?" In December of 2001, sitting at the same conference table, he told me about the deafening silence that followed in response to his question. There was no plan.

Thanks to the efforts of Jim Moseley, Jeremy Stump, Kurt Mann, Sheryl Maddux, and many others, improvements have been made in protecting our food supply. On the other hand, it has been more than five years since the Amerithrax wake-up call for America, and I worry that we have accomplished little more than to tap the snooze button. Five years after Amerithrax, America still has no plan for responding to an attack with anthrax, the most likely bioweapon terrorists will use. And even though we have made progress by increasing our smallpox vaccine stockpile from 15 million doses in 2001 to 300 million in 2007, we still do not have a plan to quickly vaccinate our citizens. Some speculate it would take weeks. My question is, "Why?" On November 2, 2004, more than 100 million Americans voted in a single day. They were able to do so because they knew where to go and what to do. The polls were primarily manned by volunteers—an electoral posse. It is amazing what can be accomplished with a posse, a plan, and a little training. The cost will not bankrupt the nation, but it will make our families, our communities, our economic future, and our nation more secure.

Our leaders fail to understand the national security implications of the biotechnical revolution. The bioweapons that I discuss in this book are the twentieth-century versions. In the twenty-first century, bioweapons will transform security as much as, or perhaps more than, gunpowder, steel-hulled ships, and aviation in previous centuries. Genetic engineering (altering existing pathogens) and synthetic biology (creating entirely new pathogens) are no longer science fiction. This revolution will change warfare, terrorism, and perhaps even criminal activity more than most can imagine. It is reminiscent of the period between the great wars of the twentieth century. With the exception of visionary leaders such as Major George Patton and Captain Dwight Eisenhower, few in the U.S. Army understood how tanks would soon revolutionize ground warfare. President Calvin Coolidge did not understand why the fledgling Army Air Corps wanted money to buy more airplanes. He asked, "Can't they just take turns flying the ones they have?"

There are things you can and should do to improve the security of your family and local community, but we all must look to the federal government for protection against the two most serious threats. Prevention of a nuclear attack is almost exclusively the responsibility of the federal government. Ensuring a proper response to a biological attack requires the coordinated effort of federal, state, and local governments, as well as some participation by corporate America, local communities, and individuals, but the fact remains that most of the bioresponse effort is still the federal government's responsibility. These are the top priorities for homeland security. It is that simple.

One other top priority is preparing the active duty military for the twenty-first century. I recommended that we reshape the National Guard to prepare it for missions within the homeland, but I did not address the role of the active duty military. Aside from providing air defense, active duty and Reserve forces should play a limited role in homeland security. With a newly structured National Guard, there would be virtually no requirement here at home for active duty forces. The active duty and Reserve forces should be exclusively focused on missions outside the U.S. However, we must expand the size of our active duty military force if we intend to maintain its current level of activity. The post-9/11 pace of operation is unsustainable with today's forces. As the former chairman of the Department of Military Strategy and Operations at the National War College, I cannot in good conscience write about the security of our homeland without expressing my concern about this issue. We did not send enough troops to Iraq to properly do the job, nor do we have enough troops today to sustain our current strategy. We must either pay the price to field the military force required to support our global strategy, or change the strategy. Either alternative is better than breaking the force, which is where we are currently headed.

We must also remember how the world has changed, not since 9/11, but since 11/9, when the Berlin Wall came down in 1989 and the Cold War ended. The cowboy movies of the 1950s and 1960s were easy to follow: there were good guys and bad guys. The good guys wore white hats, the bad guys, black. During the Cold War, America was generally seen throughout the noncommunist world (and by many citizens within the communist bloc) as the good guy in the white hat. But with the Soviet empire's collapse, the world is no longer viewed as bipolar, and the line between black and white is not as clearly defined. In today's unipolar world, many individuals in the Middle East, Asia, and Europe no longer see America wearing a white hat. In fact, many now view the U.S. as the Lone Ranger wearing gray, and in some cases, black. This is neither an assessment of U.S. policy nor a criticism of foreign perceptions. It is merely a statement of fact—a fact Americans must understand if we are to succeed in defending our homeland. In the end, the soft power of diplomacy, information, and education will be at least as valuable to our security as the hard power of the world's most powerful military force and the technologically sophisticated intelligence and law enforcement communities.

When most people hear the name Marshall McLuhan, they think of his quote "The media is the message," but I've always preferred "There are no passengers on spaceship earth. We are all crew." Long before I heard the term "homeland security," this was one of my favorite quotes. Maybe that's because I started flying airplanes at a young age, or because I was a teenager during the Apollo program. I remember those first pictures of that magnificent blue and white ball called Earth. It was the first time I thought of it as our spaceship, and us as its crew. This quote certainly had an impact on how I thought about taking care of that spaceship and our life support system.

After 9/11, however, the quote took on a new meaning for me. When United Flight 93 taxied out for takeoff on that September morning, the manifest read, "7 crew, 37 passengers." About a half hour later, technically, that manifest changed. It should have read, "7 crew, 33 passengers, 4 terrorists." Once the passengers and crew discovered the fate of American Flight 11, United Flight 175, and American Flight 77, they realized they had a mission, and somewhere over the Pennsylvania countryside, they formed a posse. The final manifest for United Flight 93 should have read, "4 terrorists, 40 crew." The members of that crew of 40 were not able to save their own lives, but in their final moments, they did save hundreds, perhaps thousands of lives in Washington, D.C. That morning, a posse of 40 heroes accomplished what the most powerful military force in the world could not.

In honor of their actions, and in the best interests of our families, we must dedicate ourselves to becoming crew, rather than passengers, in the mission of protecting America's future. The task ahead is formidable, but our posse is 300 million strong, and we can succeed. The time to begin is now.

"Let's roll."

FAMILY PREPAREDNESS: THE 85 PERCENT SOLUTION

Training
Red Cross CPR and first-aid

Plans
Sheltering-in-place
Return home from work
Evacuation
Communications
Review children's school plans
Pets

Your Home
Plug-in flashlights on every level
Battery/crank-powered radio and TV

Your Office
Mini-readiness kit and walking shoes
N95 masks
Headlamp

Readiness Kit
14-days' supply of medicines
Antibiotics? Talk to your personal physician
Medical records
3–4 days' supply of nonperishable food
Bottled water (minimum 1 case per person)
N95 masks
Pet supplies
Cash, coins, traveler's checks
Important documents
First-aid kit and manual
Flashlights and batteries
Trash bags, paper towels, toilet paper, soap
Feminine supplies
Aspirin or nonaspirin pain reliever
Antidiarrheal medication
Antacid
Contact lenses and supplies
Extra eyeglasses
Tool kit
Cell phone charger and phone cards
Matches in a waterproof container
Don't forget the scotch and the cookies!

The radiation in fallout from a nuclear detonation dissipates at a rate that is easy to calculate and remember:

- 90 percent will dissipate within 7 hours

- 99 percent will dissipate within 48 hours
  (Remember 7 x 7 = 48; well, close enough for government work)

- 99.9 percent will dissipate within 2 weeks
  (Remember 2 days x 7 = 14 days)

7 x 7 x 7

7 hours x 7 = 2 days x 7 = 14 days

Priorities
You can survive:

- 2 minutes without oxygen

- 2 hours without shelter (in extreme conditions)

- 2 days without water

- 2 weeks without food

Preparing Safe Drinking Water
First, let suspended particles settle to the bottom of the container, and then strain the water through a clean cloth. Afterward:

- Boil the water for 5 minutes and/or,

- Disinfect with household bleach—16 drops per gallon—and let stand for 30 minutes. Do not use bleach that is scented, color-safe, or contains added cleaners.

For more information
www.redcross.org
www.cdc.gov
www.tihls.org

List of Acronyms

ADIZ	Air Defense Identification Zone
ATSO	ability to survive and operate
BCP	business continuity planning
BENS	Business Executives for National Security
BEOC	Business Emergency Operations Center
BRAC	Base Realignment and Closure Commission
BWC	Biological and Toxin Weapons Convention
CBRNE	chemical, biological, radiological, nuclear, and enhanced conventional explosives
CDC	Centers for Disease Control and Prevention
CDP	Center for Domestic Preparedness
CERT	Community Emergency Response Team
CIA	Central Intelligence Agency
CORE	Citizens of Oakland Respond to Emergencies
CRAF	Civil Reserve Air Fleet
DHS	Department of Homeland Security
DIA	Defense Intelligence Agency
DNDO	Domestic Nuclear Detection Office
DNI	director of national intelligence
DOD	Department of Defense
DOE	Department of Energy
DOJ	Department of Justice
DOT	Department of Transportation
DTRA	Defense Threat Reduction Agency

EMAC	Emergency Management Assistance Compact
EMP	electromagnetic pulse
EMS	Emergency Medical Services
EOC	emergency operations center
EPA	Environmental Protection Agency
FBI	Federal Bureau of Investigation
FDA	Federal Drug Administration
FEMA	Federal Emergency Management Agency
FISA	Foreign Intelligence Surveillance Act
HEU	highly enriched uranium
HHS	Department of Health and Human Services
ICBM	intercontinental ballistic missile
JOC	Joint Operations Center
LEU	low-enriched uranium
MEL	minimum equipment list
MIPT	Memorial Institute for the Prevention of Terrorism
MTBF	mean time between failure
NIMS	National Incident Management System
NSA	National Security Agency
PCCIP	President's Commission on Critical Infrastructure Protection
RDD	radiological dispersal device
SARS	severe acute respiratory syndrome
TSA	Transportation Security Administration
UPMC	University of Pittsburgh Medical Center
USAF	U.S. Air Force
USCG	U.S. Coast Guard
USDA	U.S. Department of Agriculture
WHO	World Health Organization

Bibliography

Allison, Graham. *Nuclear Terrorism*. New York: Holt, 2004.

Barry, John. *The Great Influenza: The Epic Story of the Deadliest Plague in History*. New York: Viking, 2004.

Broad, William, and David Johnston. "A Nation Challenged: Bioterrorism; Report Linking Anthrax and Hijackers Is Investigated." *New York Times*, March 23, 2002.

Calame, Byron. "Can Magazines of the *Times* Subsidize News Coverage?" *New York Times*, October 22, 2006.

———. "The Public Editor: Secrecy, Security, the President and the Press." *New York Times*, July 2, 2006.

City of New Orleans Hurricane Plan. Internet download. (This plan was removed from the City of New Orleans Web site shortly after Hurricane Katrina.)

Commission on Intelligence Capabilities of the United States Regarding Weapons of Mass Destruction. March 31, 2005, http://www.wmd.gov/report/.

Conant, Jennet. *Tuxedo Park*. New York: Simon & Schuster, 2002.

Danzig, Richard. *Catastrophic Bioterrorism: What Is to Be Done?* Center for Technology and National Security Policy,

National Defense University (Washington, D.C.: U.S. Government Printing Office, August 2003).

Forging America's New Normalcy: Securing Our Homeland, Preserving Our Liberty. The Fifth Annual Report to the President and the Congress of the Advisory Panel to Assess Domestic Response Capabilities for Terrorism Involving Weapons of Mass Destruction. RAND, Washington, D.C., December 2003.

Gellman, Barton. "The FBI's Secret Scrutiny: In Hunt for Terrorists, Bureau Examines Records of Ordinary Americans." *Washington Post*, November 6, 2005.

Gursky, Elin. *Drafted to Fight Terror: U.S. Public Health on the Front Lines of Biological Defense* (Arlington, VA: ANSER, August 2004).

———. *Epidemic Proportions: Building National Public Health Capabilities to Meet National Security Threats.* Report to Subcommittee on Bioterrorism and Public Health Preparedness, Senate Committee on Health, Education, Labor and Pensions (Arlington, VA: ANSER, September 23, 2005).

Hart-Rudman Commission Report (Phases I, II, and III), http://www.au.af.mil/au/awc/awcgate/nssg/.

Henderson, Donald, Thomas Inglesby, and Tara O'Toole. *Bioterrorism: Guidelines for Medical and Public Health Management* (Chicago: American Medical Association Press, 2002).

Horwitz, Sari. "Old-School Academy in Post-9/11 World: New Focus Is on Terrorism, but Training Is Struggling to Keep Up." *Washington Post*, August 17, 2006.

Larsen, Randall. "The Real Threat: Bombs," op-ed. *Wall Street Journal*, August 16, 2006.

———. "70-20-10," op-ed. *Wall Street Journal*, May 25, 2006.

———. "Years After 9/11 . . . No One Is in Charge of Fighting

Our Two Biggest Threats," op-ed. *Washington Post*, May 20, 2005.

Lee, Christopher. "Report on FBI Tool Is Disputed: Justice Dept. Criticizes Post Article on 'National Security Letters.'" *Washington Post*, November 30, 2005.

Lichtblau, Eric, and James Risen. "Bank Data Sifted by U.S. in Secret to Block Terror." *New York Times*, June 23, 2006.

Minow, Newton. "Seven Clicks Away," op-ed. *Wall Street Journal*, June 3, 2004.

Moore, Harold, and Joseph Galloway. *We Were Soldiers Once . . . and Young* (New York: Harper Perennial, 1993).

Moore, Molly. *Woman at War* (New York: Charles Scribner's Sons, 1993).

The National Security Strategy of the United States of America, 2004 (Washington, D.C.: U.S. Government Printing Office).

The National Strategy for Homeland Security, 2004 (Washington, D.C.: U.S. Government Printing Office).

The National Strategy to Combat Weapons of Mass Destruction, 2004 (Washington, D.C.: U.S. Government Printing Office).

The 9/11 Commission Report: Final Report of the National Commission on Terrorist Attacks Upon the United States (New York: Norton, 2004).

O'Rouke, P. J. *Parliament of Whores: A Lone Humorist Attempts to Explain the Entire U.S. Government* (New York: Vintage, 1992).

Sheffi, Yosef. *The Resilient Enterprise* (Cambridge: MIT Press, 2005).

Stein, Jeff. "Can You Tell a Sunni From a Shiite?" op-ed. *New York Times*, October 17, 2006.

Stewart, James. *Heart of a Soldier* (New York: Simon & Schuster, 2003).

U.S. Congress, Office of Technology Assessment. *Proliferation of Weapons of Mass Destruction: Assessing the Risks.* OTA-ISC-559 (Washington, D.C.: U.S. Government Printing Office, August 1993).

"U.S. Cybersecurity Chief May Have Conflict of Interest." *Washington Post*, June 29, 2006, p. A5.

Williams, Peter, and David Wallace. *Unit 731: Japan's Secret Biological Warfare in World War II* (New York: Free Press, 1989).

Acknowledgments

The first thanks must go to Racquel Cooper. For eighteen months she has assisted with all of my op-ed articles, white papers, reports, monographs, and most importantly this book. Without her unparalleled skills in editing and research, few, if any, would have reached publication.

Dan Ambrosio of Grand Central Publishing and my agent, Wendy Keller, had faith in my ability to tell this story and the vision and talent to help me write it for a broad audience. I cannot imagine a better team to have guided me through the process.

Dr. Dave McIntyre, the director of the Integrative Center for Homeland Security at Texas A&M University, and my co-host on public radio's *Homeland Security: Inside and Out,* is a colleague and, more importantly, a friend. Since 1998 we have discussed, debated, agreed, and disagreed on an incredibly broad range of national and homeland security issues. No single individual has played a more important role in helping me ask the right questions.

Since the summer of 2000, Drs. Tara O'Toole, Tom Inglesby, and D. A. Henderson from the Center for Biosecurity–UPMC have served as mentors, educators, associates, "adult supervision," and friends. This book would not have been possible without their incredible support and encouragement. Drs. Luciana Borio, Gigi Kwik Grönvall, Eric Toner, and Beth Maldin provided technical expertise, support, and words of encouragement that kept me going.

Extraordinary thanks go to four colleagues: Bob Ross (Captain, USCG, ret.), one of the few visionary strategists in homeland security, Linda Millis, the talented director of the National Security program at the Markle Foundation, Dr. Peter Jutro, deputy director of the Environmental Protection Agency's Homeland Security Research Center, a rare combination of scientist and national security strategist, and the Honorable John Train, a prolific national security and business writer who has been appointed to senior advisory positions by both Democratic and Republican presidents. Their insights, suggestions, and editorial comments helped to shape the direction and tone of this book.

For those individuals who assisted with various sections of this book and who have been mentors, teachers, and friends for many years, I say thank you: Dr. Bob Kadlec, Dr. Elin Gursky, Lloyd Salvetti, General Dennis Reimer, and General Bill Begert. And special thanks to Jerry and Sandy Busby, Dr. Stanley and Barbra Brandon, Bruce and Barbara van Voorst, and Alane Andreozzi for volunteering to serve as readers and commentators.

Special thanks to Keith Robertory, manager, Preparedness Planning and Development, American Red Cross, for reviewing Chapter 9.

I owe a great debt of gratitude to Dr. Ruth David, president and CEO of ANSER, who in March 2000 offered me the opportunity to pursue my studies of homeland security on a full-time basis.

For Ms. Irene Jacoby, formerly of the National Legal Center for the Public Interest, my heartfelt thanks for convincing me to publish a monograph (of the same title) in 2005 based on a series of congressional hearings in which I served as an expert witness. Irene's encouragement and editorial skills were invaluable. I also wish to thank the National Legal Center for the Public Interest for allowing me to use parts of that work in this book.

To the women in my life who have for decades supported my passion for my work: JoLana, Dana, Tami, and Lana, I love you and owe you more than I will ever be able to say or write. And finally, my mom, Madonna Wise—all that I am and all that I hope to be, I owe to you.

Index

ability to survive and operate (ATSO), 190, 197

ACLU. *See* American Civil Liberties Union

"active interrogation," 102-104

ADIZ. *See* Air Defense Identification Zone

aircraft (defense), 28-32, 218-219

Air Defense Identification Zone (ADIZ), 138

airlift capacity, 217-219

Alexander, Lamar, 132

Alghamdi, Hamza, 54, 131

Alhaznawi, Ahmed, 50-51

all-hazards plan, 206-209

Almidhar, Khalid, 153

America. *See* United States (US)

American Civil Liberties Union (ACLU), 155

American homeland, 81-86, 89, 91, 224

American Hospital Association, 113

Americans, 20, 146-147, 149

Amerithrax, 49-50, 51, 55, 275

Anderson, Jack, 164, 170

André, John, 160

Andrews Air Force Base, 113

anthrax, 45, 50-55

antibiotics, 215, 259-260

Ashcroft, John, 149, 150, 154

At Dawn We Slept, 271

Atlanta, GA, 214-215

atom bomb, 59

ATSO. *See* ability to survive and operate

Atta, Mohammed, 50, 52, 54, 126, 130, 193

Aum Shinrikyo cult, 78-79

automobile accidents, 22-24

Bachus program, 48

Bacillus anthracis, 2, 48

Bacillus globigii, 1-4, 42, 48-49

Baker v. Carr, 146

Base Realignment and Closure Commission (BRAC), 177-179

BCP. *See* business continuity planning

Beamer, Todd, 25

BENS. *See* Business Executives for National Security

BEOC. *See* Business Emergency Operations Center

Bhopal, India, 64, 70, 140

bin Laden, Osama, 4, 33-34, 41, 151, 199

biocatastrophe, 87

biodefense
America preparing, 42-43
benefits/goals of, 117-120

biodefense *(cont'd)*
    director of, 182–188
    no one in charge of, 108
    organizational structure of, 109–110,
      112
    properly designed system for, 120
    Push Pack program in, 115–117
    spending initiatives required for, 107
Biological and Toxin Weapons
    Convention (BWC), 46–47
biological warfare, 43–46, 55, 69–70
biological weapons, 38, 42–58, 141
    epidemic brought on by, 43
    homeland security threatened by,
      55–57
    priority spending needed for, 92–93
    protecting America against, 39–40,
      106
    al-Qaeda capabilities in, 49, 53
    scientists knowledge of, 47–48
    smuggling, 10
    Soviet program of, 47
    terrorist-style lab for, 48
    terrorists with, 259–260
biometric information, 148
biotechnology, 4, 276
bioterrorism, 14, 55–58, 93
bombs, 18–20, 68, 152. *See also specific types*
borders, 12
    intelligence operations within U.S.,
      175–176
    securing, 11–12, 134, 137–149
    transporting weapons across, 140–142
Bouquet, Henry, 43
BRAC. *See* Base Realignment and
    Closure Commission
Brown, Michael, 8
"bug-to-drug in 24 hours," 118–120
Bush Administration, 159, 274
    FBI mission changed by, 172–173
    military approach of, 158–159
    research reactors plans of, 95–96
    spending priorities of, 6
Bush, George W., 83, 270
business continuity planning (BCP),
    190–211

Business Emergency Operations Center
    (BEOC), 213–214
Business Executives for National
    Security (BENS), 215, 225
business processes, 194–195
BWC. *See* Biological and Toxin Weapons
    Convention

calculations, 68–73
Cantor Fitzgerald, 194–195
CBRNE. *See* chemical, biological,
    radiological, nuclear enhanced
    conventional explosive
CDP. *See* Center for Domestic
    Preparedness
cell phones, 256–257
Center for Domestic Preparedness
    (CDP), 228
Centers for Disease Control, 111
Central Intelligence Agency (CIA), 2–3,
    127
CERT. *See* Community Emergency
    Response Team
charitable institutions, 88
chemical attacks/weapons, 63–65,
    70–71, 78–79
chemical, biological, radiological,
    nuclear enhanced conventional
    explosive (CBRNE), 42, 141
Cheney, Dick, 1–2
Chertoff, Michael, 76, 97
China, 44–45
chlorine gas, 64
Chou En-lai, 20
CIA. *See* Central Intelligence Agency
Citizens of Oakland Respond to
    Emergencies (CORE), 241
civilians
    airline defense systems for, 29–32
    experiences of, 233–234
    intentional attacks on, 161–162
    preparing local communities,
      211–216, 244–245
    terrorists acts condemned against, 89
Civil Reserve Air Fleet (CRAF), 217–219
classified information, 164–171
cleanup, radioactive, 60–61, 66, 250–251

Clinton, Bill, 88, 158-159, 166, 170, 178, 274
color code system, 267-268
communication systems, 236-237
communities, 211-216, 240, 243, 244-245
Community Emergency Response Team (CERT), 241
computer issues, 74
Congress, 176-180, 184
containment, 82, 88
    overreactions requiring, 90
    as single unifying strategy, 91
    spending recommendations for, 103-105
    strategy of, 86, 106
    of terrorism, 87
contractors, 98-99, 199-200
conventional explosives, 72, 140
Con-Way, 202-203
Coolidge, Calvin, 276
Cooperative Threat Reduction Program, 62
CORE. See Citizens of Oakland Respond to Emergencies
core functions, 206
corporate America, 189-190, 209
corporations, 190, 196-197, 199, 223
counterterrorism, 172-173
CPR, 247-249
CRAF. See Civil Reserve Air Fleet
credit cards, 264
crimes, 159, 162-164
crisis, 191, 197
critical infrastructures, 67-68
cross-jurisdictional support, 232
cultural barriers, 236
cyber warfare, 73-76

danger, 40, 55-57, 68-73, 92, 269-270
Danzig, Richard, 47, 57
Daschle, Tom, 2
DBD. See director of biodefense
DCI. See director of central intelligence
defense systems (contractors), 29-32, 94
Defense Threat Reduction Agency (DTRA), 48, 64

deliberate planning, 191-195, 203
Dell computers, 219
Department of Defense, 74, 103, 116, 183-184, 185
Department of Homeland Security, 97, 99, 267-268
destruction, America's, 41
Dhani, Ahmad, 89
director of biodefense (DBD), 182-188
director of central intelligence (DCI), 184
director of national intelligence (DNI), 182
dirty bombs, 66, 141
disaster planning, 240-241
    5 P's of, 200
    asking right question for, 211
    CRAF model for, 217-219
    evacuation in, 255-256
    families needing, 246-249, 268
    outside contractor used for, 199-200
    prior planning needed for, 213
    process of, 201
    returning home in, 254-255
    for small corporations, 199
    transportation plan in, 249-256
disaster response, 231
disasters, 13
dissipation rates, fallout, 250
distribution problem, Push Packs, 115-117
DNDO. See Domestic Nuclear Detection Office
DNI. See director of national intelligence
documents, electronic copies of, 264
domestic intelligence, 150-151, 171-176
Domestic Nuclear Detection Office (DNDO), 96
domestic terrorism, 55
drug war/trafficking, 144-145
DTRA. See Defense Threat Reduction Agency

education
    executive, 120-125
    homeland security, 3, 122, 125

education (*cont'd*)
  leaders requiring, 8-9
  security, 123-124
  spending not increased for, 109
Einstein, Albert, 16, 77
Eisenhower, Dwight D., 200, 276
electromagnetic pulse (EMP), 61
EMAC. *See* Emergency Management
    Assistance Compact
emergency management, 8
Emergency Management Assistance
    Compact (EMAC), 216, 234
emergency plans (checklist), 34-35,
    186, 191, 251
EMP. *See* electromagnetic pulse
employers, 145-146
enhanced conventional explosives,
    67-68, 72-73, 140
Environmental Protection Agency (EPA),
    252-253
EPA. *See* Environmental Protection
    Agency
epidemic, 43
Epidemic Proportions (Gursky), 110
evacuations, 9-10, 238, 255-256
executive education, 120-125

fallout (radioactive dust), 60-61, 66,
    250-251
families, disasters and, 246-249,
    268
FBI. *See* Federal Bureau of Investigation
Federal Bureau of Investigation (FBI),
    172-173
Federal Drug Administration, 119
federal government
  information system needed by,
    128-129
  insufficient funding control of, 109
  nuclear attack responsibility of, 96
  support from, 227-237
Federal Reserve System, 177
FedEx, 198, 219
first-aid kit, 264-265
First Amendment, 165, 170
first responders
  food for, 214

frequency spectrum increased for,
    235-236
  interoperability of, 228
  procedure standardization assisting,
    231-232
  spending increases for, 90-91
FISA. *See* Foreign Intelligence
    Surveillance Act
5 P's (planning), 200
flashlights, 265
Floyd, Charles (Bo), 248
flu pandemic, 56
food, 214, 261, 275
foreign intelligence, 180
Foreign Intelligence Surveillance Act
    (FISA), 151, 175
forensic capabilities, 50
formula, danger, 40, 68-73
Fountains-on-Estates, 241
Freed, Kathryn, 238-239
Freeh, Louis, 128
frequency spectrum, 235-236
funds, wasted, 80, 109

Galloway, Joseph L., 192
gamma detector, 96-97
Gates, Bill/Melinda, 220, 225
Geneva Conventions of 1949, 159-160,
    163
Giuliani, Rudy, 1, 12
Goldwater-Nichols reforms, 182, 183
good neighbor approach, 231
Gorelick, Jamie, 149, 152, 153, 154
Goss, Porter, 184-185
government, 26, 98-99, 102
grants, 229
ground-based defense systems, 32
Gursky, Elin, 108-110

Hamilton, Lee, 62, 150, 181
Hanjour, Hani, 130, 212
Hart-Rudman Commission, 274
hazardous cargo, 25-26
Henderson, D. A., 107, 220, 224
HEU. *See* highly enriched uranium
highly enriched uranium (HEU), 58,
    61, 70

LEU exchanged for, 105-106
as low radiation emitter, 99
research reactors with, 61-62
Highway Watch program, 14-15
Hiroshima, 59
Home Depot, 198
homeland security, 149. *See also*
    American homeland
America's spending on, 81
asking the right questions about,
    15-16
biological threat greatest danger to,
    55-57
border security and, 137-149
changing thought about, 16-17
contractors and, 98-99
corporate America involved in,
    189-190
dangers to, 269-270
education needed for, 3, 122, 125
federal governments role in,
    227-237
funds wasted in, 80
industrial complex, 97-98
information definition in, 127
massive spending programs for, 91
national media covering, 9
New Orleans reporters of, 7-8
new thinking required for, 137-149
perspective required for, 23-25
private sector response in, 213
proposal for, 222-224
al-Qaeda and, 4-5
reserve corps for, 112
strategies for, 81-86, 91, 273
success stories in, 237-242
thinking enemy and, 76-77
top priorities in, 276-277
wrong questions asked in, 4-6
Homeland Security: Inside and Out,
    12, 236
hospital beds, 113
hot tubs, 262
House Homeland Security Committee,
    38
human nature, 243
Hurricane Floyd, 255-256

Hurricane Katrina, 6-9, 191-192,
    198-200, 236, 258
Hurricane Rita, 13, 237
Hurricane Wilma, 10
hydrogen bombs, 59-60

ICBM. *See* intercontinental ballistic missile
identification, 131, 134-135, 145-146
illegal immigrants, 143-145
imagination, 77
Immelt, Jeffrey, 189
Indian tribes, 44
industrial chemicals, 64, 71
industrial complex, 97-98
in-flight emergencies, 35, 211
information (systems), 74, 127, 144
    federal government needing, 128-129
    United States attack capabilities of, 75
    as weapon against terrorism, 126-135
inhalation exposure, 46
Intel Corporation, 209-210
intelligence. *See also* domestic
        intelligence; foreign intelligence
    available, 130-131
    community reorganization, 184-186
    operations, 175-176, 180-181
    sharing of, 152-153
Intelligence Authorization Act, 166
Intelligence Reform and Terrorism
    Prevention Act, 127
intercontinental ballistic missile (ICBM),
    108-109
international environment, 4, 270
international security, 37-38, 85
international terrorism, 163-164
internet phone service, 257
interoperability, 228
Interstate Highway System, 80
Islamic terrorists, 4-5
    intention factor of, 40-41
    long-term strategic vision of, 20-21
    rock and roll initiatives against, 89-90
    using charitable institutions, 88
Israelis, 35-36

Jackson, Michael, 76
Japan, 44-46

JOC. *See* Joint Operations Center
Johnson, Barry, 240
Johnson, L. Z., 228
Joint Operations Center (JOC), 213-214
Juvenal (Roman poet), 170

Kaczynski, Ted, 66, 269
Kadlec, Robert P., 188
Kean, Thomas, 62, 181
keep it simple, stupid (KISS), 272
Kennan, George, 82, 86
Kennedy, Edward, 175, 188
Keyes, David, 73, 75
KISS. *See* keep it simple, stupid
Kobe earthquake, 207

landlines, 257
Lapson, Diane, 238, 240
law enforcement agencies, 50, 124-125,
    158-164
layered defense systems, 24-25
leaders, 8-9
legal standards, 162-163
letters, anthrax in, 53-54
LEU. *See* low-enriched uranium
Lincoln, Abraham, 122, 137
logistics, 219
long-term strategic vision, 20-21
Loomis, Alfred, 220
Louisville, KY, 204
low-enriched uranium (LEU), 61,
    105-106
Lutnick, Howard, 194-195

Marine Expeditionary Unit (MEU), 183
Maryland Defense Force, 235
mass distribution, 116
McGraw-Hill Homeland Security Summit
    and Exposition, 26-28
McGraw, Steve, 232, 263
McLuhan, Marshall, 278
McVeigh, Timothy, 25, 41, 66, 67, 140,
    269
mean time between failures (MTBF),
    30-31
media, 9, 164-171
medical capabilities, 112-115, 118

MEL. *See* "minimum equipment list"
Memorial Institute for the Prevention of
    Terrorism (MIPT), 229-230
MEU. *See* Marine Expeditionary Unit
military, 46, 203, 205, 233-234
    approach, 158-159
    medical capacity, 113-114
    organizations, 191, 196-197
military-industrial complex, 97
military-style chemical weapons, 63, 71
Miller Brewing Company, 213
Miller, Judith, 160-161
"minimum equipment list" (MEL), 31
MIPT. *See* Memorial Institute for the
    Prevention of Terrorism
Moore, Harold G., 192
Moore, Molly, 166
Morgan Stanley, 192-194
Morrill Act, 122
MTBF. *See* mean time between failures
Mueller, Robert, 128, 171, 173
Mullet, Randy, 202
Murphy's Law, 210

N95 mask, 262-263
nanny-state, 10
NASCAR-quality helmet, 22
National Counterterrorism Center, 129
National Defense Education Program,
    123
National Emergency Resource Registry
    (NERR), 212
National Guard, 233-234
national identity system, 132-134,
    146-149
National Incident Management System
    (NIMS), 230-231
nationally standardized identification,
    131
national public health system, 107,
    111-112, 118
National Response Plan, 213-214
National Rifle Association (NRA), 148
National Security Act of 1947, 150-151,
    182-184
National Security Agency, 74
National Security Letters, 156, 157-158

national security program, 63
national standards, public health with, 116
National War College, 15, 83, 121, 137
Nazi death camps, 271
NERR. *See* National Emergency Resource Registry
New Orleans, 7-8
NIMS. *See* National Incident Management System
9/11, 53
    attacks of, 22
    hearings, 149-150, 152
    intelligence available prior to, 130-131
    U.S. economy attacked on, 272
The 9/11 Commission Report, 153-154, 165-166
911, 226
not-for-profit corporation, 220-225
NRA. *See* National Rifle Association
NTI. *See* Nuclear Threat Initiative
nuclear attack, 94, 96
nuclear bomb, 60
nuclear defense, 105-106
nuclear deterrence, 103
Nuclear Non-Proliferation Treaty, 21
nuclear power plants, 61-63
Nuclear Threat Initiative (NTI), 62, 95, 225
nuclear weapons, 38, 58-77, 141-142
    danger assessment of, 70
    priority spending needed for, 92-93
    proliferation of, 94-95
    protecting America against, 39-40
    al Qaeda getting hands on, 273
    radiation types from, 249-250
    radiological detectors for, 101
    smuggling of, 93-94
    terrorist organizations and, 6, 58-59, 142
Nunn-Lugar Cooperative Threat Reduction program, 86, 105
Nunn, Sam, 62, 63, 113, 114

Oklahoma City, OK, 229
organizational structure, biodefense, 109-112

organized crime, 145
organized militias, 234-235
Osterholm, Michael, 201
O'Toole, Tara, 2, 51, 52, 113-114
our own worst enemy, 77
overreactions, 34, 90, 272
oversight commission, 176-182

pandemics, 111, 202, 244
partnership building, 211-216
"passive scanning," 102-103
The Patriot Act, 156
Patton, George, 276
PCCIP. *See* President's Commission on Critical Infrastructure Protection
"peace dividend," 79
Pearl Harbor, 39, 273-274
perceptions, 34
personnel, key people, 206-207
perspective, keeping, 23-25, 35-36
pets, 263
Pickard, Thomas, 150
pilots, 35
piracy, 164
plague-infected fleas, 45
Plaugher, Ed, 235
plutonium bomb, 58-59
polio, 41-42
posses
    electoral, 275-276
    prevention, 14-15
    push pack, 214-215
    Sowell forming, 237-238, 240
    of trained volunteers, 116-117
    World Trade Center with, 238-240
potassium iodide, 260
Powell, Colin, 16, 57, 121, 161, 185
preclinical detection, 118-120
prescription medications, 257-260
President's Commission on Critical Infrastructure Protection (PCCIP), 73
prevention strategy, 94
prior planning, 213
privacy, protecting, 147
private citizens, 243
privately funded programs, 220-221

private sector
  database linking in, 129
  government jobs v., 98–99
  homeland security needing, 213
  security role of, 224–225
problems, 3–4
procedures, standardization of, 203–
    205, 231–232
proposals, 222–224
public health, 107–111, 116
Push Packs, 14, 115–117, 214–215

al-Qaeda, 4–5
  attack orchestrated by, 50
  bioweapon capabilities of, 49, 53
  enhanced conventional explosives
    demonstrated by, 67
  nuclear weapons in hands of, 273
  winning war against, 84–85
questions (right and wrong)
  asking correct, 270–271
  good plans begin with, 211
  homeland security asking, 4–6, 15–16
  Hurricane Katrina and, 6–9
  problems not solved with, 3–4

radiation emitter, low, 99
radiation types, 249–250
radioactive dust, 60–61, 66, 250–251
radiological detectors, 101, 102
radiological dispersal devices (RDD),
    65, 141
radiological weapons, 65–66, 71–72, 141
RDD. *See* radiological dispersal devices
readiness kit, 246–247, 253, 257–268
Ready Watch program, 242
REAL ID Act, 134, 147
Red Cross, 212, 247–249
reload factor, bioterrorism with, 57–58
Reno, Janet, 152, 153
*Report on Weapons of Mass
    Destruction,* 38
Rescorla, Rick, 192
research reactors, 61–62, 95–96
reserve corps, 112
Reserve Officer Training Corps (ROTC),
    123

The Resilient Enterprise (Sheffi), 209
resources, 220–225
Responder Knowledge Base, 229–230
retail businesses, 116
Rice, Condoleeza, 256
Ridge, Tom, 86–87
Robb-Silberman Commission, 95, 105
rock and roll, 89–90
Roosevelt, Franklin, 135
ROTC. *See* Reserve Officer Training
    Corps
roving wiretaps, 155
rule of 2s, 260

Safir, Howard, 12, 236
San Diego, CA, 45–46
sarin, 78
Schoch-Spana, Monica, 243–244
Schwarzkopf, Norman, 167, 186, 201
science/technology, 102
scientists, 47–48
secure government building, 3–4
Securities Act of 1933, 176
Securities Exchange Act of 1934, 176
security
  of American homeland, 89, 224
  America's education for, 123–124
  border, 11–12, 134, 137–149
  of chemical industry, 65
  in corporate America, 209
  from information, 144
  in international environment, 270
  new threats to, 271–272
  at nuclear power plants, 61, 62
  private sectors role in, 224–225
  protecting borders for, 140–142
  strategic thinking for, 121
  wasteful shortsighted programs in, 25
  White House/CIA lapses in, 2–3
Sedition Act of 1918, 39
Senate intelligence committees, 179
17-kiloton bomb, heat from, 60
Shallah, Ramadan Abdullah, 88
Sheffi, Yossi, 209
sheltering-in-place, 9–10, 249–253
shoulder launched missiles, 28–32
situation awareness, 7

smallpox, 43–44
"sneek and peek warrants," 155–156
Social Security, 178–179
"Solar Sunrise," 74
Soviet Union, 47, 62–63
Sowell, Donald, 12, 237–238, 240
spaceship earth, 278
spending programs, 90–91
  America's homeland security, 81
  biodefense requiring, 107
  biological/nuclear weapons and,
    92–93
  of Bush Administration, 6
  containment strategy
    recommendations for, 103–105
  education and, 109
  for homeland security, 91
standardization procedures, 203–205,
  231–232
standards, public health, 110
state inspectors, training program for,
  210
Stotlar, Douglas W., 202–203
strategies, 273
  of containment, 86, 106
  homeland security and, 81–86
  for national security, 121
  National War College teaching, 83
  of prevention, 94
  single unifying, 91
subways, 265
success stories, 237–242
suicide attacks, 124–125
superpowers, 38–39
supplantation, 109
supply chains, 207–209
surge capacity, 218–219
survival, 261
system, biodefense, 120

task force, 90–91
technology, 4, 37–38, 220–221
Tenet, George, 274
terrorism
  America's economy targeted by, 33–34
  businesses target of, 190
  as crime, 159

  defeating/containing, 86–87
  information systems weapon against,
    126–135
  innocent civilians and, 89
  international, 163–164
  Israelis dealing with, 35–36
  new legal standards against, 162–163
  primary goals of, 26
  probability assessment for, 32–33
  shoulder-launched missiles used in,
    28–32
  understanding risk of, 24
  United States response to, 79
  at World Trade Center, 192–194
terrorist attacks, 12, 21, 59–60
terrorist organizations. *See also*
  al-Qaeda
  biological attack capabilities of, 69–70
  with bioweapons, 259–260
  chemical attack capabilities of, 70–71
  enhanced conventional explosives
    and, 67–68
  HEU and, 61
  imagination weapon of, 77
  information systems feared by,
    126–135
  limiting capabilities of, 87
  nuclear weapons and, 6, 58–59, 142
  two approaches to, 158–164
terrorist-style lab, 48
Texas State Homeland Security, 231–232
text messaging, 256
"They are not done yet," 20
thinking enemy, 76–77
thinking, new, 16–17, 137–149
Thirty Years War, 159
Thomas, Clarence, 165
Thompson, John, 75
Thompson, Larry, 153
Tokyo, 79
Townsend, Frances, 76
toxic vapors, 79
Train, John, 270
transportation plan, 249–256
Transportation Security Administration
  (TSA), 134
trauma counseling, 240

traveler ID's, 134–135
Treaty of Westphalia, 159
Trotsky, Leon, 190
TSA. *See* Transportation Security
    Administration
Tsonas, Cristos, 50
Turner, Ted, 95, 225
Tuxedo Park, NY, 220–222
Twain, Mark, 171
typhoid-laced dumplings, 45

"uncontained failure," 29
United Flight 93, 278
United States (US), 14, 63, 75, 79,
    93–94, 278–279. *See also* American
    homeland
  biodefense preparations of, 42–43
  corporate security in, 209
  domestic intelligence capabilities of,
    171–176
  economy, 33–34, 272
  electoral posse in, 275–276
  greatest threats to, 37–38, 41
  homeland security spending in, 81
  information in, 126, 144
  nuclear/biological weapons and,
    39–40, 106
  polio vulnerabilities of, 41–42
  security education in, 123–124
  terrorism targeting, 33–34
  War on Terror struggle of, 3–4, 21,
    84–85
  world changing for, 277–279
UPS pilots, 204, 219
uranium bomb, 59
US. *See* United States

variola virus (smallpox), 119
volunteers, trained, 116–117
von Clausewitz, Carl, 121
von Moltke, Marshall, 202

"the wall," 149–158
Wal-Mart, 197–198, 219
war, 158–164, 167
War of the Worlds (radio broadcast),
    244

War on Terror, 3–4, 21, 84–85
warrantless search, 156
Washington, George, 160
water, 261–262
weaponized bioagents, 46, 49
weapons
  biological, 42–58
  crossing borders, 140–142
  danger comparisons of, 68–73, 92
  information systems as, 135
  technological advances of, 4
  understanding threat of, 40
weapons-grade nuclear material, 62–63,
    94, 102–104
Weiss, Stanley, 225
Welch, Jack, 187
Welles, Orson, 244
We Were Soldiers, 192
We Were Soldiers Once . . . and Young
    (Moore/Galloway), 192
White House, 1–3
White, John, 114
William of Ockham, 272
Wilson, Woodrow, 39
WISE. *See* World Islamic Studies
    Enterprise
A Woman at War (Moore), 166
Woods, Michael J., 156
Woolsey, R. James, 57
world, changing, 277–279
World Islamic Studies Enterprise
    (WISE), 88
World Trade Center, 229
  bomb exploding at, 18–20, 68, 152
  posses formed at, 238–240
  terrorism at, 192–194
World Trade Center (movie), 243
World War II, 44–46

Yeltsin, Boris, 47
Young, Andrew, 180
Yousef, Ramsey, 18–20, 25, 68, 140, 159,
    193

al-Zawahiri, Ayman, 49